Essential Information for e-Commerce

Source	URL	Topic
Cyberatlas	www.cyberatlas.com	Statistical information about the Internet
Cnet	www.cnet.com	Online e-commerce news
ZDNet	www.zdnet.com	Online information on Technology
W3	www.w3.org	World Wide Web working group setting the standards for HTML, XML
Media Metrix	www.mediametrix.com	Internet advertising information
Internet.com	www.internet.com	Internet information
IDG	www.idg.net	Online information
Datamonitor	www.datamonitor.com	Internet information
Net Stat	www.netstat.net	Internet information
Techweb	www.techweb.com	Technology information
Smart Valley	www.svi.org	Telecommuting information
KDNuggets	www.kdnuggets.com	Data mining information
Ad Relevance	www.adrelevance.com	Internet advertising information

Software and Hardware for e-Commerce

Source	URL	Software/Hardware
IBM	www.ibm.com	Variety of software and hardware for e-commerce
Microsoft	www.microsoft.com	Variety of software for e-commerce
3Com	www.3com.com	Networking products
Cybercash	www.cybercash.com	Online payment services
Allaire	www.allaire.com	Cold Fusion Web software
Sun Microsystems	www.sun.com	Staroffice
Java	java.sun.com	Java language Web site
Macromedia	www.macromedia.com	Web site software
Bluestreak	www.bluestreak.com	Interactive banner ads
Real	www.real.com	Webcast software

Online Services for e-Commerce

Source	URL	Service
U.S. Patent Office	www.uspto.gov	Online trademark forms
Netopia	netopia.netscape.com	Online e-commerce sites
First Source	www.firstsource.com	Online e-business assistance
Webreference	www.webreference.com	Web site building help
Securities and Exchange Commission	www.sec.com	Online information for SEC Filings
Stock Trans	www.stocktrans.com	Assistance for companies issuing stock
Network Solutions	www.networksolutions.com	Domain name registration
Security First Network Bank	www.sfnb.com	E-bank
American Incorporators	www.ailcorp.com	Online incorporation
Verisign	www.verisign.com	Certificate security
Digi-net	www.digi-net.com	Online shopping
Ideapro	www.ideapro.com	Online shopping software
I-escrow	www.iescrow.com	Secure payment service
Nasdaq	www.nasdaq.com	Stock information
NYSE	www.nyse.com	New York Stock Exchange information
Ad Force	www.adforce.com	Online advertising management
Fedex	www.fedex.com	Online delivery service
UPS	www.ups.com	Online delivery service

Online Examples of e-Commerce

Source	URL	Service
Macmillan USA	www.MCP.com	Publishing
Amazon.com Inc.	www.Amazon.com	Online retailer
Ebay.com	www.ebay.com	Online auctions
Yahoo.com	www.yahoo.com	Search engine
Ask.com	www.ask.com	Ask Jeeves search engine
Travelocity	www.travelocity.com	Travel Site
Webcast.com	www.webcast.com	Online Webcasts
Egghead	www.egghead.com	Online retailer
I Village	www.ivillage.com	Women's network
Spiff Storm	www.geocities.com/spiffstorm/spiffstorm.html	Online Web site
Hot Jobs	www.hotjobs.com	Online career ads
E-trade	www.etrade.com	Online brokerage
Google	www.google.com	Search engine
Expedia	www.expedia.com	Travel site
Shockwave	www.shockwave.com	Gaming site
Outpost.com	www.outpost.com	Shopping site
Tucows	www.tucows.com	Free software
Fat Brain	www.fatbrain.com	Online publishing
AOL	www.aol.com	National ISP
Entry Point	www.entrypoint.com	Push technology
Geocities	www.geocities.com	Free Web sites
Chrysler	www.chrysler.com	High Tech Web site
MPlayer.com	www.mplayer.com	Gaming site
Nullsoft	www.winamp.com	Digital music

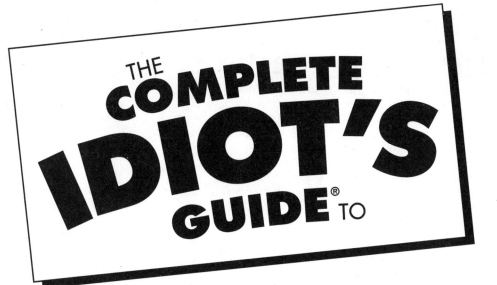

THE COMPLETE IDIOT'S GUIDE® TO

e-Commerce

by Rob Smith
Mark Thompson
and
Mark Speaker

que®

A Division of Macmillan Computer Publishing
201 W. 103rd Street, Indianapolis, IN 46290

The Complete Idiot's Guide to e-Commerce

International Standard Book Number: 0-7897-2194-5

Library of Congress Catalog Card Number: 99-63887

Printed in the United States of America

First Printing: *01/10/00*

00   99   98   4   3   2   1

Trademarks

Warning and Disclaimer

Associate Publisher
Greg Wiegand

Acquisitions Editor
Angelina Ward

Development Editor
Marta Justak

Managing Editor
Thomas Hayes

Editorial Team
D&G Limited, LLC

Indexer
Craig Small

Technical Editor
Michael Watson

Production Team
D&G Limited, LLC

Cover Designers
*Dan Armstrong,
Barbara Kordesh*

Designer
Kim Scott

Illustrations
Judd Winick

Contents at a Glance

Contents

vii

17 Offline Marketing for Online Businesses   257

18 The Marketing Goldrush: Data Mining   269

xiii

XV

About the Authors

Rob Smith is an enigma. He is a guy who spends his time consulting on technology and strategy to the CEOs and boards of large Fortune 500 companies, yet will leave mid-meeting and grab a plane to hack together a network for a small company that needs a hand. He says the small start-ups give him perspective and the chance to try out what he writes about before he endorses it. He is a founder of Exordium Technology Corp. (www.exordiumtech.com), a technology think tank and consulting firm, and Technocats.com (www.technocats.com), a "trasher" tech lab that tears apart and analyzes applications and hardware. He is also the co-founder of e-commerce companies RouteCool.com and TheStoneGarden.com. This ex-hacker is a graduate of the University of Calgary and is the co-author of *Easy Networking* and e-books *The New Exordium* and *Privileged Information*. He loves to talk and write about technology, but be careful, he's like a dog with a bone—try to take away his techno toys, and he bites.

Mark Thompson began teaching and consulting on information systems while a student at the University of Lethbridge in Lethbridge, Alberta, Canada. As the Senior Network Planner for Western Canada with Metronet Communications, Mark played a key role in the development of a national voice and data network. Known for his easy-going, comical style, Mark has written dozens of manuals on personal computing and networking, as well as delivered hundreds of lectures and seminars on networking technology. He is a founding partner of www.learnlots.com.

Mark Speaker is currently the president of 2MN8 Inc., a company focused on delivering home networking education. He was previously responsible for the implementation of a leading-edge system that modelled the communication network of the first competitive local exchange carrier in Canada, Metronet Communications. Mark is a founding partner of www.learnlots.com.

Introduction

What an incredible journey we are all about to embark on. This thing called the Internet is only the foundation of an entirely new way to build, conduct, run, manage, and operate a company. We call it a foundation because we are standing at the base of a technological volcano of opportunities that is about to blow. Forget all those old business school models that extolled the virtues of various types of organizational charts. They no longer apply. They are gone. Kaput.

Welcome to the new world of business, and the dawning of the era of advanced corporate technology, virtual corporations, and virtual employees.

Here's a scary thought. The greatest risk to any traditional business today is the fact that it conducts business as usual. We don't think you should take our word for it. Stroll into any major traditional retailer and ask whether they feel threatened by the Internet. The honest ones will tell you that they take the threat very seriously and are doing something about it.

What about the rest of the business world?

If you think that because someone makes steel or runs a coffee shop that the Internet won't affect them, then think again. Remember the competition? Yeah, the guy down the street. Well, he just hired an 18-year-old Internet whiz to rebuild his organization for the new millennium, and word has it he can buy, process, and sell both coffee and steel for a fraction of the price that those places can—and he's not even opening an office.

You don't have to concern yourself with this, though, because maybe you don't make steel or sell coffee and because you're the one holding this book.

So get ready because we're the definitive book on e-commerce. From secure socket layers to holding your own IPO streaming Web conference, we are going to tell you what all the hype is about, and why it's a lot more than hype. Plain and simple, it's business survival.

Who Should Buy This Book

Entrepreneurs and CEOs who want to understand how to move their business onto the Internet, how to redesign their corporations to take advantage of e-commerce, or how to build a brand new e-business should buy this book. These people should also buy it:

➤ Individuals who are considering starting an Internet business

➤ Anyone that wants to know where the world of e-commerce is going

➤ Shareholders who want to know what their company is doing in response to the Internet risk

➤ Investors who want to know where the best e-commerce investment will be

➤ Information technology professionals who want to know how the Internet will impact the way their businesses operate

➤ Anyone who is looking for a new business opportunity

How To Use This Book

The Complete Idiot's Guide to e-Commerce is broken into five sections. Earlier sections feed into later sections, and there are useful hints, tips, and Web site locations that you can surf to. If you own a business and are thinking of, or have already started to conduct business online, this book is full of helpful information in the first chapters that can bring you up to speed on some of the latest developments and pitfalls of the world of e-commerce. If you are starting an entirely new online business, then these first chapters fit very well with the later chapters that look at some of the new e-commerce business models and new ways of doing business. If you work for a large organization, then the entire book will give you enough high-level understanding of this new e-world and enough detail to make those mission critical information decisions.

We don't think that every business will use all of the concepts in this book, but as a business owner, the more information that you have, the better your decisions will be and the more successful your organization will become. Our goal is to give you some new concepts to consider and a better understanding of what the new e-businesses of tomorrow are thinking today. So, we suggest starting at Chapter 1 and going straight through to the final chapter that brings everything together in what we call the "definitive e-commerce business model." We think you will find something useful in every chapter.

Part One: What Is e-Commerce?

Part one covers a general view of what e-commerce is and what has led to this new buzzword. It also looks at why Internet companies are worth so much, how to build virtual corporations, and how you can make your own company or idea the next great e-commerce "killer App."

Part Two: Opportunities in e-Commerce

This part describes some of the newest opportunities in the e-commerce world and how to build an e-business, including automated supply chains and real-time, back-office systems. It also looks at electronic funds transfers, data mining, virtual workers, and customer service using the Internet.

Part Three: e-Marketing

In this part, we take some of the concepts from the first part and the e-business building tools in the second part and tell you how to market your business both on and off the Internet. This will include discussions of Internet advertising, promotion, public relations, and how data mining will help all of these. We'll also give you details about some of the newest Internet marketing models.

Part Four: e-Strategies: Managing the e-Corporation

In part four, we'll go beyond the Internet to give you the tools you need to run an e-business. We'll discuss resource planning and knowledge management and help you to understand where the land mines are on the Internet and how to avoid them.

Part Five: Pulling It All Together

In this part, we bring it all together with the definitive e-commerce model that will apply to an e-business. Whether you are changing your existing traditional business or building a new virtual corporation beside the Information Superhighway, this section will show you how to do it step by step.

Glossary

Just so you know how to "out buzz" the tech down the hall, we've compiled a comprehensive glossary of e-commerce. Now you can buzz with the best of them.

Conventions Used in This Book

The book contains a number of sidebars that have provided additional information to help you create a great e-commerce company.

Surfs Up

This sidebar contains hyperlinks to relevant Web sites that contain examples of the concepts discussed or additional information about the topic.

Success Stories

In the Success Stories sidebar, we discuss and sometimes hyperlink to the Web sites of companies that have successfully implemented the concepts we are discussing.

Stats and Facts

This sidebar provides some additional, pertinent statistical quotes, as well as some definitions about some of the newer and more exotic technologies.

Part 1

What Is e-Commerce?

In this first part of the book, we will cover what e-commerce actually is and what is driving this new e-commerce revolution. We'll study the factors that have caused Internet stocks to go through the roof and what you might be able to do with your own company to move onto the e-commerce onramp to the Internet.

We'll go into what is considered e-commerce and what pieces of e-commerce relate to the Internet. However, there is a lot more to e-commerce than the Internet, and we'll explain what that is.

Later in this section, you'll find out what a virtual corporation is and how you can build one or take your existing company virtual. We'll also discuss the concept of the "killer app," and what it means to your new e-commerce business including some pitfalls lurking in the killer app world.

In the last chapter, we'll provide you with some of the laws of the e-commerce jungle as well as some of the land mines and how to avoid them.

So fasten your seat belt and get ready to ramp up the e-commerce learning curve really fast.

What Is Driving the e-Commerce Revolution?

In This Chapter

➤ Faster computers

➤ Faster connections

➤ Critical mass

➤ Global access

➤ Lower transaction costs

Faster Computers

Do you ever feel the need for speed? We have come to expect that our computers will move fast. So fast, in fact, that we get upset if we have to wait more than two seconds for the thing to respond. Manufacturers of computers have responded to our angst. Intel is well into the 600 MHz chips and is working on the next generation of processor. Moore's law predicted that the speed of processing power would double every 18 months while the price of chips would stay the same, and so far it seems to be holding true.

But why would computers need to be faster? The answer is that technology is changing rapidly in a vicious circle with computer speed. As the computers get faster, the current technology runs more efficiently, and changes are incorporated in the design of software that requires even more power. First, it was graphical user interfaces, then networking, then the Internet, and now high-definition TV and stereo quality streaming content. If we doubled the speed of the Internet and the computers attached to it, it still wouldn't be enough to satisfy the technological thirst of our world.

We feel the need for and in fact demand more speed from vendors with each new technology that hits the Internet. As well, the success of increasing chip speed has led to innovations that are changing the very fundamentals of the way we do business. Businesses are now thinking about how they can serve their customers from inside their own systems by using the Internet as the communications tool of choice and backing it up with real-time automated systems inside the company. The acceptance of e-commerce is only a symptom of our ability to successfully process transactions for a relatively low cost. The concept of the paper office was always out there, but it seemed like an unattainable ideal for many years. This was simply because to achieve this goal, we would have required a significant change in the very foundation of the way business works. The Internet was simply the catalyst that companies realized would gain them the benefits of moving to the paperless world without all the high cost of massively integrated systems. Remember that in 1990 to achieve today's computing power would have cost many thousands of dollars per computer, but today those computers cost less than a thousand dollars each.

The Fall of the Mainframe

Another piece of the speed puzzle was what the software actually did for a company. Early in the history of computing, mainframes wandered the virtual world until one decade they became extinct as the asteroid called the personal computer (PC) hit their world. Now, users had the power to process information and the rise of personal software took hold. Mainframe programs that had to be run at night and took a room full of staff were replaced with small, custom-built software that managed many of the same tasks faster and more efficiently. As chip power grew and the costs stayed static, the mainframes were the realm of the large corporations that just couldn't shake the Big Blue (IBM) sales team.

Eventually, someone connected all these new PCs together, and users were able to share data without printing reports. The result was an incredible jump in the level of productivity as distributed software applications became the status quo. Now, users had computing power at their fingertips and specialized programs for centralized processing. The smaller and less costly server had replaced the mainframe. This information model is still the most prevalent in the business world, although some are trying to move to a "thin" client architecture that sounds very much like the old days of the mainframe.

Now with increasing power, thanks to Moore's law and software that was starting to be specifically designed to run in a distributed environment, companies could finally see light at the end of the tunnel. The holy grail of the paperless office was within reach. Of course, there were still problems such as a wide range of software and proprietary standards in hardware and operating systems that didn't communicate with each other. Building on the goal of getting a transaction such as a sale to go from order to G/L without human intervention was the last step in the process to achieve the paperless goal. This was the point of Enterprise Resource Planning software or ERP. Its goal was to make the management of resources throughout the organization a complete and integrated process usually with a single company's software.

Thin Client

A thin client is a computer with very minimal hardware devices. It still contains processing power, but the bulk of the storage and processing is run on a networked server. In these types of businesses all the applications and storage are performed centrally. This reduces the overall cost of the network clients and allows for greater centralized control of data processing. The thin client can be thought of as a dumb terminal that took some extra classes.

The Internet's Need for Speed

When the Internet finally caught fire, the concept of speed was an issue. 14.4 modems were slow and painful when graphics were being loaded, and if too many colors, animation or large text files were loaded, the result was that the computer ground to a halt while the transfer occurred. Once again, chip speed accelerated along with modem speed, and the Internet became a useful tool instead of a hard-to-use curiosity. Large graphic files, animation, and even programming functionality in applets could be loaded and run efficiently over regular telephone lines or fast cable modems. Companies that were already progressing toward integrated systems and distributed architecture were now starting to connect their internal networks to the Internet.

It didn't take long for someone to think about the possibilities of all those people connected together using standards and browser software that could process code. It was like a crowd of a million people had all gathered together in one location to share and exchange ideas, but no one bothered to open a really good food and drink kiosk. That is until guys like Jeff Bezos (Amazon.com) rode up in their virtual book-mobile.

Imagine the concept of the world's population shopping online anywhere in the world, using progressively faster technology. You could easily show a picture of a product and price list and get them to place an order. But what if the system then transferred the information to your ERP system? Or better yet, what if your ERP software supplier retooled his entire integrated package so that it would work with the standards of the Internet? That way, since it had to communicate using Internet standards, you would not only be able to process transactions, but you could now communicate with your suppliers, given that their software vendors were also compatible with the standards of the Internet.

All of a sudden your system could integrate with your suppliers' system without requiring an interpreter, and instead of you carrying an inventory, you could now look at your suppliers' on-hand stock in their system and have them ship the product direct to your customers. Or even better, have them show your customer their inventory, made to look like your inventory, and let the customer order directly from the supplier while making it look like they were ordering from you. In that way, you essentially became an information pipeline manager between the supplier and your customer. This whole ability to communicate with anyone and the ability to build an online business became known as e-commerce.

Changing the Way We Shop

Research by Shop.org and The Boston Consulting Group (BCG) estimated that online e-tailer revenue would be approximately $9 billion for the last two months of 1999.

The whole key to any of these systems succeeding was the speed of the personal computer. Without it, only a handful of people would surf the Internet, and its appeal would have been limited. Luckily, computer speed and pricing did follow Moore's law, and the popularity of the Internet grew. Now, companies big and small are building on the Net and starting the long task of establishing brand awareness among these new global users. The outcome has been a dramatic change in the business world. Not only are computers getting faster, but many organizations are finding the process of becoming an e-commerce business akin to making a jump to hyperspace in a spaceship. Battle the evil empire that is your competition while retooling your corporate engine; then hit the hyperspeed button by building an Internet site and pray that the course you have charted doesn't have an asteroid lying in the middle of it. That asteroid can be any one of the dozens of land mines that lie waiting on the Information Superhighway.

Faster Connections

Of course, the Internet would just be a fancy e-mail system if it were not for the changes to its infrastructure that occurred over the past few years. Today, everyone can connect together simply because of the work done so early on by the United States Defense Department and companies like 3com. They pushed the relatively simple concept of sending small electronic packets of data from one computer through a wire to a second computer. Protocol has defined the way this data was transmitted and with companies like Microsoft adding the concept to their new operating systems, the ability to communicate grew easier with each passing year.

10

Backbone

The backbone of the Internet are the cables that link all the main connection points, each one called a point of presence or POP, to the Internet. The vast majority of Internet traffic is carried on fiber optic cables that can route billions of packets each day.

Internet Service Providers (ISPs) flourished as a natural progression from their days as bulletin board operators. Bulletin boards were simple servers that everyone could dial into and get free software or send messages. They were notoriously easy to set up but generated almost no revenue because it was difficult to show ads and users were rarely willing to pay for access. When the concept of the Internet was rolled beyond the universities and research facilities, the natural progression for a bulletin board operator was to add a bank of modems to their computers and get a leased, high-capacity phone line to the Internet from the phone company. Although costly, the newly created ISPs could purchase bandwidth in bulk from the phone company and resell it back to its users. Thus started the birth of thousands of ISPs, of which many would succumb to the advance of the phone companies into the world of the Internet Service Provision.

As the years progressed, some ISPs became more adept at providing better access to fast Internet connections while many of the firms that did not attain critical mass failed. Consolidations occurred, and the shakeout of the ISP world had begun. During this period, advances were made to make better use of the copper lines entering most people's homes and to increase the speed of modem technology to permit much faster access. Today, the old copper infrastructure is rapidly being replaced with fiber optics (see Figure 1.1).

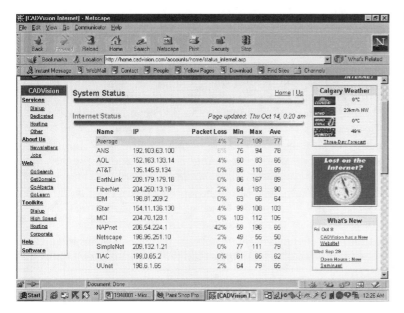

Figure 1.1

This figure shows the networks that make up the Internet backbone, as well as status information, like the percentage of packets lost.

The Internet and the Cable Companies

The next great speed advancement in the Internet was the use of cable modems distributed by the cable TV companies to users that were already wired with coax cable. This superfast access capability came with a higher price tag than the average ISP, but file loads were delivered as fast as a direct connection to the Web server.

Factors that impact the overall access speed of the Internet include:

➤ The size of the files that are being loaded.

➤ The speed of the Web servers that are delivering the content.

➤ The speed of the connection between the server and the Internet.

➤ The capacity and speed of the Internet backbone

➤ The speed and capacity of the connection between the Internet and the ISP.

➤ The connection between the ISP and the user

➤ The speed of the user's modem.

➤ The power of the user's computer.

If there are delays at any point, then the user will see a slowdown in response times. All of these factors have led to the growing use of the Internet for a variety of purposes. Businesses conduct research and exchange information; adults surf for information, entertainment, and shopping; children do research for schoolwork and gain access to gaming sites; and governments use the Web to disseminate information to the people. None of this would have occurred if the speed of computers and the speed of access had not grown to the point that using the Internet was as simple and convenient as using your networked computer at work.

Still More Need for Speed

We are once again standing at the edge of more dramatic increases in computing and access power and once again it's not a moment too soon. E-businesses are now pushing full steam ahead to bring even more spectacular content and applications to the Net, such as video on demand, digital quality music, advanced graphics and animation, and new complete software applications that will operate entirely over the Net. Finance, banking, connecting to your home area network, delivery of entertainment, shopping, education, and virtual employment are going to greatly add to the volume of traffic and the ongoing requirement for greater speed and capacity over the next few years. Innovations that take advantage of these impending changes, such as Web TV, Mp3 music format, special graphic animation systems like flash and shockwave technology, and the use of Java servlets (server side) functionality will be the areas of the greatest growth over the next few years. The opportunities for e-businesses to capitalize on the power of the Internet to conduct business have never been greater and the barriers to entry never lower.

The Value of Critical Mass

Metcalf's law that the utility of a network increases exponentially as each new user joins is a relatively simple concept that has been known since the first humans joined together into a community. Some of the greatest benefits of belonging to a group arise as a direct result of just belonging to that group. If you have a network but only one machine on it, the benefit of being on the network is very low. If, however, you add another machine and e-mail software, the value of being on the network just increased.

Now imagine if you added millions of computers on that network. All of a sudden we have created a utility that is so essential that we cannot live without it. It establishes a standard simply because of the volume of users. This concept is known as critical mass, and it is what e-businesses try to achieve when they start an online business or migrate their existing business over to the world of e-commerce.

Critical mass doesn't just apply to networks, it also applies to all types of groupings including the grouping of cells that make up your body. Just as there is a point where having enough of the right cells makes a human being viable, technological innovations and e-businesses also have a point where the volume of users makes them viable. Of course, if you don't manage the critical mass well, it can disappear and take the entire network, business, or body with it. In humans, nature handles the management of the critical mass of cells very well during the "start-up" phase, but in businesses the entrepreneurs take the place of nature, and the decisions that are made can either make the e-business viable or not. Nature has a definite advantage in this regard because it has had millions of years to perfect the start-up of life, but the downside is that it has no way to leverage this ability. Humans, on the other hand, have a magical learning curve that they can jump upon by learning about the task of starting up an organization from others. As a business leader, studying what successful companies have done will get you far up the e-commerce learning curve and partnering with other like-minded start-ups will further accelerate this process. It's all a game of leveraging your knowledge assets.

The Role of PR in Critical Mass

Gathering critical mass is the world of public relations, promotion, and advertising. Partnering with suppliers provides the opportunity to create a product offering that will encourage the creation of critical mass. Using advertising and promotion to attract visitors generates "traffic," and traffic can be leveraged into capital and even more traffic. Having a phone line was a great time saver and an essential part of everyone's life, but now thanks to a killer app called the Internet, having a single phone line is not enough. This is especially true when you start adding on functionality like telecommuting, online banking, and fax machines. The addition of these services onto an existing phone network has driven up the demand and volume traffic on that network without changing its basic functionality. So, critical mass for a new phone network can be generated through advertising that encourages people to make calls or by creating new uses for the network. The same is true for e-businesses. You can advertise to your customers to encourage them to visit your site, or you can add new functionality that everyone wants to use. This second method, if it creates critical mass, is called becoming the standard.

Sun Staroffice

You can download for free Sun Microsystem's new free software "staroffice" that provides similar functionality to Microsoft Office at www.sun.com.

Java is a standard; Windows is a standard; Microsoft Office is a standard; and HTML is a standard. They are standards because everyone uses them to the exclusion of other similar products. But being a standard doesn't guarantee longevity. Sun has released for free a competing software to Microsoft Office. That software, Linux, is a free operating system that rivals Windows, and HTML will soon be replaced with XML by its own creators.

Standards do change, and usually the market will opt for the best standard most of the time. In most cases, two competing applications or products that are considered competitive but different will go head to head to gain acceptance. In the old days the products competed on the basis of price and options. Pricing has now been removed from the equation thanks to the concept of creating critical mass by distributing the product for free. This means that two similar products that are distributed on the Internet will have to compete on the basis of what functions the application offers to the user.

Creating a Standard

You can, of course, tip the scales in your favor by partnering with other organizations to promote your product as the new standard. Another thing you can do is promote or advertise your product or distribute the product for free with other offerings. Microsoft Windows is the standard operating system primarily because it is distributed with new computers in agreements that Microsoft has made with vendors. Microsoft can also use this association to bundle other types of software with Windows, such as Internet Explorer.

However, the "product" that is offered doesn't have to be software. Providing content on your Web site or building a community online can be the "product" with the same principles about partnering and advertising to gain critical mass still applicable. You can distribute content, cross promote, or advertise with a partner for the benefit of both parties. MSNBC is an example of cross promotion through partnering where two large organizations, NBC and Microsoft, have joined to form a Web site where traffic is generated from both Microsoft's online Web site and through NBC's television broadcasts. More common partnerships include the using of one site's content on another site.

14

Learnlots.com

`Learnlots.com` is a Web site that supplies "how to" information for free on the Internet. When it establishes a partnership with another online company, that company will add a link to the `Learnlots.com` Web site. What makes the process unique is that the access to the `Learnlots.com` Web site will have the look and images of the referencing Web site (called a Webskin). That way customers at a company like `Firstsource.com` will still think they are on the Firstsource Web site.

The benefit of critical mass to an online Web site is that if you can get millions of visitors, you can earn money through the sale of advertising, click-through micropayments, or through sales commissions on products purchased by your visitors on a click-through. Critical mass also tends to add longevity as long as you continue to supply the base product for free and continue to provide repetitive value to your customers. However, where benefits accrue to one organization, another will be waiting around the corner to try and steal those benefits through competition.

Partnering Your Way to Critical Mass

One of the easiest ways to obtain critical mass is to partner. Partnering with other organizations extends the reach of your product beyond the traditional markets in which you operate. Everyone partners to gain critical mass—car companies use privately owned distributorships; Microsoft uses the computer retailers; McDonald's uses franchises; and authors use a publisher. In some cases, the payment will flow from one party to the other but in other situations, no money will exchange hands. Instead, the deal will be for the mutual exchange of something valuable like traffic (see Figure 1.2).

Global Access

The Internet didn't just provide extensive benefits because of its ability to communicate across North America. It provided significant benefits (or critical mass) because of its global nature. Countries, governments, businesses, and people all over the world are becoming wired to something that used to be exclusively American. The little Internet has become a global network capable of communicating with more than 100 million people, and this global reach has not only made the Internet more valuable as a utility, it has also made it more valuable as an informational tool. Now, anyone in almost any country can use this universal mechanism to communicate for personal reasons or to conduct business. This ability to communicate immediately, complemented by the worldwide courier services that are available to ship product, make the concept of being a global company much easier to achieve. In fact, just about any company that is on the Internet is already a global company.

Figure 1.2

The figure shows a survey that lists some of the Web sites with the heaviest traffic.

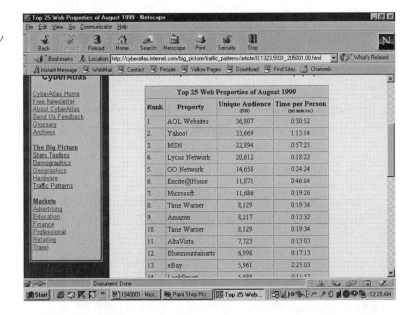

Top 25 Web Properties of August 1999			
Rank	Property	Unique Audience (000)	Time per Person (hr:min:sec)
1.	AOL Websites	36,807	0:30:52
2.	Yahoo!	33,669	1:13:14
3.	MSN	22,894	0:57:25
4.	Lycos Network	20,612	0:18:22
5.	GO Network	14,658	0:24:24
6.	Excite@Home	11,871	0:46:04
7.	Microsoft	11,686	0:19:26
8.	Time Warner	8,129	0:19:34
9.	Amazon	8,217	0:13:32
10.	Time Warner	8,129	0:19:34
11.	AltaVista	7,723	0:13:03
12.	Bluemountainarts	6,998	0:17:13
13.	eBay	5,961	2:25:03
14.	LookSmart	5,684	0:11:53

Traffic

When you visit a Web site, you are traffic and when you visit certain types of Web sites you become "lots" of traffic. Traffic is defined as the number of people who visit a Web site; however, when you visit some Web sites, you are counted as traffic at the site you are visiting as well as at the Web site that loads the banner ad, push content, etc. Traffic gives the world an indication of the number of visitors to a Web site, and this information can then be used by the site to charge for advertising, by investors to predict the company's value, or by advertisers to choose the best site to place their ads.

The continued growth of worldwide technology means that barriers to trade must fall to keep pace with the economic growth in the United States. Our ability to use technology to turn our businesses into e-businesses means that the rest of the world will have to mirror this growth in technological development in order to compete. This will arise as United States companies start exporting their technological expertise beyond their borders, much like Amazon.com is doing in Europe. Inside the U.S., more and more companies will continue to appear on the Internet with new product offerings, new applications, new content, etc.

Global Partners

Another advantage that global access provides is for two businesses on opposite sides of the world to partner. This is advantageous for organizations that can now communicate directly with suppliers in another part of the world to obtain better pricing or to track supply. For instance, a clothing manufacturer can now order cloth direct from the supplier instead of from a distributor and hopefully receive a lower price. Companies that stick to the old distribution lines will eventually supply product at costs significantly higher than their techno savvy competitors. Proprietary advantage will also disappear in a stampede of products that perform identically to the originals. Although branding will be the key to differentiation, it will not guarantee corporate survival.

The opportunities are endless. Global shopping, world-wide distribution, cross-border partnering, and distributed production are just some of the opportunities available to e-businesses. The ability to communicate with your Singapore, London, and San Francisco offices simultaneously in a variety of ways will give global corporations advantages unavailable to traditional companies. These advantages include lower cost of remote management, lower travelling expenses, and faster collaboration on projects managed from a central location.

Lower Transaction Costs

E-commerce provides the opportunity for traditional and new organizations to build structures that significantly lower the standard transaction costs for anything that they might sell. Electronic processing of any data is not free; however, some businesses are willing to bear this burden to provide other businesses with online applications that help them perform some of their day-to-day functions. For instance, if I have a store across the street from a library that has a public Internet connection, then I can set up a free e-mail address and not pay a single cent for it thanks to other online companies. I could do the same for building a Web page (see Figure 1.3). In reality it's unlikely that you would do this for your business, but you technically could conduct e-business transactions for absolutely no cost. The point is that e-commerce doesn't have to include multimillion dollar budgets to produce benefits for the small business.

Figure 1.3

Geocities is one online company that provides free Web space for building free Web pages such as the one shown.

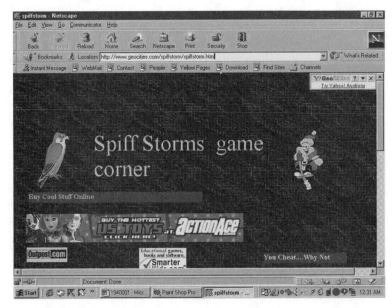

Lowering the cost of the way you do business is just one of the many advantages of technology—from simple tasks such as accepting orders online to complex tasks such as automating the entire back office of a large multinational organization along with its supply chain. Computers allow businesses to perform operational tasks more quickly and efficiently than humans. The staff can be directed to those tasks that computers are less capable of handling efficiently like development, sales, and management. The use of computers in this way lowers the transactional costs significantly by either reducing total overhead expenses or by the per unit transaction costs.

The Internet also provides companies and individuals with the opportunity to completely change the way they conduct business. It allows them to disseminate information and applications online and link with widely dispersed partners to add additional functionality and value for their customers. This allows them to build a "community of value*" that provides a discernible value to the membership of that community. The size of the community can then be used to attract advertising, link to online shopping sites in exchange for commission, or place direct links to other Web sites in exchange for micropayments or return traffic.

Of course, the ultimate business model is to be the first on the Net with a new application and to capture the status of a technological standard. That's called building a "killer app" as defined by Larry Downes and Chink Mui* in their book of the same name.

From the book Killer App *by Larry Downes & Chunka Mui, Harvard School of Business Press.*

Killer Apps

Downes and Mui identify what a killer app is and how to build one using the 12 rules of building a killer app. In short, a killer app is some form of technological breakthrough that as a result of certain characteristics becomes the standard that everyone uses, such as Windows. Other examples include the telephone, automobile, personal computer, and Internet. Downes & Mui also indicate that you can build the next killer app if you follow some basic rules and avoid some basic land mines lurking on the Internet. However, if you succeed in owning the next big technological change, such as the flying car for under $30,000, then you will likely capture the business success that goes with owning a market.

The key to the success of a killer app such as the PC has always been affordability for the masses and reliability. Even difficult products, such as the technology of today, can be accepted by the masses if the basic functionality of the product is easy to use, affordable, and reliable. It doesn't matter that you can fix a PC or install a network, as long as you know what makes a killer app a killer app, and as long as you make it accessible to your customers whether they are children or rocket scientists.

Killer Apps

Visit the killer app Web site at www.killer-apps.com to "speak your mind" in killer app forums or check out the "digital strategies center."

The Benefits of e-Commerce

The benefits of successfully retooling your company or building a new one are phenomenal. These benefits include access to a rapidly expanding market that is +100,000,000 people, state of the art technology that provides you with new ways to deliver your message and brand your image, instantaneous worldwide communications without long-distance charges, and the massive potential of the ability to interact with users in their very own home at an almost zero transaction cost. Companies at the forefront of this revolution, regardless of their industry, will succeed well into the new millennium, and their shareholders will be amply rewarded. The task, however, is not as easy as upgrading your computers to the next generation of faster machines. Instead, it will be a series of gut-wrenching decisions that may make or break your organization. The one thing that is clear is that waiting to be run over by Walmart or Amazon.com is never a healthy, long-term strategy. Either run and hide by repositioning your company, or turn on your e-competitors with your virtual sword held high.

The Least You Need To Know

➤ How faster computers are driving the e-commerce revolution.

➤ How faster connections are driving the e-commerce revolution.

➤ Why critical mass is important to e-commerce.

➤ What opportunities are presented by Internet globalization.

➤ How e-commerce leads to lower costs.

➤ What is a killer app?

The Sky Is the Limit: Internet Market Valuations

In This Chapter

➤ What you need to know about Internet stock

➤ Why Internet stock prices are so high

➤ Raising money for your e-commerce company

➤ Building a prospectus

Big Money, No Return

In 1999 Amazon.com released its annual report for the 1998 operating year. The aggregate market value noted in the report was in excess of $11 billion dollars; however, current estimates put the market capitalization at $22 billion. For a company that started from scratch in 1995, this growth rate is phenomenal. Amazon was the leader of the new wave of "e-tailers" (online retailers are often called e-tailers) exploding on the market back in 1997. Although Amazon initially started as a distributor of books through the Internet, they now sell electronics, conduct online auctions, and sell books, video, and music (see Figure 2.1).

Figure 2.1

The Amazon.com Web site provides extensive financial information about the company.

Amazon Customers

According to the Amazon Web site, its cumulative customer accounts are 10.7 million as of June 30, 1999.

www.Amazon.com

So to have a massive market value of $11 billion, Amazon must earn a great deal of money, right? Wrong. According to Amazon's financial statements for the year ending December 1998, Amazon.com lost in excess of $124 million. That's a great deal of money to lose, and yet the market value of the organization is still astronomical. They are not alone. For example, Ask Jeeves is a search engine that uses proprietary software to analyze grammatically correct English questions, such as "What is a dog?" in order to conduct Internet searches (see Figure 2.2). Ask Jeeves listed on the stock market in July, 1999 and within one day created a market net worth of just less than $1.6 billion. Its net income reported in its SEC filing documents on June 30, 1999 was not actually an "income" at all; rather, it was a loss of $10 million dollars for the prior three months.

These are only two of a long list of "money-losing" Internet companies that are posting record market valuations and stratospheric stock price increases. Compare this performance to the stock performances of the big blue chip organizations whose share prices are staying level or are falling, even though their profitability is stable. To understand why this is occurring, we have to understand how these stocks are issued and valued by the market.

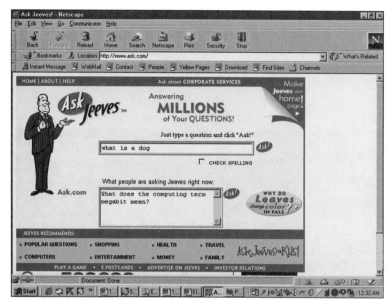

Figure 2.2

Ask Jeeves, the Internet search engine, is another Internet company that recently had a very successful IPO.

Stocks 101

Stock, as we know, is the piece of paper we receive when we buy a piece of a company. When a company decides that it wants to raise some money to fund its growth through the building of new plants, warehouses, or Web sites, it can borrow from the bank, or it can issue stock. Investors buy stock based on the anticipation of a return that is greater than leaving the money in the bank.

When a company is ready to issue stock, it goes through a relatively complex operation and series of requirements to do an initial public offering (often referred to as an IPO). At this point, the company receives a listing on a stock market (it gets a symbol and the right to sell the stock) and then issues a specific quantity of stock to the market at a certain price per share. Investors buy the stock, and depending on the demand, cause the price of the stock to rise or fall from its original issue price. Figure 2.3 shows a flow chart of the IPO process.

Underwriters are the large brokerage firms and banks that manage the process of issuing the stock, and in most cases, exclusively

Investor Information

To see a copy of the Amazon annual report, surf to www.amazon.com and use the About Amazon link to locate investor information. To view Ask Jeeves information, surf to www.ask.com and use the About link to locate investor information and SEC filings.

release the stock to large institutional investors first. The ultimate price or value of a share is dependent upon many factors, but in theory, it should reflect the net worth of the company's assets, its current net income level and forecast net income levels (which provides the basis for a return on investment calculation), and its potential future growth as measured by both the potential net worth of the company and its potential revenue stream.

Figure 2.3

The IPO process.

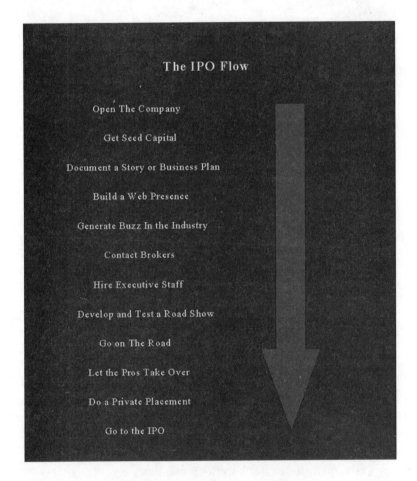

The IPO Flow

Open The Company

Get Seed Capital

Document a Story or Business Plan

Build a Web Presence

Generate Buzz In the Industry

Contact Brokers

Hire Executive Staff

Develop and Test a Road Show

Go on The Road

Let the Pros Take Over

Do a Private Placement

Go to the IPO

How To Lose Money and Still Be Worth a Billion

You may be curious as to what then drives the stock value of these companies through the roof, even though they are losing money. The answer is traffic. Traffic is Internet terminology for visitors to your Web site. Visitors, if they are managed correctly, will ultimately generate revenue. Initially, for most Web sites, this revenue is in the form of advertising, but it soon grows into sales commissions from affiliates and ultimately actual physical sales margins on product.

A comparable parallel example is advertising rates for newspapers. A newspaper that has a circulation of 200,000 people can charge hundreds of dollars per day for the ad revenue. The cost of producing the paper, of which the bulk is the actual newsprint, is covered by subscriptions. But the overhead cost of gathering the content, such as reporters' wages, is covered by the advertising. If the circulation of that paper rises, then so will the advertising rates because more readers will see the ads. What the newspaper is actually selling to the advertiser is traffic, or people reading the newspaper and potentially seeing the advertisement. With hundreds of ads in the paper, a revenue stream can produce significant profits.

How to Make Money the Internet Way

Now, let's say that you start a Web site on the Internet, and, after promoting it, start to generate traffic. Remember the newspaper numbers? Well, in general, a simple linking site can often generate thousands of hits within the first few months of operation.

Now, imagine the revenue from advertising for repeated exposure to traffic levels in the millions. Amazon receives in excess of 12 million visits or "hits" per month, and Yahoo boasts 65 million users. That's a lot of exposure for a company looking to advertise. Yet, the cost to Amazon of producing and displaying an ad is minimal compared to the cost of producing a newspaper. If you were an investor and you had the opportunity to invest in a newspaper or Amazon before it went public, which would you choose and how much would you value the stock? The original Internet IPOs, such as Yahoo and Amazon, started a stock market feeding frenzy that has not ceased (see Figure 2.4). However, it is becoming more difficult to achieve these record gains as investors start to question the value applied to these stocks. Can a company that is losing millions of dollars per year actually ever generate enough cash to grow?

Learnlots.com

Learnlots opened its Web site to the public in July 99 and by September was generating hits numbering 50,000/month.

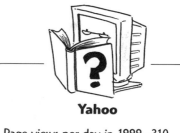

Yahoo

Page views per day in 1999—310 million.

Figure 2.4

There's lots of places to get information on a stock feeding frenzy like canoe.ca.

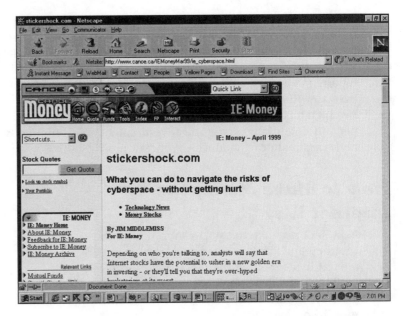

What Good Is a Traffic Jam?

Advertising revenue is only the tip of the iceberg. The real value of online exposure is the potential to tie that market into online retailing, or e-tailing. Millions of visitors can generate a great deal of advertising revenue, but just a fraction of those people buying products can generate a huge revenue volume that can easily dwarf ad revenues at the busiest traffic sites. For example, Lycos, the information search engine, had in excess of 30 million "unique visitors" according to statistics from Media Metrix for the month of July 99. Amazon was further down the list at just slightly more than 12 million visits. Yet, the market capitalization of Amazon was approximately $22 billion in September 99 (see Figure 2.5) while Lycos's market capitalization was approximately $3 billion. These figures reflect Amazon's potential to generate significant online revenue from its investments in distribution and e-tailing infrastructure.

Statistics

A great site for various Web statistics is www.cyberatlas.com.

Amazon has consistently reinvested the money it has raised in equity markets into systems and infrastructure, such as highly automated warehouses and e-commerce software. The result has been the turning of a community of book buyers into a community of shoppers, which has caused the investment community to sit up and take notice. Stock and market capitalization values are based on the potential growth of a company's net worth or the potential growth in revenue. An extremely efficient retail distribution network that does not have the overhead of expensive retail stores (yet has millions of visitors a year) should be worth a great deal. This is what drives the stock value of companies like Yahoo and Amazon so high. But it is not the only thing that inflates prices.

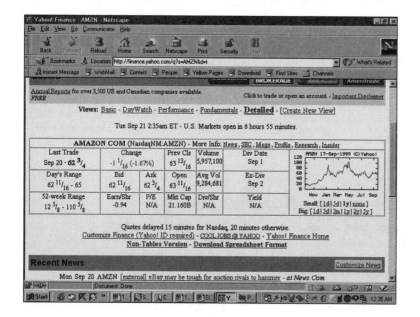

Figure 2.5

Yahoo provides free online financial stock quotes for all companies listed on various stock exchanges.

Hype, Greed, and Other Ways To Drive Up Stock Value

A wave of Internet IPOs combined with a rising stock market has created a circle of value that is adding significant upward pressure on Internet stock values. The *Wall Street Journal* reported a total of 380 IPOs in 1998. These IPOs generated a total of $35 billion in new capital for these companies. This year, more than half of the new IPOs according to *USA Today* are Internet-based.

Puffing Up the Market by Inflated Stock Prices

When a company issues stock, the underwriters attempt to place a per share value on the offering when it is released into the market. This pricing is based on values that the underwriters think will generate enough interest to sell out the issue. When the issue is released to the market, the underwriters will take their share of the stock and sell it first to their best institutional investors who, in turn, may release the stock into the open market. This is usually why some IPOs hit the open market at significantly higher levels than the initial pricing.

Day Traders

Day traders are stock traders who buy and sell stock on the same day hoping to make a profit before the stock market closes.

The second reason that a stock takes off after issue is due to pent-up demand driven by past successes. The IPOs of Yahoo and Amazon, for example, have underscored the potential profit that can be made from the initial rise in price. When Ask Jeeves (ASKJ) went public, the stock skyrocketed from a $14 per share issue price to more than $77 dollars in a single day. It has since fallen back. Stock price increases like that can lead day traders (stock traders who buy and sell a stock on the same day) to make exceptional profits over a short period of time. This potential profit attracts seasoned investors and stock neophytes alike, which creates upward pressure on the stock price and adds value to the pressure already created by the concept of traffic.

Everyone's Jumping on the Bandwagon

However, even companies that are established can benefit from the high Internet valuations. Existing retail organizations that are leveraging their expertise in procurement and distribution can easily move to the Internet and benefit from the move with increasing shareholder value. However, not all companies that move to the Internet will experience the same benefit. Sometimes, it can be difficult for companies to move past their entrenched market image to capture the heart and imagination of the market, which is a critical factor for new Internet IPOs. The key appears to be the willingness of the organization to develop more than just a virtual retail space. Building communities of value is one key to the process, as is the addition of new e-commerce initiatives, such as the redesign of distribution systems or the implementation of real-time back office systems.

Securities and Exchange Commission Information

Most annual reports and all prospectuses have some form of business plan incorporated in them. To view SEC filing documents including prospectuses, surf to www.sec.gov or look into the investor links on most Web sites, such as www.Yahoo.com or www.Amazon.com.

So—How Do You Issue Stock?

There are a number of steps related to the issuance of stock that e-commerce companies must carefully consider. Two critical steps in the process are the eventual creation of audited financial statements and the creation of a business plan, complete with the admission of potential risks. The business plan should also include the identification of key staff and a clear definition of your "killer app" (see Chapter 6, "Killer Apps").

Hey, We Don't Have a Track Record!

Investors seek information on an organization to help them define the potential future success that the organization will have. This information helps to establish a potential risk level in the investor's mind and a forecast level of return that he can anticipate. New Internet companies usually have no track record for either the organization or the application. How can an investor evaluate a new start-up company with a new killer app if no one else has ever done the same thing? The answer is that they use a mix of evaluating what history is available, traffic patterns, and what the business plan says. If an online retailer has built a Web site that attracts a consistent traffic flow, then the investor can use this as the basis for evaluating the success of the organization, but only with reference to what the company plans to do with the traffic, what competition is out there, etc. However, just because a company has a limited history does not mean that it will be unable to raise money. In fact, the pressure is on the investor not to miss the next Amazon.

Develop a Good Story and Start Writing It Down

A "story" in start-up investing lingo is the business plan of the organization. Internet business plans usually cannot rely on an industry comparison or a past track record of the company simply because neither exist. Half of the battle of raising capital or completing a successful IPO is to have a good clear story that usually includes a "killer app" (discussed in Chapter 6). The more clear and precise the plan is, the greater the demand that will be created for the stock. A plan that includes limited financial information can include other types of info to help the investor evaluate the company or the idea.

Other Information in Business Plans

➤ Who is the Org?

➤ Goals

➤ App details

➤ Any market information

➤ Executives' backgrounds

➤ Risks

➤ Financial information

A Good Outline Is Essential

After you have created an outline of the information that you are going to include in the business plan, start filling in the information immediately. Make sure that your document is in a format similar to those used by successful start-ups in their IPO prospectus. Start this process when the business is still in the development stage. The benefit from starting early is that by the time you are ready to raise second level capital or do an IPO, you essentially have a prospectus that you can provide to potential investors. If you have a rough prospectus already created, you can save yourself an incredible amount of effort and expense. The document should look professional and should be delivered to investors with a "road show" or executive presentation.

Putting on the Ritz

Testing a road show involves writing, directing and producing presentations of varying length from five minutes to three hours and trying to pre-answer as many potential investor questions as possible. Testing also involves choosing key staff to make the presentation, ensuring that they are equipped with all the market information that is available, that they clearly understand the plan, that they know how to close a deal, and that they have practiced the presentation numerous time in front of video cameras and test groups.

A Corporate Shopping List—Fundamental Requirements To Attract Investors

➤ Computer equipment

➤ Answering service

➤ Development software

➤ Communication to the Internet

➤ Low traffic Web hosting

➤ Domain name registration

➤ Trademarking

➤ Patent registration

➤ Application development staff

➤ Web development staff

➤ Web content and graphics

➤ Phones, travel, supplies

➤ Administration staff

➤ Executive staff

Just before your road team leaves, ensure that your Web site is running. It doesn't have to be completed, but it does have to have some information and functionality that investors and other parties can look at. The first stop for your team should be personal visits to affiliated companies that you would like to partner with, such as search engines.

Personally visiting your partner sites makes a more favorable impression, as opposed to phone calls, and this favorable impression can start what is called a "buzz." Industry buzz about a new company is a very powerful ally when your road team has to approach second level investors. As you create a buzz, people should be able to surf to your Web site to get more information about your company or to see your Internet application. The goal is to create that buzz just prior to approaching the investment community for second level financing. If the lag time is too great between creating the buzz and raising second level financing, the buzz may die out, and the job of selling the organization will be more difficult. If the buzz is growing, then the likely reception from the investment community will be at least one of interest.

Locating Seed Capital for Your Business

Seed capital is the first financing that you will require to assist your company to construct the basic pieces to move to second level financing. In an Internet company, there are a number of tasks that need to be funded at the start.

The seed capital will have to be enough to carry the organization through to the second level financing.

A timetable for implementation must be developed to ensure that the cash doesn't disappear before the second level financing is obtained. Often, the seed capital is obtained from family or friends, and sometimes it is obtained from venture capital firms. Seed capital raised is usually exchanged for voting stock, and a board of directors is also appointed from the investors. The board should be chosen for their experience and expertise because they will help to define the business plan and may provide valuable contacts and support. Executives may provide work in exchange for an equity position in the organization. This will greatly aid in reducing the largest expense.

Building a Presence in the Marketplace

Creating a buzz is only effective if you have a presence. This means that the organization must build an actual operation, whether it's a physical operation with an office, phones, and development lab, and so on, or it's a virtual operation with only a Web site. The point is that interested people need a place to go to get more information. Often, the most cost-effective presence is an informational Web site. These low traffic Web sites are primarily placed to highlight an application, product, service, or company. The Web site will disseminate information to interested users and help to spread the buzz by making it easy for people to find the information and pass on the location of this information to others. You should also ensure that the site is registered with all major search engines.

Hiring the Right Executive Staff Will Save Headaches Later

Any company needs staff. Depending on the ultimate size of your organization, your key individuals or executive team will be an important piece of the overall team that will be an integral part of the business plan. Their background is essential to the success of the IPO because their experience or fit for the organization will be reviewed very closely by investors to reduce any perceived risk. If the risks to the organization are too great, the investors will not provide the financial backing that you require.

Key Personnel

Most companies promote their key executives. To see an example of key employees, go to www.ezonenetworks.com and follow the Corporate Services link to Key Personnel.

Your executive team should be experienced in their field with a proven and familiar track record. They should also have the correct blend of experience. If your killer app is highly technical, then your executive team's experience should reflect technical backgrounds, such as electrical engineering degrees, application development management, and so on. If your Web site depends on promotion and marketing, then the

Learnlot's Capital Expansion

In 1999 Learnlots.com opened a Web portal to provide Learnlets, which are step by-step instructional tutorials on a variety of topics. They raised initial seed capital from business associates and used that capital to travel to the affiliates and the investment community with the goal of raising second level financing of $2 million and to start the process of building their Webskin technology. This amount represented the funding required to expand the content of the Web site and to generate enough traffic for the next step in the process—the preparation of the IPO. In September 1999, the second level financing was complete.

executive staff should reflect this value with their experience in marketing and business development. Many organizations recruit top-level executives only for their reputation and experience. Some of these CEOs don't even become involved in the day-to-day operations of the organization, but are simply paid for their presence at board meetings.

NASDAQ

The NASDAQ Web site has some excellent information available for the companies that are moving to an IPO. This information clearly details the requirements for the issuance of stock, including the usage of brokers to raise the capital. You can find the Web site at http://www.nasdaq.com.

Approaching the Market— Private Placement

After you have obtained some seed financing, created a presence, collected information on the business plan and the company, and started the process of building your killer app, the next step will be to start approaching the financial community to raise second level financing. Venture capital firms or wealthy investors usually supply second level financing, also called interim or bridge financing, venture capital, or private placement financing. Many retired CEOs are involved in this type of financing through their investment companies, as are many large technical organizations like Microsoft or Intel. The role of these individuals varies from company to company with some people demanding controlling ownership (the right to make decisions) and other people investing as silent partners. Some investors require voting stock, while others invest with no voting stock.

The decision of which type of investor to bring into the organization depends on a number of factors. If you have created a significant buzz about your product or service, or you have developed a significant traffic level, then you will have more options about which type of investor will provide funding. If you do not have a widely known application, then your choices will be limited. This is the fundamental reason why it is important to create a buzz and traffic to your Web site prior to attempting to raise capital.

Be forewarned that you will be required to give up some of your stock ownership to these investors and the amount of control they will exercise over your organization will depend on their level of involvement. It is standard practice to issue Class "A" preferred shares to initial investors. These shares are usually convertible to the common stock that will ultimately be listed on the open market. The common shares are called "widely dispersed," and they are the shares that are listed on the stock exchange and traded by the public on the open market. Preferred shares provide the seed or second-level investors with the right to protect their investments before common shareholders.

However, by having a say in the organization usually with a place or a "seat" on the board requires the ownership of common or voting stock. That way the seed or second-level investor can influence and monitor the progress and direction of the firm. This often results in complex stock structures with different classes of stock that imply different rights and obligations. In these instances, a class "A" stock will have different rights than a class "B" stock, such as the option to convert to class "B."

The primary purpose of second-level investors is to provide the funding necessary to take the organization to the next level of funding, which is the IPO. The funding obtained at the second level will be used to grow the organiza-

Standard Prospectus Table of Contents

➤ Introduction

➤ Business strategy

➤ Development (what has been built or owned)

➤ Market or industry (if it is available)

➤ Areas of growth

➤ Risk factors

➤ Executive officers and directors

➤ Legal proceedings

➤ Stock

➤ Financial statements

➤ Notes to the financial statements

➤ Report from the auditors

➤ Management discussion of financial statements

tion by hiring the staff necessary to fill out operations such as marketing, investor relations, back-office and development, and to build traffic levels to the Web site through promotion and advertising. The company will incur very large expenses related to preparing for a stock issue. The business plan will have to be turned into a prospectus and printed often at a cost of many thousands of dollars. The road show team will run up significant hotel and travel expenses as it generates investment interest. Advertising, such as banner ads, and the development and execution of promotional programs including travel expenses, press releases, displays, and development, will all require extensive capital.

Completing the Story

After your second level financing is in place and you have the staff in place necessary to complete development on the Web site, you can start the process of taking the organization public. There are a number of things that must be completed prior to issuance of stock on a market like NASDAQ.

One of the things that must be completed is the prospectus, based on the business plan that you have gathered to date. You also need a set of audited financial statements inclusive of balance sheet, income statement, and a statement of changes in financial position and notes.

The prospectus and the audited financial statements provide the basis of the documentation necessary to go to the market with an IPO. Of course, each stock exchange has a complex series of rules and requirements, and some of the money raised in the second level financing should be used to hire the lawyers and brokerage professionals to take on the task of issuing a successful IPO. These professionals are a great asset in the battle to issue stock, but they are not entirely necessary. There are organizations that will assist you in issuing stock on major markets without the exceptionally high fees extracted by traditional brokers (see Figure 2.6).

Letting the Pros Take Over or Getting Help

Once you are ready to issue your initial public offering of stock, you can involve an investment banker or a brokerage firm. They will take your preliminary prospectus, financial statements, and other information and determine whether the concept can be sold to the market. If they decide that the stock is marketable, they will provide one of two types of agreements. They will agree to guarantee the sale of the stock by purchasing it all or they

Red Herring

A red herring is a prospectus that is distributed prior to the IPO to generate interest. It is called a red herring because it has red print in the margins and at the top.

Figure 2.6

W R Hambrecht is one company that assists Internet companies with their IPOs.

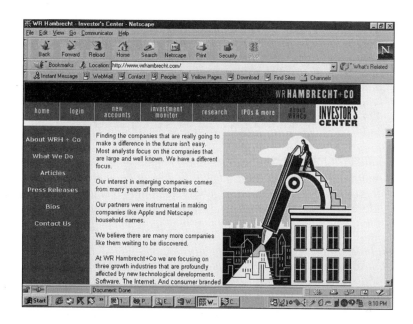

will agree to distribute the stock on a "best efforts" basis. Companies like Goldman Sachs or Solomon specialize in taking companies to the market in IPOs. They have the contact with market stock analysts and the expertise to complete the formalities of the issue, such as the printing and distribution of both a final prospectus, as well as red herrings.

These companies will also assist in the completion of the process by setting up a series of analyst meetings so that your road team can make presentations (often called a "dog and pony show"), manage filing with the Securities and Exchange Commission (SEC), combine with other brokerages in a syndicate to distribute the stock, and release information and analysis after the stock has been issued. They will be compensated by a spread between the issue and sale price or set fees that are deducted from the money raised in the issue. The entire process of issuing stock is complex and costly; however, if the story or business plan is solid, then the task will be made easier with the assistance of investment bankers or brokerages.

NASDAQ Market Value

1995 $1.1 Trillion

1999 $3.1 Trillion (July YTD)

Nasdaq Web site

This Decade Hits the Highest Level of Investment Ever

Another thing that is driving up the value of the stock market is the greatest volume of total investment capital ever in our history. This massive volume of money that is searching for a home is the result in increasing retirement savings in all age groups and the ease of investing provided by online services like E-trade.com.

Another record that has been set is the number of individual investors in the stock market. This is a result of the large proportion of the population in the 30–50 age range, who are involved in investing in the stock market. They also have the highest per capita disposable income ever.

The combination of the highest level of disposable income in the largest number of middle-aged individuals has lead to an excess of capital searching for investments in the market. This is one of the factors that has lead to astronomical Internet valuations, in addition to the other factors outlined throughout the chapter.

The Least You Need to Know

➤ Why Internet stock prices are so high.

➤ How to determine the value of traffic.

➤ How to develop a good story or business plan.

➤ How to approach the market.

➤ What is creating a buzz?

➤ What is seed capital?

➤ What to consider when hiring staff.

➤ How to build a presence.

➤ How to raise money with a private placement.

JIMMY JACK'S ONLINE BAIT SHACK

The Next Great e-Commerce Company—Yours

In This Chapter

➤ Implications of e-commerce

➤ e-Commerce enabled operations

➤ The future direction of technology

➤ Technology strategy

Any Company Can Capitalize on e-Commerce Today

Just how difficult is e-Commerce? It can be as simple as building a Web site or as complex as reengineering your entire company—and given that e-commerce technology changes at breakneck speed, just keeping pace with the changing world will be a full-time task. Since it is impossible for any single individual to keep pace with all the changes to technology that are occurring today, you may require the assistance of staff, consultants, outsourced services, and suppliers. Just one aspect of e-commerce, such as the Internet, requires extensive knowledge of Web languages like HTML, XML, or Java. And then there are the thousands of applications you might need to know, such as search engines, Web servers, communications, and networking—all of which are significantly different than the internal technology structure of most organizations.

It is vital to position your organization to take advantage of any changes in technology that may be applicable to your company. Make no mistake—buying the newest of everything can be a very inefficient use of your cash if the benefits from the

XML, HTML, and the World Wide Consortium

To understand the future of the Internet, surf to the W3 consortium Web page at www.w3.org.

technology are not yet available to the organization. In fact, applications such as Web casts (see Figure 3.1) are interesting to study, but at this time yield little in the way of material benefits to the average organization due to their limited quality. However, other technological changes, such as building a Web site, are both immediately applicable to most organizations and financially beneficial.

Figure 3.1

You can see a variety of Web casts on sites like zdnet.com.

Web Casts

A Web cast is a streaming of bits of data between a server and a client computer. The data bits can be sound, video, or text, and they are usually used by technology companies to promote new products.

Understanding Technology— The Key to Your New e-Business

The task of restructuring your organization requires that you clearly understand the implications of e-commerce, as well as the technology. Since it is unlikely that you have the time to do it alone, you will need to hire a technically competent staff. However, if you've tried to hire technical people before, you know that in this environment the best e-commerce experts are difficult to find, difficult to hire, and difficult to keep. This is doubly true of individuals who have crossover expertise between e-commerce and operations such as logistics.

One thing that will greatly aid in this task of managing your technical resources is for the people at the top of the organization to understand e-commerce, which is the goal of this book. You will need to understand concepts, such as building a community of value, that may be lost on the most technically competent Web designer. However, for one single person to understand everything—from how to issue an IPO to how to code a servlet in Java—is asking far too much.

Informit

To see the volume of technical jobs posted on the hundreds of Internet job boards, try surfing to http://www.informit.com/jobs. We searched on the keyword "technology" under the computer listing and found more than a thousand jobs.

Any organization can benefit from e-commerce, including those organizations that already have an existing Web presence; perhaps they can benefit from a review of their old operations. Corporations expend a great deal of resources in servicing their customers through retail locations, service departments, and call centers. But this old style of operating structure is predicated on the notion that communications and distribution will never be efficient enough to operate centrally.

The Role of Communications in the e-Business

In fact, during the 80s, a movement away from the centralized strategies of the prior decades was well underway with the move to satellite offices, complete with stand-alone accounting departments. Actually, some large organizations had entity charts that had hundreds of legal entities. However, organizations rapidly realized that they could again capture significant savings by re-centralizing their operations to gain advantage in areas such as data storage, call centers, hub distribution, and centralized management. The results were a more efficient use of resources and stronger overall profitability.

However, a problem existed with communications and delivery. Without decentralized sales and distribution outlets, there was no way to effectively market or communicate with the end customers. When the Internet became a tool used by the average household, the opportunity for manufacturers to talk directly to the customer opened a world of opportunity. Retail outlets could be made redundant or at least more efficient since the customers could get information about the products sold and have them shipped directly to their home or office. Service returns could be reduced, thereby increasing customer satisfaction by providing better information to the customers. Distribution could be outsourced to courier companies that delivered products faster and cheaper than the manufacturers' own distribution network.

Online Services

To see an online brokerage, surf to
www.etrade.com.

Service organizations have also learned to capitalize on the new age of communications by providing online products, such as virtual brokerages for selling stock, information and news services, and integrated help services such as the major search engines. Essentially, we have moved from the industrial age where we learned to turn raw material into finished products with a high level of efficiency, through the technological age where we learned to store and manage information, and finally into the age of rapid, global communications.

The Age of Communication

So how will this new age of communication affect your organization? It will depend on what type of organization you operate and how good your understanding of this new world of e-commerce is. Manufacturers that have an extensive network of distributors and sales staff may find that direct selling to customers through the Internet is more profitable and provides a greater growth potential than capital spent on distributor network expansion. However, if manufacturers rush to set up a sales Web site and do not clearly understand concepts like "communities of value,"* it may result in those manufacturers being relegated to act only as suppliers to their competitor's Web site (see Chapter 6, "Killer Apps," for more extensive coverage of communities of value).

Local information providers who can successfully extend their reach on the Internet may find themselves out of business if they attempt to hoard or make proprietary any information that is currently freely distributed. Software companies that build applications but refuse to distribute them as freeware over the Internet in order to capture critical mass will find themselves without the ability to attract enough users to be profitable. So, it is vital not only to understand the technology, but also to understand the concepts of e-commerce in order to remain competitive and strong in the next century.

e-Commerce Enabled Operations

Structuring your current operations so that they are e-commerce-enabled is a task that is made far easier if the operations are brand new. Companies that start with a blank sheet of paper have the best chance of building operations that take full advantage of the current e-commerce environment. This doesn't imply that companies that want to reengineer their current operations will fail. In fact, you could argue that experience and existing company efficiency reduces the potential of failure, as opposed to the blank page theory.

* A phrase coined by Downes & Mui from the book *Killer App*

Keeping Innovation Alive

Anyone who has ever custom built a house knows that after the first few months of building, he will start to see things that could be done better. The same concept applies to building or reengineering e-commerce applications. Often, the most successful new organizations are those that are designed by using a blank sheet of paper by individuals with a variety of talent and experience.

However, to encourage innovative thinking, some ground rules should be required, such as never allow anyone to say "it can't be done" or "that's not the way it's currently done." The response to these statements should be that you will choose the best ideas, regardless of their origin or history, and that every problem has a solution. It should be the ultimate benefit to the company that will drive whether or not the solution is feasible.

Sears Successfully Makes the Leap into e-Commerce

One company that has successfully moved to Internet retailing is Sears. It has opened an e-commerce retail presence, but has also incorporated its own payment technologies, using Sears credit cards and delivery methods through partner distribution points and even a Spanish site (see www.sears.com).

Understanding e-Commerce Can Save You Money and Headaches

Enabling your existing operations requires an extensive understanding of e-commerce applications that may directly impact your company. You need to understand the functionality of any new technology and how these functions will impact your current corporate procedures. For example, many organizations installed proxy servers on their networks that allowed multiple users to share modem pools or a router connection to the Internet. The executives clearly understood that access to the information contained on the Web was vital to creating innovative operations. What they didn't expect was that their employees would spend an excessive amount of time surfing the Web at the expense of company productivity.

A second example of the application of technology is the use of Internet video to conduct online meetings. Companies decided that video technology would promote communication

NetMeeting—Not Your Regular Online Boardroom

To obtain a copy of the NetMeeting software, surf to www.microsoft.com, search for netmeeting, and follow the download link.

between employees. The capability to use software, such as NetMeeting to conduct "video phone" meetings, does encourage communication. The problem is that it also uses most of the bandwidth on the corporate networks and causes them to grind to a halt. You have to estimate the impact of a new technology on your resources and decide whether this impact is going to provide a benefit greater than the expense of the technology.

The Future Direction of Technology

Another thing you have to decide is the future direction of the technology. In order to foresee the future of a particular technology, you need to clearly understand its implications on the market and second-guess its level of future user acceptance.

An awareness of what the technology means to the current market is an excellent starting point, and the best source for information on new technologies is the Internet. Even though it is fundamental to stay abreast of new technology, it should not become the sole focus of your executive team. Their familiarity with the direction of technology is important, but others can more efficiently compile and report on such change, and a number of companies offer such services.

These organizations can also provide you with a direction that they think the technology will take, although you will have to be careful of hidden agendas. For example, asking a Microsoft Solutions Partner for information about the future of a Microsoft product is unlikely to reveal any usable information. However, asking the Linux guys why you should buy their product instead of Microsoft NT will likely yield very good information about the future direction of the Microsoft product. In both cases, the individuals who are answering will have a bias toward their own product. The greatest difficulty arises when a new technology is introduced, but no one has analyzed its performance, functionality, or usefulness. For these types of situations, you will have to rely on the information provided by test labs, eZines (see Figure 3.2), or consultants.

After you have studied changes in technology and the applicability of these changes to your company's operations, the next step will be to decide whether you are capable of integrating these new technologies into your operations. Resources have to be made available, including staff, equipment, and outsourcing. You will have to decide whether you need to raise funds to implement the technology and raise these funds if required. Then you will have to map out the internal processes affected and the changes to those processes. You will also have to implement the technology and review the success of the implementation. Finally, you will have to continuously study changes to the technology and other associated technologies. You should always have a contingency plan ready to help bail you out and implement a replacement application if necessary.

A perfect example is network technology. Whether a company installs either Linux or NT is a decision that must be decided today by many organizations. There are pros and cons of both systems; however, a decision to use one of these systems while completely ignoring the other may prove to be a very costly decision. If Linux replaces NT as the dominant standard (and it does have strong support), then investment in NT may be an expensive decision. However, if Linux is chosen as the corporate technology of choice, the risk is that its critical mass will not be attained, and you will have invested in the wrong technology. A more likely scenario is that you will invest in one technology or the other, only to have an application on the Internet change the entire way that networking works.

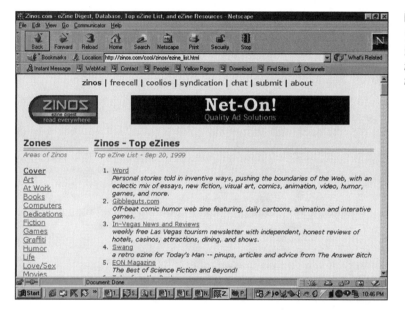

Figure 3.2

You can get updated information from Web magazines, more commonly known as eZines.

New e-Commerce Applications

There are a variety of new programming applications ready to be released into the market. However, an application in the language of e-commerce doesn't just refer to programs or programming languages, but also refers to the entire way that a type of business is conducted electronically. For example, search engine software is a relatively simple application program, but a search engine Web site includes a number of programmed applications, such as free e-mail and messaging software all combined in one location (see Figure 3.3).

This combination of regular applications is itself an e-commerce application. It is an important distinction because if you only consider e-commerce as the programming of or implementation of a programmed application, you are missing a significant piece of the e-commerce puzzle. E-commerce applications do include actual programs, such as shopping cart software used to create online orders at retail Web sites, but also include concepts such as real-time systems, virtual corporations, and critical mass. One of the new applications that may soon be released on the Internet includes a free suite of software that is comparable to Microsoft Office 2000 but is free to use and copy. Other applications include free help sites that have thousand of step-by-step instructions on thousands of topics, low cost, direct-to-home Internet connections that bypass the Internet Service Providers like America Online, or Web TV that requires only a keyboard, TV, and small processor hub.

Figure 3.3

There are a variety of applications available on the Web portals like Yahoo.

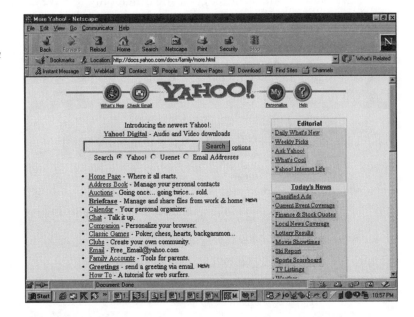

Evaluating New Technologies

Each of these new applications may or may not have a direct impact on your business. Accepting a new technology may put you way in front of your competitors, or it may simply allow you to keep pace with them. Others applications may be very interesting but will provide limited or no benefit to your organization. There is even the threat that a new technology may not be accepted at all, and if a company has invested heavily in that particular technology, the company may even go bankrupt.

Each new application that enters the marketplace must be carefully evaluated for its applicability to your company. Sometimes it is best to let your young, technically hip staff play with the applications first and then report to you on their functionality and usefulness. In fact, some organizations have positions that do nothing but this type of evaluation. Your staff's ability to understand the connection between these new technologies and such concepts as resource efficiency and impact on business strategy will be limited. However, you should encourage them to give their insight and opinions, and you should carefully review this input before you or your board of directors makes any decision about technology.

Technology Strategy

Every organization regardless of its size should have a technology strategy in place reviewed and approved by the board of directors. The implications of the tech strategy are so important that they should never be exclusively left to a chief information officer or technical leader. If you are uncertain of the technology, then you can mitigate the risks by obtaining the second opinion of an outside consultant (see Figure 3.4).

A technology strategy is nothing more than a goal for the entire organization and a map of how to get the company from where it currently is to that goal. Along the way are markers or smaller goals with scheduled times attached. The strategy should be periodically reviewed to measure how close you are to the smaller goals (also known as benchmarks or milestones).

It is important to remember that since technology changes so rapidly, these strategies should be developed and approved quickly and changed or updated frequently. Technology companies sometimes use a running strategy or one that is never fixed, and most sophisticated organizations employ a strategy technique that places a set time frame on the use of a new technology. Then once the application is installed or implemented, it stays in use for a set period of time, such as two years, before any upgrades or changes are made.

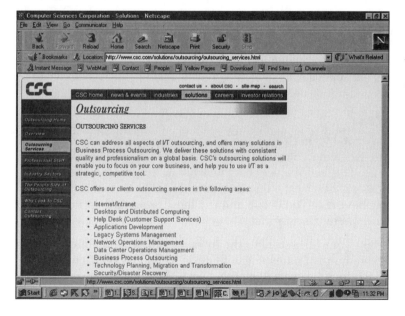

Figure 3.4

CSC is a company that provides staff to organizations seeking to outsource some tasks.

Another more costly way to reduce the risk to the company from changes in technology is to outsource to organizations that specialize in leasing technological solutions. It is important to understand that not all new technology implemented by the organization will be successful, but if you test a group of technologies carefully and clearly understand the implication of each technology on your company's operations, the likelihood of failure will be significantly reduced.

The Technology Template

The technology template is a series of standards that the corporation has decided will be the long-term technological environment of the organization. For example, I may want to develop applications for my employees, and therefore I may set as a long-term standard that the corporate Intranet will be the primary delivery mechanism for these applications. This establishes a way for the company to analyze new technology. If it doesn't work on the intranet, then it has failed an important hurdle in the analysis process. However, it should not be the only measure of acceptance. For example, a new type of application delivery mechanism that is cheaper than the corporate intranet, such as delivery over the Internet, may prove to be a more beneficial solution to the organization. Testing technology on the basis of a number of parameters is important for any organization.

All of these standards when combined will help you define a technology template that can be used to provide some level of assurance that a new application is appropriate for the company. It doesn't guarantee that the technology won't fail; it simply provides you with some assurance that the technology is likely to provide a benefit to the company. It is also important to understand that even with a comprehensive template, some new technologies will not be easy to assess and will have to be studied by the corporation. The best solution is to develop a technology test lab or contract out these services. A template can be provided to the testing facility, and they should be able to return an opinion of applicability.

Where Do You Start?

When you've finally convinced yourself that you want your company to be an e-commerce powerhouse, where do you start? You start by looking at where you are and where you want to go. This is not a very easy task because it requires something that no book can provide: business savvy. It's the whole reason you are in business in the first place. You either have it or you don't, and the most important application of business savvy is deciding where you want to go.

Whether you decide to take your little store to the Internet will depend a great deal on whether you have the resources and expertise to do so. If you do set that as a goal for your company, the path to get there will be filled with Web site development, computer upgrades, distribution agreements, e-commerce technology, and i-commerce strategy. On the other hand, you may just simply want to make your back office more efficient so that product flows more quickly to your customers. This goal may be as simple as implementing a new order entry system and using Internet courier delivery application (see Figure 3.5).

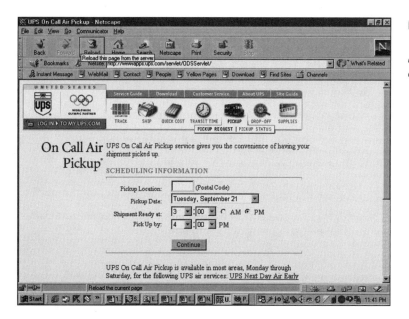

Figure 3.5

UPS provides worldwide delivery services using an online order system.

The best place to start is to decide how you would like your operations to change based on the concepts outlined in this book. You can then map a path to this goal by setting mile markers, such as restructuring your internal operations, building a Web presence, doing application development or partnering, and obtaining partners and affiliates. Always ensure that you do not stretch beyond the capacity of your resources or else you will make timing mistakes that may be costly or critical. These mistakes may include generating buzz and traffic before the Web site is available, approaching the market with an IPO before your Internet application is ready, and generating online sales without a fully functional back office to take orders or implement a technology before it has attained critical mass.

Developing Strategies

A strategy is essentially a game plan—one that is going to increase your chances of a win. The process involves setting a single corporate goal and then establishing smaller goals that will lead to the attainment of the corporate goal (called a strategy map). You will also need to place times or dates beside these smaller markers so that you are aware of how close you are to your goals (or the path).

The Least You Need To Know

➤ Any company can capitalize on e-commerce today.

➤ You must clearly understand the impact of e-commerce.

➤ The new age of communication will directly impact your company.

➤ You must carefully analyze new technology and its future direction.

➤ You can build a technology strategy.

➤ Technology templates define the technical standards for the organization but are only one tool used when evaluating an application.

e-Commerce Defined

In This Chapter

➤ e-commerce versus i-commerce

➤ Why e-commerce is so important

➤ How to build a Web presence

➤ What are back-office systems?

➤ An e-commerce example (and one that isn't)

---

e-Commerce versus i-Commerce

e-Commerce is derived from the phrase electronic commerce, and i-commerce is derived from the phrase Internet commerce. The world today uses both phrases interchangeably, but in practice i-commerce is a subset of e-commerce. For example, if I enter a customer order in my computer and it automatically generates both an electronic invoice and an electronic sales journal entry in the general ledger, that's considered e-commerce. If I e-mail the invoice to my customer via the Internet, as shown in Figure 4.1, that's considered both i-commerce and e-commerce. Most of the general press coverage today is focused on i-commerce or doing business on the World Wide Web; however, most of the industry press is dedicated to the wider concept of e-commerce.

Figure 4.1

You can email an invoice to customers as one way to conduct e-commerce.

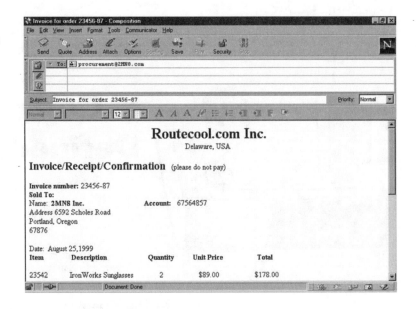

Why the Difference?

It helps to keep things organized if we consider e-commerce as "business conducted exclusively through an electronic format" and i-commerce as "business conducted through an electronic format on the Internet." Both elements are vital to the survival of any organization in the next millennium. The systems in your company that electronically communicate with each other are e-commerce systems, and they should be able to function effortlessly with any Internet applications that you are planning to use. However, e-commerce isn't just about conducting business on the Internet; it also refers to any electronic functions that assist a company to conduct business. These functions can include electronically managing old paper-based tasks such as creating accounting journal entries, or manufacturing tasks such as an automated assembly line or order entry (see Figure 4.2).

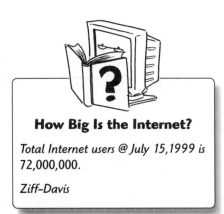

How Big Is the Internet?

Total Internet users @ July 15, 1999 is 72,000,000.

Ziff-Davis

Who Put the "e" in Commerce?

Many progressive companies are performing some level of e-commerce. A small company that types an invoice on a word processor is conducting some business electronically. So the buzz around e-commerce doesn't pertain to anything new, because companies have been using computers for decades. It has gained massive press attention recently only because of the explosive growth of the Internet and the pressure on all companies to join this cyberlinked world. Companies like ebay, whose home page is shown in Figure 4.3, are succeeding on the Internet and forcing other companies to give serious consideration to the jump to cyberspace.

Figure 4.2

An online invoice in Navision will automatically create journal entries.

Figure 4.3

ebay is a successful online auction site that uses e-commerce.

The primary factor that has made the growth of the Internet so strong is that so many people have joined the Internet community. This large group of users (called critical mass) has drawn the business world like horses to water. After all, what business can refuse a large group of people located in one place? Well, not physically in one place, but more spiritually in one place. The Internet is essentially a community or gathering place. We all go to the Internet to get, give, or exchange information, and the communal nature of the Web is the main attraction for corporations hungry for opportunities to advertise or sell.

The Internet goes one step further than your average communal information watering hole. It maintains detailed and very highly controlled information about who is at which part of the watering hole. This makes it very easy for corporations to target their advertising to their customers by either placing the advertising where their customers "hang out," like banner advertising (see Figure 4.4), or by attracting customers to their side of the watering hole, called "generating traffic."

Figure 4.4

Banner advertising like this at the bottom of the Web page is one form of online advertising to reach your target market.

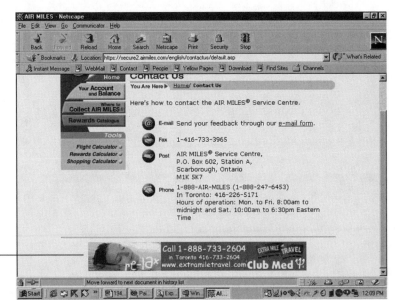

Banner ad ——————

What's All the Buzz?

The big buzz about e-commerce today is the substantial cost savings that would occur if a company's business were entirely electronic. This includes functions such as buying and selling, shipping products, or producing financial statements—and all without human intervention. This is the real "e" in e-commerce. Humans, of course, will not disappear entirely. They will simply move to other tasks that generate real value, such as personalized customer service, sales, corporate development, or new product research. They will no longer do those tasks that can be handled faster and more efficiently by a computer, such as creating journal entries, sending purchase orders, or confirming shipments. If a company uses computers extensively to perform internal functions, we say that they are *"e-commerce ready or capable."*

One of the biggest underlying costs in any organization is labor and the support of that labor by maintaining office space, travel expenses, phones, and so on. Most of the individuals working in organizations throughout the 70s and 80s did not generate any actual revenue. These positions *supported* the generation of revenue but did not *earn* any revenue. To make matters worse, the majority of tasks were related to communications such as typing memos, managing information, or producing reports.

The Internet started as a way for large computer installations to share electronic information, but it rapidly attracted individual users who were able to share personal electronic communications, like the e-mail shown in Figure 4.5. It didn't take long for companies to realize that they could communicate over this network with their satellite offices and reduce their long distance expenses, travel charges, mail costs, and the typing pool (first human casualties). i-commerce was born.

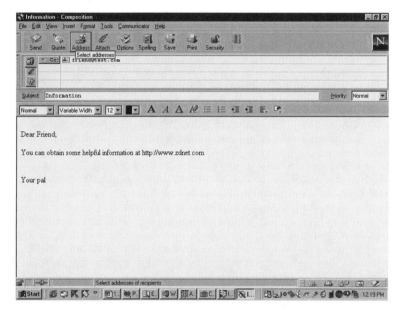

Figure 4.5

An e-mail is an excellent way to communicate with other people electronically.

Go Play on a Busy Highway

The Information Superhighway (as the Internet is sometimes called) is easily accessible for anyone with a computer and a phone line. By connecting to a local ISP through a modem, any user can become a member of the Internet community and is able to send and receive information at a very low cost. Even access to the Internet through an ISP can be obtained for free (see Figure 4.6).

There Is No Free Lunch

OK, OK, nothing is free. Any free Internet connections, email services, Web page hosting, etc., usually come with limitations that force the "free" subscribers or users

53

to view advertising whether they want to or not. But, in exchange, anyone can access and use these services, and in some cases, free services even make more sense than the pay services. For example, if I travel the world, I can usually find free access to the Internet through a library or a cybercafe, but I won't be able to get my email unless I use one of the worldwide free email services such as Yahoo mail (see Figure 4.7).

Figure 4.6

Access to the Internet can be obtained for little or no money from companies like Net Genie.

What's an Internet?

A net or network is two or more computers that are connected together so that they can communicate. An Internetwork is simply a collection of these networks. So the Internet is nothing more than a collection of networks connected together so that the computers on each network can communicate with each other. Large volume telephone lines and fiber optic cables provide the link for all these computers, and the total capacity of a line is called its bandwidth.

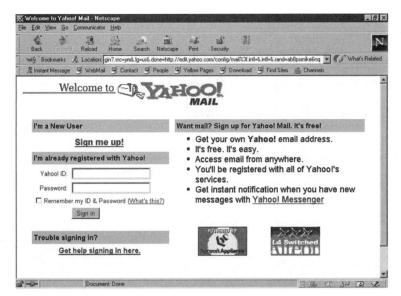

Figure 4.7
You can obtain a free email account by using the Yahoo Freemail service.

The Main Uses of the Internet

➤ Email

➤ Viewing information in a Web site

➤ Presenting information in a Web site

➤ Shopping

➤ Newsgroups

➤ Chat

➤ Obtaining information through forms

➤ Providing information through forms

Byte Me Zine

e-Commerce Related Activities

(number of PCs used in millions)

	Jan-99	**Jan-98**	**% Increase**
e-commerce purchases	20.1	11.6	72%
e-commerce purchases incl. financial	26.0	16.3	60%
All shopping activities	29.7	21.8	36%
Total e-commerce (shop,finance,buy)	37.2	26.4	41%

Ziff-Davis Inc.

The first step in choosing a name for your company is to research whether it exists on the Net. We will skip the lessons on name choice, marketing, how to run a company, and so on. You can get this info from a variety of books.

Email

An ISP agreement to host a domain should allow your organization to set up multiple email IDs with your own domain name. If your original email was mycompany@ISP.com, it can now be changed to yourname@mycompany.com, or webmaster@mycompany.com, or sales@mycompany.com., or all three. Email can also be set up as aliases, where email sent to these addresses all goes to the same mailbox. Multiple email boxes present the impression of a larger company but also helps separate mail when the company eventually does grow.

Searching the Net

We can now search for our new proposed name in a number of ways. There are a wide variety of search engines available on the Internet, some of which are shown in Figure 4.8. There are the big search engines such as Yahoo, Netscape, Infoseek; new search technologies like Web Ferret or Google; or search services like AskJeeves. The big search engines search in one of four ways:

1. Some engines have stored all the pages of a large number of Web sites. The search will look through each page and rank them according to how many times the keywords appear.

2. Other search engines look at the few keywords (called Meta tags) that were originally submitted when the site was set up with the search engine.

3. Some search engines use advanced algorithms or calculations to locate the most popular site.

4. Finally, some search engines list sites that have paid a fee, followed by non-paying Web sites. The problem with this technique is that if I am searching for information on "mice,"' I don't want to see the Disney site listed first.

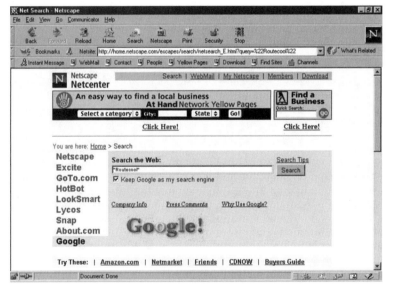

Figure 4.8

Search engines are a great place to search for the presence of a new company name for anyone trying to see whether a name is already used.

The second place to search will be the U.S. Patent and Trademark search engine located at `http://www.uspto.gov/` (see Figure 4.9). If the search turns up zero hits, indicating that the trademark is available or unregistered, you will be able to trademark the name. The U.S. government has a number of agreements with countries like Canada so that in the event of a trademark or patent dispute, the first occurrence of the trademark or patent in either country will take precedence in court. So, if you have the time, search all databases in other countries or hire a lawyer to perform this task.

Trademarks or Just Keep 'em for Yourself

You can register your organization's name as a trademark online by going to the U.S. Patent and Trademark Web site at www.uspto.gov. You must have an address or an agent in the United States.

Figure 4.9

The U.S. Patent & Trademark Web site allows you to search for patents and trademarks online.

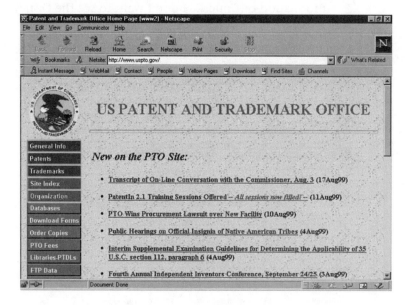

The next search mechanism is the domain name registry at www.networksolutions.com (see Figure 4.10). This search engine will allow you to see whether your domain name is available.

Figure 4.10

Network Solutions provides an online system for searching and registering domain names.

Registering a Domain Name

Now that we have confirmed that the name RouteCool.com is not is use by someone else, we can start the process of registering the name.

Incorporating a Company Online

One of the first things you can do with an Internet connection is incorporate your company online. Sites such as www.ailcorp.com provide an online incorporation service that will allow anyone from anywhere in the world to incorporate a company anywhere in the United States, and they will even act as an agent on your behalf.

Let's say that we have successfully staked a claim to Internet terra firma by getting the name RouteCool.com. We can now go to the U.S. Patent and Trademark site and register the trademark. Your domain registration should count as a legally published use of the trade name and will hopefully be enough to convince a court. (You might want to use a real trademark lawyer to be certain of all the legal ins and outs of trademark law.)

There are a few things to consider when applying for a trademark. First, you can trademark both text and graphics. A specialized symbol is often as valuable as the name so if you have a custom-designed graphic that will be the focus of your promotion (such as the AT&T Deathstar logo), it is a good idea to trademark both the graphic and the text. Second, the trademark will have to apply to a class of goods or service, and you will have to pay hundreds of dollars for each class (and there are hundreds of classes). Third, you will have to pay the fee via credit card. Finally, once the application has been accepted, it will have to be reviewed, which could take weeks.

Now that you have a domain name and have started the trademark registration process, you can incorporate the company online at an online incorporation site. These sites are numerous and can usually be located through the links on a state-sponsored Web site.

Spoof...Now They're Gone

"Spoofing" is a term used to describe an Internet activity in which an unscrupulous company mimics another Web site (see Figure 4.11). The site may look like a real government Web site, but, in fact, it will be a false site designed to get your business. Some sites are designed only for the purpose of obtaining your credit card information. Be very careful on how you access sites and be even more careful about supplying credit card information. We suggest either calling the company or government agency to confirm the site URL, using clearly identifiable sites like www.microsoft.com, government sites that end in .gov, or connecting by using secure technology such as SSL or certificates. (For more information about security see Chapter 11, "Show me the Money.".)

Now that we have started the process of creating our e-commerce company, we can start working on the actual business. Remember that prior to this point you should have identified what your company was going to do and who your market would be. This process should have resulted in the company name and some initial agreements to do business with suppliers, etc.

Let's say that our game plan for going to the Internet is a contract to sell books for a publisher. I could potentially send emails to everyone on the Internet in an attempt to advertise the books. This technique is called "spamming" (see Figure 4.12), and is considered to be the Internet equivalent to junk mail. Another much less intrusive and more lucrative i-business model is to present the information to the public and try to get them to come to your Web site. Trying to get customers to come to your site is called generating traffic, and it is a key concept in most of the e-commerce business models that we'll study later in the book.

Figure 4.11

A spoof site is a Web site that uses a domain name similar to the name of a high traffic site.

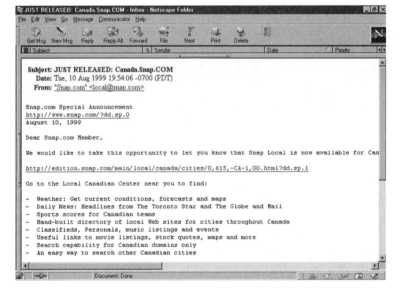

Figure 4.12

Email spam is the equivalent of junk mail and is usually used to sell products.

Spam...Email, Not the Lunch Meat

The act of sending bulk email is called "spamming," and it often results in the termination of your Internet account at your ISP or a darn good torching (otherwise known as "flaming"). The term "flaming" is used to describe the act of sending thousands of pieces of "hate email" back to a "spammer" site. If a few hundred flamers do this, it may be enough email to collapse your ISP's server and make your ISP very, very angry. We don't recommend spamming or flaming, although there are companies and individuals on the Net that do nothing else.

Traffic Jams

When is a traffic jam a good thing? When it happens on the Internet and the site they are coming to is yours. Each server on the Internet has a limited capacity for hits. That is, they have a set limit to their bandwidth, and if everyone tries to access a Web site at the same time, they will likely receive the equivalent of an Internet busy signal, or a "site is not responding" message. This occurs because the pipe that brings visitors to your site only has a limited capacity. For example, if you decide to promote your site during the NFL Superbowl, make sure that your server can handle the traffic during halftime.

Mechanics of the Net

The Internet, as we already know, is a collection of networks that are linked together. There are a number of key elements that function together to make the Internet work. First, assume that we have two networks and that we would like to connect them in an Internet. The first thing we have to do is run some sort of communication medium, like a wire, between them. This would not be difficult if they were located in the same building, but we can't string wire between two cities. Luckily, the phone companies have already done this, and they can supply one of these high-speed lines right to the server of both networks.

The second piece of required equipment is the hardware that will allow the networks to communicate. One type of connection to a high-speed phone line is a high-speed modem, but for a direct connection to the Internet, the piece of hardware needed is called a router. A router is essentially a computer that takes the message from one network and sends it out on the Net to another network using an IP address. Another key function of a router is to know the fastest way or route to get to the other network.

The Wizardry of IP

When we said that the Internet is a collection of networks all linked together, we meant linked by high-speed phone lines. When an ISP (Internet Service Provider) sets up a network to connect to the Internet, it gets a high-speed line from the phone company (such as a T1 line) and requests an IP address (or group of addresses) from a central IP registry organization, as shown in Figure 4.13. The IP address is like an Internet phone number that allows communications devices on the Net, called routers, to locate your ISP's network. When the ISP's router receives the message, it forwards the message to your computer or emailbox.

Figure 4.13

Here is an example of IP addresses for an NT configuration.

I Am Master of My Domain

A domain name is a Web name that is centrally registered and belongs exclusively to you or your company: www.2mn8.org or www.amazon.com are examples of domain names. When you register a name with a domain registry organization, the name is linked to an IP address on your ISP internal network. You then contract with your ISP to host your domain. Hosting will allow other users of the Internet to view your Web page by typing in your domain name as shown in Figure 4.14. You can order a domain name and search the database for names that end in .com, .net, or .org by surfing to www.networksolutions.com.

Figure 4.14

You can enter a domain name in the URL search box of your browser to find a Web site.

On each machine that is connected to the network, software called a protocol operates as a network language (of sorts). This, combined with a piece of hardware called a
network adapter (connector to the network) and a little configuration, will result in
messages being sent to or received from another computer. "To" and "from" IP
addresses are attached to each message sent on the Net, and all routers look at or
"sniff" the messages that pass by until they locate their own IP address. The router
will analyze and hand off to a Web server those messages that will be allowed
through the network firewall. *(For a great reference book on networks try* Easy
Networking *published by Que.)*

Firewalls

A firewall is a piece of software that analyzes an incoming network message and
compares the IP address or message content to a database of approved parameters. If the IP address isn't listed (or is listed on a blocking list) or the message
contains text that is not allowed, then the message will be dropped. If the message passes the parameter test, it will proceed to the correct computer.

Usually, all these pieces of the Internet puzzle are managed by your ISP (Internet Service Provider).

Domain Hosting

Another service that your ISP will provide is domain hosting. Domain hosting allows other Internet users to connect to your domain name by entering a URL such as `http://www.aol.com` in the URL search box on their browser. This will cause the central domain registry and all the Internet routers to send the message to your ISP.

After you have established a Web hosting agreement with your ISP, it will allocate storage space on its server that will be accessed each time a request comes in. You are now ready to create your first Web page, or home page, and load it into this "storage space." Web pages are created by using one of the many Web design software packages like "Quicksite" (see Figure 4.15), or Microsoft's "FrontPage," or by utilizing the services of a Web designer. Most, if not all, Web pages utilize the main software language of the Internet, Hyper Text Markup Language (HTML), although many now use other languages and software in addition to HTML (such as Java by Sun Microsystems or Coldfusion by Allaire).

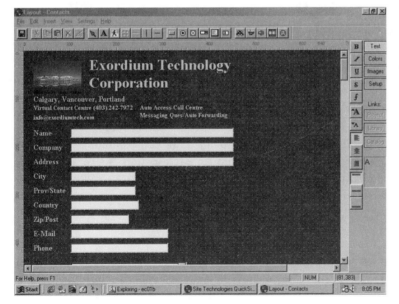

Figure 4.15

You can design an HTML Page using HTML editing packages like Quicksite or Frontpage.

After the Web page HTML file has been uploaded to your ISP's server, other users of the Internet will be able to see the page by typing in your URL, which stands for uniform resource locator (such as `http://www.routecool.com`). Your company is now conducting i-commerce as well as e-commerce. Electronically, your customers can see your Web site to get information about your company or products, as well as to send emails.

Links

After you have created a home page and provided your customers some place to go on the Internet, you can continue to add pages of information. You access these pages by creating links on your home page that allow visitors an easy way to view another page. One way is to insert a text hyperlink that will allow visitors to click on the actual text and link to the other pages. Often, these links are part of the functions of an image. Images such as GIFs (Graphical Interchange Format), JPEGs (Joint Photographic Experts Group), or image maps often include tags or links that will link to another page on your Web site when the graphic is selected (double-clicked by the mouse). You can also link to other

Index.html

When you create a home page, the file name attached to the first page is index.html (or htm). When the domain is accessed through a browser, it will always go to this page first.

sites on the Internet or link to email addresses. This is a very powerful tool that is an important component of any e-commerce model, as we will see later.

Image Map

An image map is a special graphic. Well, the actual graphic is nothing special, but by using mapping software such as the software available at http://www.softseek.com/ Internet/Web_Publishing_Tools/HTML_Image_Mapping/, you can segment or define areas on the graphic and create different links for each section. When a visitor selects a section of the image, the browser will process the link associated with that area.

A Form Takes Shape

You can also add a page that allows your visitors to send information without using email. A form is a special type of Web page that uses various types of on-screen boxes to permit your visitor to enter or choose information. An example of a form is shown in Figure 4.16. When the visitor completes the form, the information is sent to your email box. This is another extremely powerful tool that is also a key ingredient of any e-commerce model. Most of the "shopping carts," credit card payment pages, or registration pages are forms. The creation of a form is not difficult and most Web site software will offer this functionality. The tricky part will be in entering the processing parameters that will be provided by your ISP.

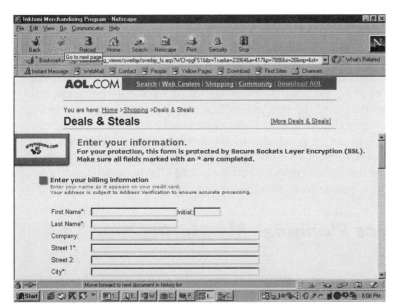

Figure 4.16

This figure shows an HTML form used to enter shipping information on AOL.

e-Commerce—More Than Just Web Sites and the Internet

Most of what we have discussed is i-commerce functionality. E-commerce is a term that has a much wider definition. We know that if business is conducted electronically, we are doing e-commerce, but when we use the term e-commerce today, we are primarily talking about companies that use computers to perform all or the majority of the back-office functions with minimal or no human intervention.

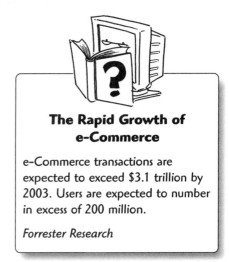

The Rapid Growth of e-Commerce

e-Commerce transactions are expected to exceed $3.1 trillion by 2003. Users are expected to number in excess of 200 million.

Forrester Research

Hold On...Back the Office Up

The term "back office" refers to functions that support the operation of an organization. Answering phones, creating orders, producing financial statements, and so on are all part of the back-office functions. They are critical to an organization but can often be performed by computers with greater efficiency, accuracy, and at a significantly lower cost than by humans. Humans are still required for personalized service functions such as sales, support, etc., but the best-designed Web site can even eliminate these functions without any negative impact on sales.

Convergence of Systems...Not Planets

Dunrite is an e-commerce company and Ohdarn ... is not. What makes the Dunrite Corp. so successful is that the systems used to operate the back office without staff are *convergent*. That is, they operate together in unison and in real time, one transaction at a time. For this model to be successful, all software must work together seamlessly without human intervention, and the computers that run this company must be powerful. This doesn't imply that you have to buy everything from one software vendor. On the contrary, it is usually a good idea to avoid this type of dependency. The most important aspect of designing an e-commerce operational model is an exceptional ability to organize the operations of a company and clearly understand how all the pieces of the corporate puzzle work together.

Enterprise Resource Planning—Monitoring Your Resources

ERP (Enterprise Resource Planning) describes the modeling of the operations of a business by back-office software. The goal is to eliminate multiple systems and the links between the systems by implementing one integrated solution. An integrated system is one that processes information without the need to send it to another type of software. An example is a customer order that generates a sales journal entry automatically in the GL.

Most ERP software does not integrate well with other systems. For all systems to converge, standards must be established and agreed to by all the software companies. The Internet is successful because it has been constructed by using standards.

So, this is what the buzz on e-commerce is all about. And, if you don't believe that it is important—just remember that your competitor down the street is already halfway to becoming an efficient e-commerce company, and when they're finished, they'll probably start a price war...just for fun.

The Least You Need to Know

➤ How to obtain information through forms.

➤ How the convergence of systems works.

➤ What is a critical mass on the Internet?

➤ How to generate traffic and the importance of doing so.

➤ Links can make your Web site more informative and interesting.

The Virtual Corporation

The Virtual Corporation Defined

What is a virtual corporation? The main difference between a virtual corporation and a regular company is the degree to which the operations of the company are electronic. A truly virtual company does not carry inventory and has no staff, but still generates revenue. How? By utilizing the power of new systems and the Internet. In Figure 5.1, you can see a simple example of a company that developed a Web site with a single link to an online retailer who pays either a commission or a micropayment for sales or hits. After the Web site is running, no additional intervention is required to operate the organization, and if a visitor to that site links to an affiliate's retail site and then makes a purchase, the virtual company will receive revenue. Amazon.com is one company that pays a commission for sales referred to its site in this manner. In this example, the virtual company does not carry any inventory or utilize any staff. However, to generate significant revenue, it will require Web site promotion as well as bookkeeping to track revenue or file tax returns. Both of these tasks may require staff and other physical resources (unless these functions are outsourced).

Figure 5.1

The figure shows the Web page of a simple virtual company.

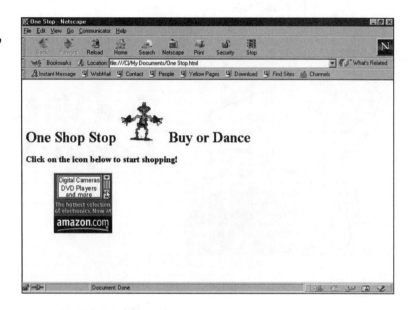

The word virtual is often linked to "virtual reality" gaming systems that provide an electronic world to play in. With the use of goggles, specially designed gloves, and body sensors, you can achieve the sensation that you are inside the game in a false or "virtual" reality. The virtual company is much like the artificial world created by these gaming systems: It has a structure and it conducts commerce, but without a physical location or people. The concept of an entirely virtual corporation is an unattainable goal for most organizations and deserves the same level of respect as the paperless office. However, many companies are starting to incorporate virtual concepts into their operations as part of a general movement toward e-commerce.

Virtually an Oxymoron?

The term virtual reality is almost an oxymoron or a phrase that "contains contradictory or incongruous words" (Webster's). Reality is either real or it is not. We say it is "virtually real" because the systems are approaching reality or the image of being real. But when we talk of a virtual company, we are discussing a company that is already real but is going backwards to "almost becoming" a company in the modern sense of the word. A company that is almost a company or "virtual," is moving away from having physical operations such as offices, staff, or physical assets.

Why Build a Virtual Corporation?

Do we really need to build a virtual company? Let's turn the question around and state it as "Do we really need to invest money to reduce our costs?" Believe it or not the answer is often "no." There will be thousands of businesses next year that will spend more on e-commerce than they will ever receive back in profit. Many of these companies would be better off financially if they invested their money and focused their operations on tasks that provided the greatest return on investment. However, there are hundreds of thousands of companies that can redirect staff toward value-added tasks, such as sales, through the greater use of automation. They can also reach new customers in other locales or more effectively communicate with their existing customers by using the Internet. The bottom line is higher sales as a result of implementing some level of e-commerce initiatives. So, although you may not need to "build" a new virtual corporation, using the concept as a long-term goal can produce significant financial rewards for your organization.

The Top 10 Benefits of e-Commerce

➤   Higher revenue

➤   Reduced overall labor costs

➤   Reduced inventory expense

➤   Faster external access to internal information

➤   24X7 (24 hours a day, 7days a week) customer support features

➤   Faster information dissemination

➤   Reduced communication costs

➤   More valuable goodwill and shareholder value

➤   Better external information gathering

➤   Reduced operating expenses through supply reductions

The Top 5 Costs of e-Commerce

➤ Higher per capita salaries for more sophisticated staff

➤ Higher technology costs

➤ Ongoing system upgrade costs

➤ Promotion for companies that are expanding their area of operation

➤ Coffee expense...lots and lots of java...in fact just install a Starbucks

Building a Virtual Corporation

Building a virtual corporation from the ground up is far easier than converting or reengineering an existing corporation. The greatest single benefit from building the company from scratch is that you will not have to deal with legacy systems or systems that the organization is currently using. When reengineering a company for e-commerce, these old operational systems usually have to be connected to the newer i-commerce systems or have to be retooled to provide real-time processing capabilities. This is such a difficult process to complete when combined with your staff's unwillingness to change that some organizations start entirely separate companies to manage new e-commerce development (sometimes outsourcing these functions can also be financially beneficial).

e-Commerce Software

By the year 2002, $2.8 billion will be spent on e-commerce software with the largest amount going to supply chain management software.

DataMonitor

The first step in building a virtual corporation, after completing the business plan, should be to clearly define what tasks your company will perform to complete its business on a daily basis. This "mapping" of operations can be done quickly to show the general tasks necessary to conduct a single transaction. However, don't dwell on unique hypothetical situations: KISS it (keep it simple, silly). These tasks should also follow the overall business plan that you develop to define what your company will do. For example, if my company's business plan is to sell a specific set of products on the Internet, a "high-level" map of the process may include such tasks as the following:

1. Order new product from vendor.
2. Receive and update inventory availability.
3. Warehouse the product.
4. Process customer orders.
5. Deposit receipts.
6. Pick and ship the product.
7. Confirm delivery.
8. Pay the vendors.

The second step in the e-commerce development process is to decide which of these tasks can be automated. Systems can automate tasks # 1,4,5,7, and 8, but to "virtualize" the inventory management tasks in 2,3, and 6 will require either outsourcing the function back to your vendor or a third party, or the installation of some very expensive warehouse robotics. Most vendors will deliver the product to a third party at your request. This function is called "drop shipping" and although on the surface it appears to be an easy way to reduce inventory, it may require a higher rate of compensation to your vendor. This higher rate must be less than your own costs of storage and processing for you to successfully increase your margin or per order profit. In those situations where your operation is small and your vendor will ship only in bulk, a third-party warehouse and shipping service may be appropriate.

A Virtual Example

The basic e-commerce supply chain model is the start of the "virtualization" of organizations, and many companies are starting to take advantage of the cost efficiencies to be gained. In this model, as shown in Figure 5.2, a customer can place an order by viewing real-time information about an inventory over the Internet at the same time

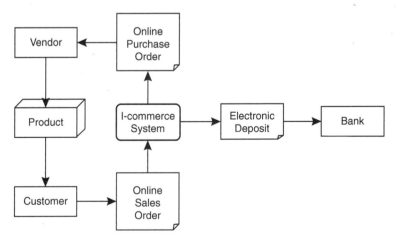

Figure 5.2

The figure shows a flow-chart of a supply chain.

that a vendor is notified that your inventory has to be restocked or that the shipment should be sent to the customer.

Managing and Displaying Inventory

Your first construction project beside the information highway can be an online store. Start by adding links to Web sites that meet two criteria:

1. They will help you attract visitors to your site.
2. They will pay a revenue stream for hits or sales.

Next, to attract customers to your online store and generate revenue you will need to provide them with a reason to visit the site. This will be provided, for example, by a store that will carry goods that can be purchased by visitors to the site through online shopping software. These transactions can be processed without any human intervention to manage the inventory, the Web catalog, or orders. To successfully achieve this goal, you will require a system that can manage both a real inventory stored in a warehouse and a virtual inventory stored at your vendors or partners. The virtual inventory will be either a direct link to vendors who want to use your Web site to sell their product or an online posting mechanism for partners who don't have sophisticated systems. The real inventory will be an actual supply of goods. In both scenarios, you will need a way to manage the financial aspects of the business, such as accounting for sales and inventory. As well, all information should be real-time, and all inventory systems should be capable of storing and uploading images of the products that are sold.

Accessing Information Not Stored on Your Web Site

There are two ways to present "content" or information on a Web page. The first is to put it on the Web by creating and uploading new HTML pages (see Figure 5.3). The second is to purchase software that will load the content for you. The first method requires extensive staff to create the new Web pages while the other method automatically loads dynamic (changing) information. To automatically load information will require software capable of accessing a dynamic file or a database of information, as well as software to load the information on the Web site. Most current back-office inventory systems are based on relational databases and are already dynamic or, more simply put, when a product is purchased, the inventory numbers change automatically. The trick will be to have this information loaded to your Web page in real-time so that posted inventory levels and pricing remains current as shown in Figure 5.4. Of course, another option is to build the database as part of your Web site.

A Way Out There...Like Way...Way Out There

XML stands for Extensible Markup Language, and it will be the new standard for Internet communications designed to eventually replace HTML in the coming years. Documents

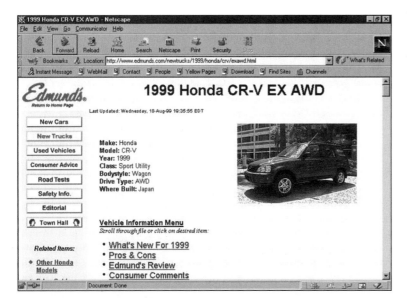

Figure 5.3

The figure shows a static HTML page.

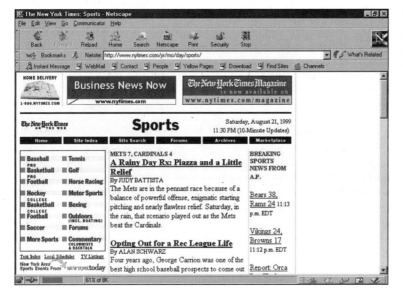

Figure 5.4

Dynamic HTML pages are often used to load breaking news stories.

on the Web are currently distributed and viewed using HTML. XML is a wider version of HTML that allows for more flexibility in designing Web applications, while still supporting older HTML development. Corporations that exchange electronic information, such as invoices, have used EDI (Electronic Data Interchange) for many years. Development is also currently underway to combine EDI and XML so that business documents at one company will easily flow over the Internet to another company. See www.xmledi.com.

Transferring Information from Systems to Web Sites

One of the first problems that you will face is how to store, process, and manage information between your Web site and internal systems. In the previous section, we discussed the use of forms to accept information from a customer. A customer who visits your Web site is viewing an HTML page. The HyperText Markup Language (HTML) is essentially a document "displayer," and it displays information according to a set of standards. A form can also be displayed to a customer through HTML, but a form allows the customer to enter information or select information from a look-up list. When the customer uses the Submit button, your ISP's software will send the information to you as an email similar to Figure 5.5.

Internet Sales

Internet sales are predicted to reach $14 billion by 2002.

Consumers Electronic Manufacturing Association

Using a simple example, you can HTML hardcode a product on your Web page and use a link to a form page to allow your customer to enter delivery information, account numbers, etc. Then when you receive the "form" information in your email, you can enter the order into your existing back-office order/entry system. A more sophisticated system would accept the order information from the form and process it in the back-office system without any intervention. This can be as simple as copying the text in the email to an input media such as Word* or Excel* or by saving the text file as a delim-

Figure 5.5

This figure shows an email generated by a form used on a Web site.

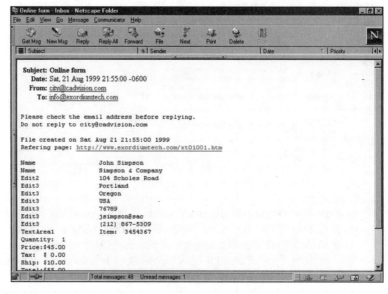

* *Trademarks of Microsoft*

ited file (separated by commas or spaces) for direct upload into an order/entry system input.

Online Shopping

There are much easier alternatives to creating an online inventory/shopping site, such as using the services of companies like Digi-Net (www.Digi-net.com) or Idea-pro (www.ideapro.com) that are online services providing any company with the opportunity to list their inventory and prices (see Figure 5.6). The information is maintained on the Digi-Net server, and when a customer completes a purchase, email confirmations are sent to both the customer and the company retailing the product. The company can then sign onto the Digi-Net server and get the customer's order information. Although these are e-commerce alternatives, they will still require the administration of the Web data by your staff through a browser.

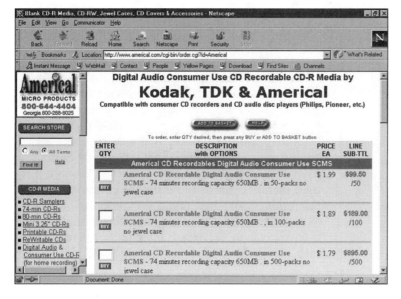

Figure 5.6

America Online inventory listing created by using ideapro.com *services.*

Online Credit Card Purchases

Let's face it. You can't take cash with you, and you can't spend it over the Internet, so you will have to use some form of online credit payment system (see the following chapter on electronic payments). Most credit card payment systems are form-based systems that are maintained on a secure server (see Figure 5.7). The data is encrypted or scrambled using software such as SSL (Secure Sockets Layer). You can tell that you

Figure 5.7

This figure shows a credit card payment form on a secure site.

Padlock

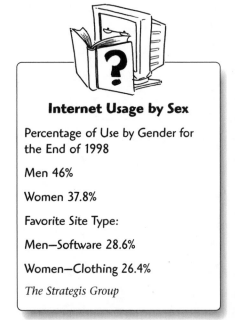

Internet Usage by Sex

Percentage of Use by Gender for the End of 1998

Men 46%

Women 37.8%

Favorite Site Type:

Men—Software 28.6%

Women—Clothing 26.4%

The Strategis Group

are using a secure site when the URL changes from http:// to https://, and there is an unbroken key or closed padlock in the bottom corner of the browser. There are a number of companies that will process these credit payments for a fee, such as Digit-net, or other services available, such as i-escrow (www.iescrow.com) that will accept credit payments from the customer but won't forward it to their member companies until the customer receives the product. Another service is cybercash (www.cybercash.com) that allows a customer to pay Internet bills to Cybercash merchants by credit card, cash, or check.

Migrating to a Virtual Corporation

The migration from a regular organization to a virtual organization can take a number of different forms. Like building a new virtual company, the first step in the process is to analyze or "map" the tasks that your company performs and then decide which processes can be automated. The next step is to decide whether these tasks will be outsourced or not and what new systems will be required to complete these tasks in a virtual manner.

One of the most difficult barriers to this "virtualization" process will be the attitude of the staff. As humans, we tend to stay with the comfort of "that with which we are familiar." Fear of the unknown is a great barrier to change and will require very careful management. Without the "buy-in" of your staff, their resistance will slow the process of change and could result in the failure of the organization to capitalize on the financial benefits of "virtualization." In some cases, this resistance has caused the failure of entire organizations.

Things That Can Be Made Virtual

Virtual office space: Employees work at home or on the road and take any available workstation or communal space when working in the office.

Virtual order entry: Orders are entered by the customers online without the assistance of any staff.

Virtual inventory: Inventory is listed online for customers, and orders are automatically sent to manufacturers or suppliers. The product is shipped directly from the manufacturer to the customer.

Virtual service: Customers are provided information through Internet search engines and FAQs (frequently asked question lists) seven days a week and 24 hours a day (7X24).

Virtual delivery: Many couriers handle the task of shipping anywhere in the world, complete with Web-enabled tracking systems and guaranteed delivery.

Virtual procurement: Purchase orders can be automatically generated either when a customer orders the product or when your own inventory falls to a certain level. Also orders can be shipped directly from the vendor to the customer (drop shipped) to eliminate the need for inventory and warehousing.

Virtual banking: Credit card information can be automatically processed for deposit by a number of financial institutions, such as www.indianabank.com.

Outsourcing

Outsourcing has been around since the earliest companies. Technically, any necessary function to the organization is outsourced if another company performs the task. Today, this usually implies hiring an external company to do the regular day-to-day tasks of the organization like accounting or computer maintenance. One downside of this concept is that the company often loses control over the task that has been outsourced. This can be disastrous if it involves a critical function such as customer service or sales. Also, more companies are finding that "farming-out" tasks to larger organizations have left them at the mercy of these external companies, sometimes to their own financial detriment. Theoretically, outsourcing should reduce the cost of doing business or at least allow you to focus resources on those tasks that provide the highest return on your investment. However, you must ensure that any outsource agreements clearly and concisely define the responsibilities of each party and the ongoing cost of the agreement. Always be prepared to bring the task "back inside" should the partnership become unfavorable.

To Web or Not to Web

When you have decided to become an e-commerce or virtual company, you will have to make some serious decisions about the path that you would like your organization to take. The most prevalent model of a current operating structure still follows the old Henry Ford assembly line theory, and most systems have been developed to manage information in a similar way. Processing information in batches is still the order of the day for most large organizations, but the problem is that computers allow us to capitalize on even more efficient business methods by combining elements from Henry's model with our capacity to process information one transaction at a time.

The old systems were designed on an old model, and now they need to be retooled. In the Ford model, limiting customer choice leads to efficiency and, in general, this rule still applies. However, thanks to faster computers, e-commerce systems, and the Internet, offering your customers more choice doesn't necessarily lead to any significant inefficiency in production. So the tough decision is do you stick with the same old systems that you have used in the past, or do you develop your business for the next millennium by retooling your systems for the e-commerce?

The Least You Need To Know

➤ Be able to define a virtual corporation.

➤ Know how to map a basic set of tasks.

➤ Be able to determine what to outsource.

➤ Choose what to automate.

➤ Know how to start building an "online store."

➤ Be able to define a basic e-commerce supply chain model.

Killer Apps

Converting Apps to e-Commerce Apps

Applications are not just programs, but concepts, products, or ways that a company conducts business or performs a task. Implementing an e-commerce program is an ongoing process of converting your regular applications into e-commerce applications. If you are very lucky, one of these might become a *"killer app."*

Back in 1998 Larry Downes & Chunka Mui wrote a book called *Killer App*. It described the creation of applications (called apps) for the world of i-commerce and described such elements as "critical mass" and "first to market." The whole concept of the book was to describe a way of looking at applications for i-commerce or the Internet. The same can be said of e-commerce. E-commerce is a way of looking at the entire environment of an organization by using some old concepts such as "the paperless office," as well as some newer killer apps concepts like "critical mass." None of these concepts are particularly new, but they are becoming increasingly important in achieving success with e-commerce.

What Is a Killer App?

Downes and Mui defined a killer app as "a new good or service that establishes an entirely new category and, by being first, dominates it, returning several hundred percent return on initial investment."* Essentially, the killer app is the next big thing, the new wave, the hot tip. It is this way because of the very simple principles that were identified by Downes and Mui called the 12 rules for building killer apps. *For more detailed information, the book is published by Harvard Business School Press and is widely available.*

Before we get to a brief overview of killer app concepts, it is important to reiterate that the killer app rules outlined in this book are not necessarily new concepts. A great deal of praise should be given to the salesmanship abilities and the "right place, right time" dumb luck of the inventors or founders of these "apps." Bill Gates is probably a nice guy, but computer operating systems were already around before he learned how to use a spoon. His success was in having IBM to distribute DOS with every PC, thereby creating critical mass, and Jeff Bezos sold his first Amazon book long after you could buy used texts on almost any university network and gaming software on any BBSs (Bulletin Board Systems). Even the Ford assembly line was an ancient concept because most of the great structures of the world used similar methods in their construction. What made these entrepreneurs and inventors successful was the combination of timing, perseverance, and a mix of the 12 rules.

The 12 Rules for Building Killer Apps

Downes and Mui identified 12 rules that they considered essential for building successful killer apps. These concepts drive many of today's most successful technology companies and can be used by both new e-commerce companies and older companies that are changing to the new e-commerce way of thinking.

Rule 1: Outsource to the Customer

Outsource to your customer is a relatively simple concept. Get the customer to run your company and don't pay her a thing. Now you can just imagine a banker throwing the combination to the vault over the desk and walking out the door. But what if he could somehow restrict the customer so that she could access only her own money. He might convince the customer that she can watch her own money and still get all the benefits of banking, like security and centralized clearing. If the banker succeeded, he could take an extended vacation and return only to count the revenue from service charges.

This is exactly what "outsource to the customer" implies. One of the most common examples of this concept in action is a bank automatic teller machine (ATM) where the customer, with the assistance of the bank computer, performs his own banking transactions while paying a fee for the privilege. Another common implementation of

*From the book Killer App *by Larry Downes & Chunka Mui Harvard Business School Press.*

this concept is the online "call center" or i-center (discussed in Chapter 10, "The Customer Is King"). The customer accesses a company Web site or i-center to obtain information about products or services, tutorials, or general help all without the assistance from a company employee (see Figure 6.1).

Figure 6.1

The Microsoft i-center provides customers with access to valuable information and online support.

Rule 2: Cannibalize Your Markets

"Build an e-business that steals customers from your current business to capture brand loyalty, reach new markets, or obtain critical mass."* This one is a very tough pill for most businesses to swallow. Hurting your existing operations for the sake of new operations is not something that has been taught in business schools. The concept is that if you don't take advantage of the Internet now, your business will suffer later. The Internet provides anyone with the ability to "take-over" a category of product or service, and the rule of the day is eat or be eaten even if it's your own leg. If you hedge your bets by attempting to cannibalize only areas of the market that you are not active in, then when someone else does sacrifice the whole market, he will become dominant. An example of this concept is the *NY Times* that is providing online information from its newspapers free over the Internet as shown in Figure 6.2.

Here's a hypothetical example. Let's say that I sell books from a chain of stores. I don't want to hurt sales in these stores, but I want new sales. Binky, the kid from the computer room, says he can build me an online retailing empire as big as a jungle. I tell Binky to go ahead and start an Internet sales company that will only ship to customers where I do not have a store and to set the prices so that they are the same as in the expensive retail outlet. After all, I don't want to hurt my existing operations. Binky quits, mumbling something about a rain forest.

Figure 6.2

NY Times offers its news-paper information free over the Internet even to its existing customers.

The next week Binky opens congo.com (this is a fictional domain name, any resemblance to any jungle domain name real or imaginary is purely coincidental). He has an old warehouse and the same titles that I carry, and he ships using a courier. He doesn't just cannibalize my operation, he eats it whole as an appetizer and spits out the bones. I, of course, could have stopped Binky in his tracks if I had been a bit more ambitious and less fearful of hurting my existing operations. The problem is that businesses see all that they have invested in a company and fear losing it or worse, ticking off the shareholders. The cannibalizing concept implies that you should make the investment in the new operation and toss the old model if it can't compete. If you are really good, you will make both concepts succeed.

Rule 3: Treat Each Customer as a Market Segment of One

This concept discusses the ability for e-companies to provide each customer with her own unique product or service. Remember in the old days of Henry Ford that customers could have any color Model T they wanted as long as it was black. Now, in today's killer app world, customers can receive exactly what they want. For example, many information supply companies with Web sites, such as online news organizations, offer their customers the ability to customize the information that they receive. Customers log on to the Web site and have the ability to customize and personalize a page that will reappear every time they sign on. They can also choose the content that they will see on this page. We will see in later chapters how this concept can be extended beyond bits of information to hard products, such as books, with the implementation of real-time systems.

This customization allows companies to perform a marketing technique called "niching" that involves breaking down customers individually by traits and rebuilding them into unique groups called "communities of value."

Rule 4: Create Communities of Value

In Downes & Mui's book they identified the concept of "creating communities of value by valuing communities."* This is another rela-

Yahoo Online News

To see a customized news page, surf to www.yahoo.com and find the My Yahoo link.

tively easy concept to understand. What companies have to do to create a killer app is gather customers together into discrete communities by creating an environment where they want to "hang out." For example, let's say that I want to gather together computer users who are frustrated with using their computers. I can create a Web page at www.IHATECOMPUTERS.com (which actually exists but is under development). Now let's say that I offer very easy-to-use tutorials for basic computer use, such as how to turn on a computer in seven clear and easy steps with graphics and online support. What I am doing is supplying both helpful information and an environment where like-minded individuals can "hang out" and later be mobilized to purchase products, perform actions like sending emails, etc.

The i-Village Online Community

One of the more successful communities of value is at www.ivillage.com. This is a site designed for and catering to women.

This is the second part of the niching concept described previously. After customers have been identified by individual traits, they are recombined into customer groups.

Rule 5: Replace Rude Interfaces with Learning Interfaces

Downes & Mui have obviously received a lot of bad service because the phrase "rude" appears to apply to any type of human-based customer service. In fact, some service organizations provide exceptional human service. Just go to Disneyland to see how hard those young kids work at keeping a smile. In general, however, Downes & Mui are correct, any human-to-human interaction has the potential of becoming rude. Their solution is to provide an electronic interface for customers. The benefit of this approach is that the organization maintains complete control over the interface, because if my customer service clerk is "having a bad day," he may take it out on my customers and indirectly on my future sales figures. An electronic interface doesn't have "bad days," and electronic interfaces not only capture information, but can instantaneously provide better responses by using this information to learn and memorize.

The authors are discussing the concept of the i-center or the electronic self-service help desk. Most large organizations have a Web site that performs these functions (see Chapter 10). The bad news is that even these automated interfaces are rude and becoming ruder.

Rule 6: Ensure Continuity for the Customer, Not Yourself

This rule says that companies will attempt to manage change for the sake of continuity in the organization. The continuity that companies are trying to hold onto is the way that they currently do business. If fact, killer apps upset this balance and can cause "the way businesses do business" to change so dramatically that older companies fail. So organizations would be better off managing the continuity of their customer's world, regardless of changes in the way business is done. The way they do this is by building interfaces to new ways of doing business that mirror what the customer is already familiar with. As long as there is this familiarity, customers will use the company's new technology instead of a competitor's.

For example, let's say that you run a brokerage. Your customers call your brokers and ask for information about a hot stock that they have heard about. They may want information such as price, market news, company data, and the broker's opinion. Most of them also use computers and the Internet. You could manage the company's continuity by discounting the need to build an online trading facility with excuses like "trading over the Internet is a fad because customers want current information and opinions from live brokers."

Your competitor, however, has probably already reasoned that most brokerage customers have computers and Internet access and by supplying broker information online along with a stock price look-up facility and a news search engine, your competitor will be able to provide an interface that the customer is already familiar with. In this scenario, your competitor will steal your customers because the customers will try the system and find more concise and current information 24 hours a day.

e-Trade Online Brokerage

To see an online brokerage, surf to www.etrade.com.

Rule 7: Give Away as Much Information as You Can

The point of this rule is that information is relatively free and available. If you are hiding or hoarding information with the view that it provides you with a competitive advantage or keeps your customers faithful, then you may have missed the boat. Downes & Mui provide a number of examples in their book of companies that "missed the boat" when the Internet grew in popularity because they faithfully treated their internal information as an asset that would provide a greater return. This includes the specifications or standards for their products.

But nothing is secret, and the first casualties of the new information order were the companies that failed to gain a "first-to-market" advantage by enticing customers with free information. Customers now have access to free information everywhere, and they will always gravitate toward free information, products, or services and away from proprietary or fee-based information services. They will even pay in other more subtle ways for this content, and since they attach a value to information, that is what attracts them to a Web site. If enough customers can be attracted, then concepts such as critical mass and creating communities of value will start to have a significant impact on the market value of the organization supplying the information.

The bottom line is that if you hope to "sell" information or provide some sort of proprietary access to the information, customers will go elsewhere. In most situations, providing free information will result in greater benefits for your organization. Consider two companies, one that provides home help information over the Net as a subscription and one that provides it for free. Company A, the pay-per-view company, signs up some customers and immediately has the resources to edit and write data. Company B, the free company, adds a way for visitors to post information for free. The Downes and Mui rule predicts that visitors to company A will be limited but profitable, while visitors to company B will be vast but nonpaying. Now let's say that Company B calls Home Depot and tells them that a "vast" number of customers come to their site for free information (maybe in the thousands) and asks whether Home Depot would like to advertise. Eventually, the growth in company B's Web site would even attract company A's customers and lead to its demise. The moral: give the information away for free and capitalize on the other benefits of critical mass.

Rule 8: Structure Every Transaction as a Joint Venture

The virtual corporation is a company without infrastructure. But how does a company without infrastructure operate? Simple, it forms partnerships and joint ventures with other organizations that do have some form of structure or with other virtual organizations. Even more importantly, it forms partnerships and joint ventures with its users. The killer app often consists of a buy-in by the users even before the corporate partners. Java, Sun Microsystem's killer app, was released on the Internet and grew over time to the status of a standard simply because the users of the Internet accepted its open standards concept and because it was free. Once the users were jumping on the Java bandwagon, it became very easy to attract corporate joint ventures.

This concept of joint venturing, as Downes & Mui point out, is now to the point where new companies with no physical structure can compete more effectively than large, older organizations simply by choosing a series of partners that provide the missing physical structure. The advantage is that the virtual corporation can change instantaneously simply by altering the mix of partners. As well, partners can be brought together on short notice to grow an app that already has growing user support. The authors state that this type of process can be made so efficient that each transaction could be structured as a joint venture. What they don't consider is that at some point you will need a partner with real assets. Luckily, most "asset based" companies are not organized enough to compete effectively with the virtual corporation. (See Chapter 4 for more information on virtual corporations.)

Rule 9: Treat Your Assets as Liabilities

Downes & Mui correctly identified that the new technology-based organization has little in the way of physical assets. This makes it very powerful competition from a financial perspective simply because the return on investment is astronomical for any revenue. If your company doesn't have any physical assets, such as real estate, there is less pressure to provide a return on that investment. The downside of course is that with no physical assets you are providing a service only and will be ineffective at competition unless you attain brand recognition.

Not all assets, however, should be dismantled. Assets that are used in production that is not threatened by digital technology should be kept. However, asset-based companies must move to the e-commerce model by building or valuing digital assets. If they don't, virtual competitors will develop these virtual assets, and the physical, asset-based company will be left on the sidelines as a supplier to a large virtual market with very tight margins.

Let's say that company A is a producer of industrial products with a significant investment in plant and equipment. Let's also assume that they have a traditional marketing network of brokers and salesmen. Company B is creating a virtual marketplace that provides customers of heavy industrial equipment with a place to view and compare information, prices from partners, and a way to communicate with the rest of the community. Their customers can order online, cutting out the middlemen and significantly lowering their costs. For company A to avoid becoming just a supplier to the market and competing with other manufacturing partners on price, they should beat company B to the digital market by creating that market themselves.

The Online Auction at ebay

An example of a digital market is ebay, which allows anyone to sell or buy products. Surf to www.ebay.com for a look.

Rule 10: Destroy Your Value Chain

A value chain "is the series of functions that create and distribute an organization's goods and services."* Conducting business in a traditional supply chain model is a risky proposition, according to

Downes & Mui. There are numerous competitors who are after your market share, and they intend to upset the market through the use of new technology. The concept of destroying your value chain is simple: take the risk and upset your partners, give away value for free, and essentially do what it takes to reposition yourself as the leader of the destruction process. Why? Because leaders control the process and can define standards or limit damage. Regardless of what your value chain is, use the power of the digital world and new technology to position the company for the future.

How Can You Destroy Your Value Chain?

➤ By giving away proprietary information or products so that they become the standard for an industry

➤ By eliminating middlemen and using the customer to create orders

➤ Outsourcing functionality to new partners (such as delivery)

➤ Automating the process where possible

Rule 11: Manage Innovation as a Portfolio of Options

Innovation is expensive, risky, and hard to put into terms such as projected return on investment or impact on shareholder worth. Borrowing a page from financial portfolio managers, Downes & Mui identify the number one method for minimizing the risk of investing in innovation, the diversified portfolio. Remember that if your company doesn't pay careful attention to innovation, it can be run over by it.

Just ask any major bookstore if Amazon is a concern. The problem is that innovation is risky, tough to quantify, and often expensive. The easiest way for a company to participate is to take a small position in the new technology so that the company is an active participant with a relatively low exit cost. Microsoft continually invests in emerging technologies as a minority partner only. That way if the technology fails, their loss is minimal. If the technology succeeds, Microsoft is a participant with an inside track. The key is that any failure will likely be offset by a successful innovation somewhere else. This is how innovation is managed as a portfolio of options.

Rule 12: Hire the Children

Finally, the authors identify one more rule for building the killer app. Hire the children does not mean giving junior the title of CEO just to keep him off the streets.

However, hiring junior to give his input into development is a great idea if he is under the age of 30. Children and young adults of this age group have been brought up in a different world than their "40 something" parents. The way they interact with technology is totally different than older adults, and their frame of reference or understanding of technology is also totally different. In many cases they drive the first initial interest in killer apps.

Children have learned by playing computer games that textual information is slow and inefficient, that interfaces should be straightforward to use regardless of what they do, that things should be fun because attention spans are short, and that somewhere out in cyberspace is what they want or need for free. These concepts are vital to the success of your killer app, and are easily understood by the children. As a killer app builder, you cannot afford to ignore their insight.

These are the 12 rules of developing a killer app as written by Larry Downes and Chunka Mui. They obviously go into greater detail, and we highly recommend the book *Killer App*. But we have also noticed that there are a number of land mines out there that will sink most of the killer apps that are currently under development.

Land mines on the Road to a Killer App

There are without a doubt a number of serious land mines on the killer app access road to the Internet. They are the following:

➤ Internet usage drop

➤ Disinterest

➤ Clutter/garbage

➤ Obvious advantage of asset owners

➤ Fragmenting of the Net

➤ Duplicate function

➤ Selling of the Net

➤ Control of the Net by industry/lockout

➤ More effective and efficient coverage—brute force advertising

Internet Usage Drop

Over the past year the volume of traffic on the Internet has risen dramatically. New users of the Internet accounted for the vast majority of this traffic. Their usage levels rise significantly in the initial year of use, sometimes to the level of an addiction. However, over time, the usage decreases and levels off. Usage can again rise if access is provided at work, but never up to the levels when the Internet was a new toy to the user. This occurs because user interest wanes and because their access process is made more efficient. They will start to go to sites only when required and only if the process is fast and efficient. This decline has been documented in studies such as the one by Greenfield Online.

Remember that this phenomenon is only related to existing Internet users and will undoubtedly become more of an issue when the growth of new users plateaus. Since this plateau is still a long way in the future, the net impact on e-commerce corporations will be minimal for company models that attract new users to the Net. If your model is based on the return of existing users, this information will have to be carefully considered during the business plan design process in order to entice your customers to return on a regular basis. The best examples of this technique are Web sites that allow users to customize the main access page for news feeds. This encourages repeat visits to the site on a daily basis to "get updated" on current news, sports scores, stock quotes, and other information. Most of the major search engines such as Yahoo provide this type of customization.

Online Web Purchasing

Percentage of people with online access who said they bought something through a Web site:

1st Quarter 1999   74%

2nd Quarter 1999   71%

Greenfield Online Inc.

ZDNET Online Information

`http://www.ZDNET.com` is an information provider that allows visitors to customize their access page.

Disinterest

One of the reasons that customers do not return to a Web site is disinterest. Customers' attention spans are very short, and if the information changes, then they will stay tuned. If the information doesn't change, then they will lose interest. Let's say for instance that you buy a new car, and it is delivered to your house. Do you drive the car at a set and constant level over the next few weeks? In fact, most people can barely leave the vehicle alone the first night but as the weeks wear on, the interest in "taking the car for a spin" diminishes. The same thing happens to the Net. People initially get hooked up and spend the first few weeks surfing, but then slowly and gradually become disinterested in surfing. They may still use the Internet, just not at the same level as when it was new. In the example of the new car, they are getting less new information that is of any value since the smell is fading, the newness of the driving experience is gone, and there are other new things that tug at one's attention.

This information is also valuable to e-builders since keeping the attention of customers is tough. How tough? Just ask television advertisers who found users switching channels during their commercials or fast forwarding past the commercials that were recorded by VCRs. The interest level of users in commercials was waning until sounds and images were more carefully constructed to quickly attract and keep viewers' attention. This is even a greater threat to the Internet since it also requires the users to expend an effort to interact, as opposed to television, which requires little effort. The best remedy for disinterest is to provide customers with something new and interesting on a regular basis, make it easy for them to use, and carefully construct the sounds and images to hold their attention. Strive to make your Web site highly entertaining while requiring minimal effort from the users.

Clutter and Garbage

One of the biggest contributing factors to disinterest by users of the Internet is the increasing level of clutter and garbage on the Net. Anyone who has surfed the Internet for information over the past few years has noticed the steady increase in Web sites that appear on search engine lists for specific searches that have very little to do with the information in the search. A large number of these sites have advertising and sales as their number one priority, providing lots of information about sponsors and products without making it easy to find the information you are looking for. Combine this with the concept of short customer attention spans, and you have a recipe for disinterest. The downside of this problem is that there is no solution. Companies hungry for business and profit will continue to pound out more and more advertising, promotional material, and links without any thought as to the overall consequence. The consequence is declining usage rates for the average user.

This does present a great opportunity for companies to capture a large piece of the market with a killer app that cleans and sanitizes the Net for content so that users get high value. This, however, flows against the premise of the open nature of the Internet and could prove to be a significant Internet land mine for future e-commerce companies.

Obvious Advantage of Asset Owners

An asset owner is anyone who owns a physical asset, such as plant and equipment used to manufacture products, or content such as movies or music. One fact that any Internet builder will have to face is that the owners of hard assets have the advantage and over time will capitalize on that advantage. The race to the Net is intense because of this very concept. If your organization doesn't own its assets, you will have to own the customers. You own the customers through branding (creating a widely known brand), familiarity (making the customers familiar with your site), and standards (becoming the standard). If you can attain these goals, then the owner of the hard assets will be relegated to the role of supplier.

However, do not underestimate the power and wealth of organizational asset owners who have the physical assets you need to conduct business. You can open a retail site, but will have trouble selling at rates less than a manufacturer's Web site. The point is that if your technological and marketing savvy and operating methodology were comparable to your suppliers, they could blow you out of the water because they own the product. If they are reading the book *Killer App*, they may just destroy their value chain and you along with it.

The solution to this threat is to own the customers by gathering their loyalty into a cohesive community. Customers will be naturally suspicious of Web sites that promote one manufacturer's product, and suppliers are unlikely to support their competitors. This single piece of information should help you compete with asset owners regardless of their wealth as long as you beat them to the market.

Fragmenting the Net

Fragmentation of the Internet is a growing problem that will command more attention in the coming years. Part of the problem comes from one of Downes & Mui's rules. Creating communities of value will cause the fragmentation of the Internet into successively smaller groups as more and more companies attempt to gather customers to their own community. Customers will feel less like moving to new communities if two requirements are provided:

1. The clutter and garbage on the Net make finding new communities difficult (familiarity).
2. Everything that they need is provided at their current location.

Customers will always venture around the Internet, and this will make trying to build a critical mass of customers into a community of value more and more difficult. Another aspect of Net building that will contribute to this problem will be the race to be "The First to Market." Each new successive venture on the Internet will continue to fragment customers into smaller and smaller groups because each venture will strive to be "New" or the first to market. Obviously, promotion will be the main growth engine of new Internet communities in the coming years. The implication is that unless the concept you are building is so innovative that customers will come to visit your site by word of mouth alone, you will have to find a promotional bankroll as big as that of a large corporation to attract enough traffic to make your venture viable.

Another possibility is that users of the Internet will hunt for goods or information internationally, but deal locally with organizations that they are familiar with. In creating communities of value, the organizations that have the ability to add a physical aspect to the group, such as a local meeting place or physical location near the group, will continue to cross-fragment the market. Members may still occasionally leave the group to surf outside, but the community app will still command the lion's share of the transactions. This assumes that two rules are not met by the organization behind the group. If it is sophisticated enough to provide for its customers, then these external excursions will be smaller in number.

Duplicate Function

As each new venture is started on the Internet, cross-over and duplicate functionality is likely to be more prevalent. Every customized Web page offers news, sports, and stock information, and they are all essentially duplicates of each other. Is Snap better than Yahoo, or is AOL better than ICQ? This duplication of function is a serious limitation to the growth of any new organization since the only way customers will change from their familiar surroundings will be through differentiation. If my Web site offers the exact same functionality as yours, I'll probably stay with my site. If your offering is significantly different, enough that I value it more, I will move. If I am new to the Net, I will most likely start at the most popular sites.

Linking Multiple Web Sites

The linking of sites can be seen by surfing to www.shop.com. On this site, a number of links are chosen that eventually lead to a retail Web site. This provides shop.com with a retail presence without the retail assets.

Duplicating of functions is not easy to manage. In the case of restaurants, more locations in closer proximity can often generate significantly more business than a single restaurant by itself. The same concept on the Internet will not necessarily offer the same benefits since the first example deals with a physical location and the second deals with a virtual location. However, partnering with your competitors to turn them into your suppliers is often the best solution. Using your competitor's site as the foundation of your own organization is the best defense against duplication. Moreover, they have already done the hard part of building their own site, and this allows you to focus on your own special add-on functionality. If the add-on brings you more clients, it will also bring your partner more clients, and everybody will win.

Selling of the Net

Everybody today wants to be an e-tailer. Just try a simple, general search for product information and see how many responses you get for online retail organizations as shown in Figure 6.3. Most general product information searches will result in links to the Web pages of companies trying to sell products. These links force users to scroll through various advertisements and propaganda before they successfully access simple product use information. This is greatly adding to the time that users have to spend on the Net to find something of value, and it has started to cause users to put down the keyboard in frustration. At this rate, the attraction and utility of the Internet is likely to diminish for seasoned users. However, to offset this decline will be the continual rise of new users and Net shoppers. This information should be considered when designing any new e-commerce company or Web site as it will have a direct bearing on traffic levels.

Figure 6.3

Here is a sample product information search. (Microsoft was 17th on the list.)

Control of the Net by Industry/Lockout

There has never been an industry that has such potential for growth as information technology, and this usually attracts the big established corporations such as Microsoft and Disney. However, large global competitors don't like to share their toys, especially with fledgling upstarts; the exception is Microsoft, whose strategy is to "buy-in" to emerging technology that fits their vision of the future. Disney rarely shares. One thing these titans do have in common is the need to control. Almost all large organizations have gained this control through size and branding, but the Internet has caused some of them to shake and shudder at the thought of losing control. This is why the most valuable Internet terra firma, such as the search engines, are being bought up by the big corporations.

The plan is not new: They use money to purchase these virtual assets and then work to control the market. Step two in the plan is to keep out the small fish by creating an overwhelming presence through advertising or by buying the smaller guys out. The Disneys of the world also have the money to buy the right knowledge assets so that just as you are reading this book, so is the Disney war department. The downside of all this is that even if the Net looks like it is free, portions are slowly being swallowed in the background by the big companies and once they have narrowed it down to the "usual country club suspects," it's back to business as usual. Unless, of course, new giant killers emerge.

Even if they succeed in controlling the Internet, so what? Well, the problem with guys like Disney is that they don't share their toys, and they are not likely to keep running things for free. Eventually with size, you will start to see attempts to capitalize on the free content of the Internet. Content is the power of the future, and copyright and trademark are a powerful ally to the big company. So, if Disney and friends own the search engines, they may not blatantly charge a service fee, but they may start charging companies to submit URLs or just relegate those that don't pay far down the result list. Most search engines already offer "services" that allow companies to list their names at the top of a search list, and this is bound to continue. So by capitalizing on their Internet assets, these large organizations can make short run gains (or long run if no competitors emerge) at the expense of the openness of the market.

More Effective and Efficient Coverage— Brute Force Advertising

Let's say that you and I were going to release the same killer app on the Internet. The only difference between us is that a major partner bankrolls my company. If the two apps were identical and entered the market at the same time, they would initially have an equal chance of becoming the "standard." However, since I am bankrolled by very deep pockets, I have the advantage of attracting visitors or generating traffic by a large international advertising campaign.

All else being equal, traffic would flow faster to my app, thereby increasing the chance of its acceptance as the standard and relegating yours to the second place. Your only hope would be to attract enough backing to capture a significant piece of the market to make the app viable. However, just because you are the first to market doesn't necessarily give you all the advantage. There are a number of search engines that are active, viable, and profitable as well (see Figure 6.4). In fact, you could change your app enough to surpass my app's popularity, depending on the change that was made. However, as more and more large organizations enter the fray, it will make it more difficult for the upstart to compete if the business models are the same or similar.

The good news is that by being aware of the world of e-commerce, you can easily out-maneuver your competitors to avoid each pitfall.

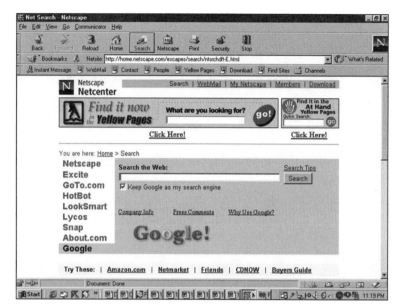

Figure 6.4

There are a number of active and successful search engines.

Avoiding Land Mines

Knowing what land mines exist and where they are is extremely important information that you can use in the development of your e-business. Steering clear of land mines or making your business land mine proof will protect you from the scenarios noted above.

1. Keep the content fresh and interesting, change it often, and provide ample help and assistance.

2. Provide new value by adding new functionality, information or offerings to your market; if you're really effective at this, you will attract new slices of the market to your site all within the same community (called creating subcommunities).

3. Become indispensable to your customers by providing applications that they must use on a regular basis, such as links to search engines, stock quotes, news, etc.

4. When dealing in physical products, be prepared to have a physical location in the future.

5. Make your business fast, efficient, easy to use, and fun.

6. Provide links that add value to the community. If you don't, then users will consider them as nothing more than annoying clutter.

7. Limit the amount of advertising allowed into your community and strictly review links and affiliate sites for content and advertising levels.

8. Use the three-click rule as a testing guideline.

9. Keep the information useful and relevant, clean the site often, and ensure that the amount of useless information is minimal.

10. Ensure that help functions such as FAQ search engines return efficient and clean answers. You can provide detailed archives elsewhere in the site with an appropriate warning of content clutter.

11. Never allow your partners to clutter your site or overapproach your customer (i.e., Spam).

12. Control access to customer information so that they will continue to patronize your site.

13. Avoid killer app competition with asset owners unless

   ➤ You have long term contracts.

   ➤ They are woefully slow or technologically illiterate.

   ➤ Your killer app is better than their offering.

   ➤ Your aim is to sell out to them or their competitor.

   ➤ The competition between asset owners limits their flexibility.

   ➤ They don't have this book.

   ➤ Your app is based on the community and not the asset.

   ➤ You're in it for the short term.

   ➤ The app is a stepping stone to take over the hard assets.

14. Avoid duplicating another killer app unless yours has better functionality, or you are attempting to steal market share or split the market.

15. Use subtle methods to sell and avoid overselling to your own market.

16. Develop an organization or killer app that has the potential to attract or recombine fragmented markets.

17. Promote your app as a standard or as a critical mass by imaging it as a community of value.

18. Partner with compatible organizations and work to lockout the big organizations by continually hitting them where it hurts with high quality free content. This could be called "destroying their value chain."

19. Counteract brute force advertising with savvy Net promotion. One advertisement during the Super Bowl will not generate as much traffic as a well-placed Internet story.

"A moron makes a mistake and continues to make it; an average person make a mistake once or twice and learns to never make it again; a genius learns from the mistakes of others." By knowing the land mines that lay ahead, you can become the genius in your market by simply avoiding them, using them to your advantage, or building a killer app that can withstand them. There are undoubtedly other land mines and pitfalls on the horizon, but by staying informed and keeping in touch with the world of e-commerce, you will greatly increase your chances of spotting them long before they will do any damage. Our best advice is to hire an on-site e-commerce guru to continuously scan and report on changes to the world of e-commerce and i-commerce and how these changes affect or alter your plans. The money will be well spent.

Knowing what it takes to build a killer app and where the land mines are will provide a solid foundation for your business plan to help you create a new e-commerce company or move your existing functions toward the e-commerce model.

The Least You Need To Know

➤ Define what a killer app is per authors Downes & Mui.

➤ Outline Downes & Mui's 12 rules to building a killer app.

➤ Identify potential land mines lurking on the killer app road.

➤ Understand how to avoid land mines and pitfalls.

The Laws of the e-Commerce Jungle

In This Chapter

➤ Moore's Law

➤ Metcalf's Law

➤ How users result in value

➤ Creating partnerships

➤ Competing with large companies

➤ Marketing to leaders

➤ Hiring innovation

The Laws of the e-Commerce Jungle

There are a number of laws that define the e-commerce jungle. And don't be fooled. It *is* a jungle out there where companies either eat or are eaten. Some of the older ones are even hunted for sport. In the midst of all this overnight growth, chaos and big apes are certain laws that apply in this jungle. Knowing the e-commerce laws can help you avoid the nasty quicksand and things that hide in the grass just waiting for your company to come along. These laws are not particularly new, but they are very relevant, and knowing them will go a long way toward helping your company survive and succeed in the wilds of the Internet.

There are a couple of things to consider. First, all laws will eventually be broken and even though you may want to religiously follow a law, remember that as the world changes, so do laws. Often, this strict adherence to a principle can lead to an inability to change quickly, which can have dire consequences for organizations. Secondly, remember that laws attempt to define a precise principle, but with the exception of mathematics or physics, laws rarely last or stay the same over time simply because the world changes. So, you need to understand these e-commerce laws and principles, but remember that there is never any black and white, just various shades of gray.

Moore's Law

In the 60s, Gordon Moore, Intel's founder, predicted that every 18 months chip processing power (as established by chip transistor density) would double while the costs stayed the same. This simple law has held true in general. Transistors were first created in 1949 at Bell Laboratories. They are simply very low-voltage, electrically-powered switches.

Placed in the chips of computers, millions of these switches control the functionality of the computer. In order for Moore's law to be true, more and more of these switches would have to be added to the CPU of the computer for it to become faster. However, if these chips were simply added inside of computers, we would be back to rooms full of machinery and the cost would not decline. What Moore saw was that the technology would advance that would allow for transistors to decrease in size and for more of them to fit on the silicon wafers of chips. Even though the cost of the plants and machines necessary to make these chips would increase, the actual cost per chip would remain constant since more and more would be produced.

Transistors

To get some detailed information on how transistors work, try surfing to http://www.lucent.com/ideas/heritage/transistor/.

This, of course, has a significant impact on the world. It keeps the cost of computers constant, which over time implies that the actual real cost, given inflation, is actually falling. Economies of scale, or buying supplies in volume, help to further reduce the cost, which makes computers accessible for almost everyone. The more people who use computers, the greater the "critical mass" and the benefit of this "mass," which we will discuss in the next law. So, Moore's law incorporates an assumption that even though it would cost more to make the chips that have increased speed, this speed is necessary to make computers more functional and therefore more widely useful. If there were no need for greater and greater speed in computers, there would be no market to justify the investment in chip technology and Moore's law would "hit the wall." We have not reached that point yet.

There is, however, a growing size and weight limitation requirement that is still pushing hardware manufacturers to obtain fully functional computers that are progressively smaller and lighter. This causes pressure to be placed on the chip manufacturers to increase speed while maintaining or even decreasing the size of chips. Smaller devices are required for everything from personal computing devices, integration cell phone computers, networking devices that must be carried by staff, and so on. So the law basically says that computers will get faster, but will remain the same price.

Metcalf's Law

Robert Metcalf, the founder of 3com, made an observation that a network increased in value with the addition of each new user and that this value could be defined as the square of the number of users.

Utility = (number of users)^2 where ^{2} denotes the square.

Often, the value of something is measured by its utility. Utility roughly equates to how useful something is. The point of the equation is not to provide a number that we can impress people with to get dates such as "Hey baby, my network is 36 utils." Instead, the utility of a network formula is used to show the concept that as each new user is added to a network, this mysterious value or worth of the network increases at a faster rate than the number of users. So, if I have a network with one user, and I add user number two, the size of the users would double or have a growth of 100 percent, but the utility would grow by 400 percent.

What constitutes a network in Metcalf's law? Well, since he was the founder of Ethernet powerhouse 3com, a network was likely a network or a group of computers connected together. We are all familiar with a regular computer network, such as the local area network in our offices, the Internet, or bank automatic teller machine networks, but there are a variety of other networks that Metcalf's law applies to. Phones are essentially networks with network interface devices (phones) attached. Other types of networks include utilities that deliver electricity or gas, pipelines that deliver oil, road systems, banking networks with ATMs, satellite TV networks with dishes, credit card networks, and so on.

Value in a Crowded Network

When Alexander Graham Bell made his famous phone call, there were two users. But, if I took the network and tried to sell it, everyone would first say, "What's a phone?" followed by "What use is it to me?" Now, imagine if I put the current worldwide AT&T network with its millions of users on the market at the same time. Which network would be worth more? And if we included the entire worldwide telephone network, it would have an even higher value. The value of the larger network is derived from the fact that everyone knows what a phone network is, and therefore appreciates its value. These larger networks have achieved "critical mass." Alexander's two-person network would have minimal value to the average person.

So what's the point? The point is that the value of a network is the square of the number of its users, and this rule also applies to applications on a network such as

Web Traffic

To see a posted count of the traffic that visits the top Web sites, surf to www.mediametrix.com. Then use the links to go into the Press Room and Press Releases.

Web sites, software, or retail sites. If you are going to build an e-commerce corporation, this point is very important. The value of the organization will grow significantly as more users are added to the company's network or community of users. This can include visitors to an e-commerce retail site, intranet, or users of a distributed application.

This sounds like an obvious statement from a sales perspective because it is obvious that if I add more customers, the value of my company will grow. But what if the application or access to my Web site is distributed for free? We would think that the value of the organization in this scenario would fall to zero, but actually the opposite is true. Amazon loses money, but is worth more than $11 billion; Yahoo doesn't charge its customers, yet is worth billions of dollars; and Ask Jeeves is worth in excess of a billion, even though it provides nothing but links to other Web sites. Their values are derived from the millions of unique visits to their Web sites each year by Net surfers. These users or "traffic" create value according to Metcalf. An example of user demographics to a Web site or traffic is shown in Figure 7.1.

Figure 7.1

Demographics or traffic measures to a Web site are very useful in evaluating a Web site's value.

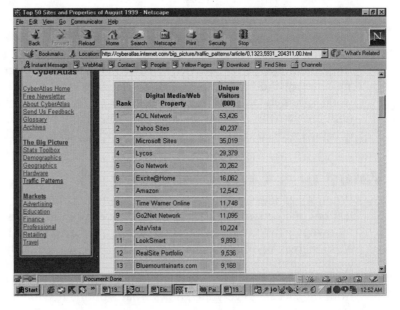

Rank	Digital Media/Web Property	Unique Visitors (000)
1	AOL Network	53,426
2	Yahoo Sites	40,237
3	Microsoft Sites	35,019
4	Lycos	29,379
5	Go Network	20,262
6	Excite@Home	16,062
7	Amazon	12,542
8	Time Warner Online	11,748
9	Go2Net Network	11,095
10	AltaVista	10,224
11	LookSmart	9,893
12	RealSite Portfolio	9,536
13	Bluemountainarts.com	9,168

How Do Users Result in Value?

The real value created by traffic is not just the potential of sales and advertising, but the potential of being the lead killer app in the category and becoming a market standard. If your application becomes the standard for a market, as in the case of the Windows operating system, competitors have a difficult time competing, and you will, in effect, control the market. This provides the ability to dictate changes and control what affiliated or compliant applications are included in with your own killer app.

An affiliated application may be a link in a Web site, a plug-in to software, and so on. What is most valued by the market is the potential to make money in the future, not through sales of the original application, but through sales of the other add-ons, such as training, affiliate sales, software, and so on. The more users that use an application, the greater the value of the application will be. Easy, huh? We'll see how this applies in real e-commerce life at the end of the book.

First to Market—Wins (Usually)

This law is only true to the extent that the first killer app to market has the greatest potential to win, but doesn't guarantee a win. What they will "win" is the chance of becoming a standard and the value associated with this position. But being the first to market does not imply that everything should be held in secrecy.

Secrecy Is Not the Answer

In fact, holding everything in secrecy usually can't be done because there are always disgruntled employees and suspicious vendors ready to spread the news. Even if you are successful, it probably indicates that you have not shared your ideas with the market. When the application is released, you will have to spend a fortune in promotion to get traffic to come and see your site, Internet users will be wary of this phony promotional buzz, and your resources will be smaller because most of your budget will be spent. Also, if you don't share your ideas with the market, you will lose out on the valuable associations that can be gained from partnering with organizations on the same wavelength.

By keeping things "under wraps," you may, in fact, be smothering your killer app to become the "killed app." A better approach is to worry less about the secrecy of your project and concentrate more on getting it to market first. This is especially relevant when we discuss applications that aim to take advantage of a deregulated market, such as the telephone market. The first to market law doesn't guarantee success to the first participant. In fact, any of the following aspects can negatively impact your "first to market" benefits:

➤ If the application is deficient to the number two entrant

➤ If you mismanage the entrance to the market

➤ If you attempt to capitalize too soon on the value

➤ If you ignore your partners

➤ If you ignore the market

The best way to get to market first is to have a clear battle plan that will take you there complete with promotional strategy. But we caution that you shouldn't dwell on the plan; quit goofing around and get down to business.

Learnlots Shares Its Information

Learnlots.com is an organization that was created to provide large Web sites with online education for its customers. Learnlots.com has created an Internet-friendly tutorial format for a wide variety of topics, ranging from how to use Microsoft Word, to how to apply makeup, or how to do a proper push-up. The founders laid the groundwork for the site by contacting publishers and other Web companies with their ideas for the new site. They were not worried that others would beat them to the market; rather, they were trying to generate a buzz in their supply and affiliate community to gather content and partners. We will discuss their business plan at the end of the book, but you can see the site by surfing to

www.learnlots.com

First Out of the Gate Doesn't Guarantee a Win

Remember that first to market doesn't guarantee a win. This is especially true if the second to market is Microsoft. The great Bill Gates Internet miss was his underestimation of the importance of the Internet that caused him to delay development of Internet Explorer. He should have studied Metcalf's law more closely because if he had, Internet Explorer would have beaten Netscape to the market and would have been distributed through that locked-in market of the Windows 95 operating system. The result would have been Microsoft's domination of the browser market, and eventually we would all have used browsers. This also would have given Microsoft a stranglehold on that pesky little upstart Sun Microsystems and its Java application. In fact, Internet Explorer was next in line behind a number of other browsers and yet today owns the top usage spot. It's not a killer app, nor does it have the status of a standard, but that's Bill's folly. If Microsoft had been first to market, just imagine what it could have done and for so much less investment.

Want to Download Netscape for Free?

To download Netscape, surf to www.netscape.com. Want Internet Explorer? Go to www.microsoft.com. Want a Java browser? Go to www.sun.com. Want Java? Go to www.sun.com.

A Small Piece of Big Action Is Profitable

In the early 90s, the deregulation of the phone industry started to generate a number of interesting developments. Smaller competitors were starting to get into the business of sending data over phone lines or their own finer networks. As phone switch-building companies developed new switches that would carry both voice and data, these smaller upstart data companies started to prepare to move into the phone business.

All it would take was fiber optic cables, network interface devices (switches), and a way to get critical mass on the network. Investors who funded the fiber networks in critical areas, such as downtown business zones, completed the first requirement. Phone network supply companies such as Nortel that built the digital switching systems handled the second requirement. The third requirement was fulfilled by the deregulation of the phone industry and rules that forced incumbent phone companies to provide access to their networks so that all calls would be carried regardless of the originating company. This created instantaneous critical mass for the new companies since they could now put a call through to any owner of a telephone. The business plan of the start-up phone companies was simple. They were to be the first to market with a new infrastructure and the latest technology in a deregulated industry that already had critical mass. They had nothing to lose.

This concept, however, doesn't just apply to large deregulated industries. It can also apply to any industry that is dominated by old, slow-moving corporations with massive infrastructures. Your company will have an advantage if you can supply the same service with better technology than a larger incumbent organization. Although larger companies usually have a larger amount of cash to compete with, they often cannot move fast enough to compete with newer technology. They also don't want to bring in new technology too fast because they are trying to protect their existing infrastructure, as was noted in the previous chapter on the killer app. That implies that industries such as banking, utilities, retailing, insurance, real estate, government, publishing, entertainment, and media are all open to the attack of the killer app. Just think about

107

all the steps that are involved for these companies to get a product from supplier to customer. Then decide how you can do the same thing faster, cheaper, and without a distribution network.

Get Partners, Lots and Lots of Partners

You *can* do it alone. You can raise the money, create an awesome killer app, and spill it onto the Internet and be an overnight Web sensation. But you probably want to last more than 15 minutes, and you probably don't have years to build the perfect app, given the previous example. The next best thing is to develop partnerships with companies that can add value to your app. This provides two main benefits. First, they can pass traffic to your killer app in exchange for traffic from your site.

Mutual Partnerships

To see an example of a mutually beneficial partnership, surf to www.learnlots.com. Learnlots.com uses a technology called a Webskin™ to create partnerships between itself and other Web sites. These partnerships work two ways, providing mutual benefit to both parties. For example, learnlots.com's first partner was an e-commerce information company called MySimon.

The basic terms of the learnlots.com's relationship with MySimon involved sending traffic back and forth between MySimon and learnlots.com. The benefit was not only increased traffic flow, but also the ability of both companies to supply their own respective communities of value with the services of the other company. In this case, learnlots.com supplied traffic from other partners to MySimon's Web site, as well as information in the form of tutorials for MySimon's customers. In addition to extra traffic, MySimon supplies learnlots.com with Internet purchasing capabilities for its other partners. Learnlots doesn't have to worry about building an online retail outlet, and MySimon doesn't have to worry about creating the information that its customers crave. Both companies get added value for their customers and increased revenue for themselves through commissions on sales and advertising.

The second thing that your partners can provide is an actual piece of your virtual organization. Let's say that you run an Internet retail outlet that focuses on selling software. You may also want to link to another Web site that provides reviews and tests of software. The goal is to provide your own user community with the added value from the second Web site without having to add and manage this functionality yourself. Now, if you continue to do this a number of times, you will build an organization with significant functionality for your customers without the overhead. The downside occurs if your partner turns out to be unreliable by providing poor service or a poor quality application.

Large Companies Are Large and Can't Move

The fact is that most large corporations are unresponsive to changes in the world around them. They have huge infrastructures with committees, budgets, and managers, that are incapable of movement. By the time they have changed, the market has moved, and the technology has become obsolete. Not all large corporations are this way. Some very inventive entrepreneurs have created large organizations that can turn on a dime. How do they do it? They follow a few basic rules:

➤ Pay attention to the world around you. The only way to do this is to actually get out into the world around you by learning new technologies, talking to companies on the cutting edge, and spending a great deal of time researching technology. There are some ways to make this process more efficient by using electronic news delivery services, by hiring research staff, or by using test labs.

➤ Test new technologies when they are available. Many companies are now using in-house and contract test labs to test new technologies for both functionality and a detailed synopsis of a particular technology's capabilities.

Changing Technology

You can get information on changes in technology through Web sites such as www.zdnet.com *or* the links at http://dir.yahoo.com/news_and _Media/Technology/.

➤ Hire technologically forward-thinking people. Individuals who think outside the box are a very rare breed. They are difficult to find and even more difficult to keep. However, good companies endeavor to satisfy these employees because they are the lifeblood of the new corporation.

Large Companies Have Less Talent

This is a growing phenomenon as new firms start attracting talent through pieces of ownership that large firms would never give up. Giving a stake to its employees is not a new concept. Many organizations have provided stock options and share purchase plans for employees for a number of years. What is new is that these plans were originally only given to senior individuals. Now the talent is becoming increasingly younger, and in order to entice the very best individuals, companies are starting to acknowledge that the young stars are the ones who need the stock options.

Attracting the "Rising Stars"

Most of the new start-up Internet companies have very limited resources. This causes them to search for talented individuals who will accept an equity position in a company in exchange for wages. However, very few established organizations accept the theory that people should be given "a piece of the action" if they don't own the business. Companies like Microsoft have never followed this old style of management. Instead, it has rewarded its employees with generous options that have resulted in a number of millionaires—many who continue to work for the benefit of Microsoft and themselves. The philosophy that no employee should ever be paid more than an executive is absurd in this rapid-paced world of technology. It becomes even more ridiculous when we realize that older executives who have risen to the top over many years do not fundamentally understand the new technological world order or their place in it.

Young "star" employees are realizing their worth and many are abandoning the old corporate structures for the new environment of the virtual organization. No limits, no boundaries, fat stock options, and generous signing bonuses are becoming the rule of the day in the technological world, and it will become even worse as the complexity of the technology grows. This doesn't apply to all technology employees and, in fact, sometimes the level of compensation does not warrant the investment. Many optioned employees are not worth the value of their options: for example, executives who are incapable of effective organization, technology employees who cannot think "outside the box," and employees with extensive experience, but none that is applicable to the current world. Companies have to be very careful in applying the equity of the organization to the talented individuals who will add significant value and then provide those people with higher levels of compensation. At the same time, companies have to strike a balance by ensuring that too little compensation is avoided, or the impact on the organization will be extensive.

Options Are an Option

Options are essentially agreements that obligate the company to sell a certain amount of stock at a certain price level. The intent is to encourage the employees to work hard so that the value of the organization will increase and thereby increase the market price of the stock by making the options valuable. At the same time, delays in the vesting of the options ensure that employees stay with the organization until all benchmarks are complete. For example, a company may give a star employee 10,000 options at the current market value of $15 each and set three benchmarks at 1 year, 2 year, and 3 years. This means that the employee will be able to cash in one third of the options, if he wants, at each benchmark. This is called vesting. The goal is to keep the star employee from leaving the organization.

The downside of options is that if the employee is a poor choice, there is no way to fire him without "paying out the options" or allowing him to continue working. Legally, unless termination is written into the option agreement as grounds for expiration of the options, the company will be stuck with the employee.

A second problem is that often organizations supply mediocre employees with excessive options. These line employees do not necessarily provide any growth potential to the organization and will often cause the "stars" to leave for greener pastures. For example, if the chief accountant has more options that the chief technology officer, the company will run the risk of losing the employee who provides a higher value. To keep employees staying with the organization, the company will have to update the option agreements to add new options to the employee compensation package in later years. Also, for the options to be of any value, the company must be, or plan to be, public in the near future.

The bottom line is that large established organizations are loath to give up share ownership to attract star employees and are even more loath to provide options worth millions to young employees. The result is that these established organizations will have a deficient talent pool in the future that will add to the risk level of the organization. By rights, the value of the organization should reflect this level of technological risk, and as investors and traders become savvier to this measure, stock values will fall. The exception will be organizations that employ talented individuals, reward them to stay, and promote this fact to the world. This is called managing intellectual assets.

Twenty Percent Know, Eighty Percent Follow

The 20-80 rule was founded by marketing specialists decades ago. They quickly realized that 20 percent of the population were likely to try a variation on a product or a new product during its introduction. They also found that within this leader group there was a subset of super leaders that adopted the newer technology first, regardless of price or complexity. The remaining 80 percent were laggards who adopted new innovations after the first 20 percent had proven the use and popularity of the product. This particular rule is very applicable to the world of new technologies such as e-commerce. Twenty percent of companies and individuals within companies will accept innovation. Eighty percent will follow behind.

111

This has never caused too much difficulty until the era of the killer app. Now, organizations that were always exceptionally stable at generating revenue are now under siege from the new upstart virtual organizations and their ownership talent. The result is that the leviathans are effectively caged by their lack of a technologically advanced talent pool. The standard solution of paying higher salaries may not succeed in attracting the talent needed to compete.

Herein lies a true dilemma; if you hire a talent pool, the board of directors must approve the outlay. What they are approving is the outlay of both cash and equity to other people. Only a board with a majority of 20-percenters is likely to approve such an arrangement. But, statistically speaking, your chance of getting the majority of individuals on a board who are innovators is astronomical. What this means is that the new killer app organizations have lightning fast reflexes and carefully developed talent pools motivated by the fact that they will become rich if they bump off your company. On the other side is your board of directors.

The 20 percent innovators are often the most valuable people to have as customers. They will tend to pay more for the technology just to be leaders. These individuals are called the cream of the market. New technologies steal these individuals away simply because they want to be the innovators in the marketplace. The downside of this for the incumbent organization is that these people usually supply a large piece of the overall corporate profitability. The second problem is that they will eventually drag the other 80 percent with them.

Targeting Market Leaders

Competing with established retailers and e-tailers is becoming a very difficult task and the odds against new online retailers are growing. Some companies have chosen to take the approach of targeting the leaders of regional buying groups in promotion and advertising by identifying their traits and actions. Placing ads on Web sites about new technology will likely attract higher income individuals in the 20–40 age target range that these companies are trying to capture. They are not interested in attracting the whole market (it's unrealistic), but instead they are interested in attracting just the leaders willing to try and accept the new approach to online e-tailing.

Nature Giveth and Nature Taketh Away

There is no perfect employee. Exceptionally smart employees can often be arrogant, sarcastic, and difficult to keep challenged, while upbeat employees can often be inefficient and unfocused; technologically brilliant individuals sometimes have difficulty thinking outside their own box, and charismatic individuals are difficult to manage.

Developing e-commerce requires a mix of all these talents. You need charismatic individuals to sell, technologically savvy staff to implement the complex technology, upbeat individuals to add drive and spark, and intellectually intelligent individuals to pull it all together and create innovation. If you choose your team members only from one type of discipline or only with one of the above personality traits, you are losing out on the potential rewards of the others. It is like building a baseball team full of great shortstops. Who's going to pitch, catch, or play first base?

e-Commerce Innovation Center

At www.cf.ac.uk/uwcc/masts/ecic is the Cardiff University e-commerce innovation center that includes case studies and examples of projects.

Diversity in Employees Is Key

e-commerce is a marriage of technology and business. The subtle nature of both must be clearly understood in order for your e-commerce company to efficiently make it to market or for your old company to become an e-commerce company without collapsing the existing business. The likelihood that your network guru is also a marketing guru is remote. Therefore, the move to e-commerce will require an assessment of your existing talent pool's strengths and weaknesses. Back-filling these weaknesses with outside talent is the best option, but to really gain significant benefits, make sure that these individuals bring a wealth of different perspectives to your operation. For example, the combination of a Web application builder, logistics specialist, and customer support specialist will produce a stronger e-commerce application than three programmers.

Staying Innovative

A sure sign of an innovator is someone who reads about, writes about, or studies advancements in his or her field and in other fields. You can easily stay on top of innovation at online technology information providers like www.zdnet.com or www.techweb.com.

Innovate, Innovate, Innovate

It is also important to recruit innovators. Innovation is a true talent because very few individuals can see the forest for the trees and even fewer can tell you what's beyond the forest. Yet, innovation is so essential to the world of e-commerce technology that ignoring it could be catastrophic to your organization. The case of IBM is a classic example of a company that nearly collapsed on itself due to a lack of innovation. Old ideologies allowed guys like Bill Gates to capture vast control over areas such as operating systems and the world of client server computing. Yet even Microsoft nearly missed the Internet innovation. Innovators are a very rare breed, and yet are essential to divining the direction of e-commerce technology.

It is important to understand that individual intelligence manifests itself in different ways. Some incredibly gifted musicians are autistic, some great artists fail math, some great mathematicians cannot write, and most of us fall somewhere in the middle. Effectively mixing the types of intelligence inside your talent pool can lead to some amazing innovation.

People Fear Change, Machines Don't Care

One fact of life is that the vast majority of people avoid change. It is a simple fact that we feel comfortable with things we know, and the only time we change willingly is when we have become bored with the existing status quo. This isn't to say that people won't change; it's just that people are usually unwilling to change as an act of free will. They often have to be enticed or coerced or forced. This has an immense impact on the development and implementation of e-commerce applications from both an internal and external perspective. Internally, employees are usually most open to change when they are young or new to an environment. That is simply because they have not had the time to build a comfort level or familiarity with their environment. They are open to gathering as much information as possible to climb the familiarity curve as fast as possible.

The second place that the acceptance of change will have an impact is with external contacts. Customers will have to be enticed to visit your e-commerce company and suppliers will be wary of any changes that they will have to make. Unfortunately, you need these individuals to accept your innovation in order for you to succeed. This aspect was covered briefly in the rules of the killer app related to "Ensuring Continuity for the Customer." The underlying reason for ensuring continuity for the customer was to avoid the reluctance of your customers toward change. If they are familiar with the new interface, then they will be more likely to use it. As for new customers, they usually have to be coerced with clever promotions or by following the leaders.

Fear of change goes hand-in-hand with the previous law of the e-commerce jungle regarding innovation. The primary reason for lack of innovation is fear of change. If we avoid change, then we will likely see only minimal benefit from innovation. This fear is also highly motivated by our own personal fear of not understanding the innovation and our growing lack of leisure time in our busy lives. Basically, change takes time and effort. Who has any of that? However, change is essentially not just to stay ahead of the competition, but to stay ahead of the workload. Pouring money into e-commerce development will yield savings in one of the most precious commodities, our time. If we free up some time, then maybe we will be more willing to study change and the vicious circle of more work, lack of time, no innovation—and more work will finally cease. This investment in technology will also yield a side benefit; since machines don't fear change, change is easier to implement. The more technologically advanced your organization is then the less you will have to deal with aspects such as the fear of change.

Fear of Change

You want to see information on change? Surf to www.google.com and type in "fear of change" to see that there are thousands of documents on the subject.

Spend on the Future, Not the Past

Companies spend an enormous amount of time and money on looking back or just staying up with change. Accounting departments spend a great deal of time and resources to produce financial statements and analyses that review what has just happened, sometimes a month ago.

Although accounting is an essential way for any organization to track its performance and even provide indications of future trends, spending resources on producing another report is one less resource available to push ahead. Accounting does, however, provide the foundation of any organization, and it is essential to implement systems that will reduce the resource requirements of this back-office system. Large companies are notorious for maintaining complex accounting structures that provide minimal benefit but use a great deal of resources.

Consistent procedures are the key to building a successful real-time accounting system. Real-time accounting systems capture information on a transaction-by-transaction basis from point-of-capture through to the general ledger without human intervention. This then allows management to obtain information quickly and in real-time so that resources can be spent looking forward.

Once you have implemented the foundation of your organization, you can spend more time looking ahead and far less time looking back. Getting your employees to change will be more difficult. Many managers protect their own personal interests by building extensive empires or undocumented complexity. Many major corporations have hundred of legal entities and as many bank accounts to manage their operations.

The same functionality easily can be managed by using a fraction of the entities and bank accounts at a significantly reduced level of overhead. Often the response from executives and managers is that the entities are needed and cannot be reduced. However, some of the largest organizations in the world operate with a handful of entities and bank accounts.

Tie It All Together

In order for a corporation to survive in the demanding, fast-paced world of e-commerce, it will require a number of things to succeed. It must have a mix of talented people who can produce a wide ranging and forward thinking viewpoint and yet have the ability to complete goals and understand complex technology. It must have a focus on efficiency that eliminates waste and redirects resources to value-added tasks while focusing the organization on looking ahead. It must gather traffic to its Web site, its products, or its innovations in order to become the leader of its industry to create critical mass and become the standard. It should endeavor to be the first to market with innovation in order to lead the competition. It should ally itself with like-minded organizations and go after the established titans' high-profit markets with a low or no overhead structure. It should not fear the big established organizations because they are slow to move and short of talent. It should hire the best people and reward them for being the best. It will succeed.

Safeway

At one time the Canadian division of Safeway Store International operated a $14 billion annual treasury flow through two legal entities and less than a dozen bank accounts.

The Least You Need to Know

➤ Moore's Law—every 18 months chip processing power doubles while the costs stay the same.

➤ Metcalf's Law—a network increases in value with the addition of each new user.

➤ It's imperative to get partners.

➤ Find the leaders in the market.

➤ Go after the lucrative markets.

➤ Big companies have weaknesses.

➤ Hire innovative employees.

➤ Companies should look ahead, not back.

Part 2
Opportunities in e-Commerce

It's wide open and new, fast, and exciting. It's the world of e-commerce, and the opportunities are endless. In this section, we will go into some of the details of what you have to do to become an e-business. First, we'll discuss the concept of real-time and integrated systems, particularly as they relate to the back office.

Then we'll discuss the supply chain and how you can automate in order to significantly drop the cost of doing business. We'll look at some of the things that Amazon.com did and provide you with some online examples that you can link to.

We'll look at how to manage your customer relationships better by using e-commerce and how to build an i-center or online customer service center. Knowing all about managing your electronic payments is critical to e-commerce, and we'll also discuss the latest technologies and security.

We'll close the section with a look at how to build and manage a virtual workforce and work environment, and the last chapter will look at the concept of data mining, including how to store, retrieve, and analyze your operational information to make better decisions.

At the end of this, you will be able to build the foundation of your new e-business and be ready for the next section on marketing in this new world.

It's Just a Matter of Time: Real Time vs. Batch

In This Chapter

➤ What real-time systems are and how they can work for you

➤ How systems can create near-zero transaction costs

➤ Why batch systems are dinosaurs compared to today's technology

➤ Real-time, back-office systems and why you need them

➤ Things you should know about information storage

Real-Time Systems Defined

There are basically two types of software: Those that process information on a transaction-by-transaction basis and those that store data for processing at a later time. The first is called a real-time system and the second a batch system. Originally, computers were expensive, slow, and required offices full of programmers and operations staff, yet to process a single transaction could often take a room full of hardware many minutes to complete.

It was during this period that the Henry Ford mass production model was inadvertently used as a basis for programming. The goal was to gain enough speed and cost efficiency to make the use of computers justifiable for large organizations. Remember that the old behemoth mainframes required a great deal of a company's resources for everything from special ventilation to permanent maintenance and operations staff. Thus, the concept of grouping the transaction data and applying a programmed routine to this batch of information was born. In this era, the computers could be scheduled to run at more advantageous times when the office staff were not present, and apply programming routines that repetitively processed high volumes of information such as month-end accounting data.

The Batch Era and the Introduction of the PC

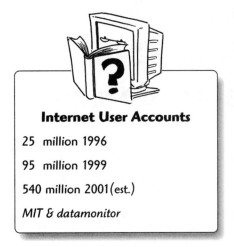

Internet User Accounts

25 million 1996

95 million 1999

540 million 2001(est.)

MIT & datamonitor

As the years progressed, the cost of hardware fell, new software and operating systems reached the market, and the speed of computers significantly increased. In this environment, these batch programs actually performed even better and allowed the programmers to focus their attention on new processes, such as capturing document data typed in letters and memos, improving data communications such as file and data transfers, and providing greater data analysis.

With the introduction and acceptance of the desktop PC, an entirely new "world order" emerged. The power of computing was instantaneously distributed to users, and software was created that allowed them to produce documents and ad hoc reports from their very own computers. Batch systems that ran on mainframes still commanded the bulk of computing resources, but new online processing such as automated banking and order entry were starting to emerge and produce significant operational cost savings. In the distance was the rumbling of a new technology called distributed computing or networking that was about to change everything.

The introduction of networking software to the general public was simply an extension of the project by DARPA to connect large mainframes at various government defense departments and educational institutions. This project was the Internet, and the distributed or "spread-out" nature of this environment gave rise to the greater use of transaction-based processing (processing information one transaction at a time) such as e-mail and file transfers. Even the basic premise of sending a "packet" of information over a network between two computers lent itself to the processing of information one transaction at a time.

Object-Oriented Code and Databases

As the cost of computers continued to fall and their speed increased, programmers found two avenues to explore. The first was the storage of data in a series of indexed files or tables called a database, and the second was the development of object-oriented code. In an object-oriented coding environment, variables (data storage capsules) are passed into an object or piece of programming code that processes the contents of the variable and returns either a new variable or some other type of output. The goal is to create an "object" that performs an action on a type of variable, regardless of the value or contents of the variable.

How the Internet Was Born

The Internet started life as a project of the United States Defense Department's DARPA (Defense Advanced Research Projects Agency). They wanted to link the computing environments of major government agencies and universities involved in defense research to a network that would provide continuous communications and processing capabilities should any part of the network be destroyed by an act of war. The primary focus was on the long-distance transmission of packets of information and the routing of these messages around "damaged" areas. The project was titled ARPANET (Advanced Research Projects Agency Network) and focused on the transmission of data over a network using a new suite of protocols called TCP/IP (Transmission Control Protocol/Internet Protocol).

In 1985 the NSF (National Science Foundation) started implementation of a new program to establish Internet access across the USA through the implementation of a high-speed, high-volume backbone called NSFNET. Then in 1989, Tim Berners-Lee developed a set of hypertext standards for CERN (The European Laboratory for Particle Physics), and the Net was born.

For example, it is easy to write a piece of code for a robotic arm that accepts a number and converts it into a signal to move the arm the same number of millimeters as the number. The small "snippit" of program code now can be referenced from elsewhere in a program or by other programs to move the arm. The alternative, which was widely used, was to code the distance into the program whenever the arm needed to move. As you can see, to make a simple change to the distance would require recoding the program. The concept of object-oriented code is an essential element of most programming performed today, and it is the basis of programming languages such as Java by Sun Microsystems. An example of Java code is shown in Figure 8.1.

Figure 8.1

Here is an example of program code for Java.

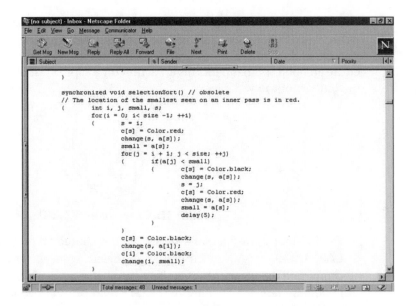

```
                )

                synchronized void selectionSort() // obsolete
                // The location of the smallest seen on an inner pass is in red.
                (      int i, j, small, s;
                       for(i = 0; i< size -1; ++i)
                       (       s = i;
                               c[s] = Color.red;
                               change(s, a[s]);
                               small = a[s];
                               for(j = i + 1; j < size; ++j)
                               (       if(a[j] < small)
                                       (       c[s] = Color.black;
                                               change(s, a[s]);
                                               s = j;
                                               c[s] = Color.red;
                                               change(s, a[s]);
                                               small = a[s];
                                               delay(5);
                                       )
                               )
                               c[s] = Color.black;
                               change(s, a[i]);
                               c[i] = Color.black;
                               change(i, small);
                       )
```

And where were all the batch programs? Alive and well, still trudging along, and oblivious to the world around them. That is until two events converged. The first was the Y2K threat, over-hype, hoax, or Armageddon (take your pick). Inside these old batch programs were the first noted Y2K threats, and this started the greatest process of software replacement in the history of computing. It is interesting to note that most of the problems originated with code that was *not* object-oriented.

The second event was a small Internet company called Amazon.com. Amazon was started in 1995 to capitalize on the growing use of the Internet to purchase books online with a credit card. Figure 8.2 shows the Amazon home page. It was always an Amazon corporate mantra that its internal systems would allow for this process to occur online and in real-time—10 million Amazon customers later, the stodgy world of retailing stopped dead in its tracks.

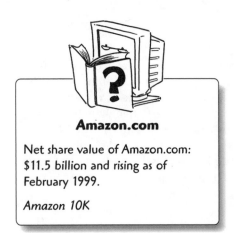

Amazon.com

Net share value of Amazon.com: $11.5 billion and rising as of February 1999.

Amazon 10K

The customers at Amazon enter their orders for books online as easily and efficiently as if they were shopping at a store. They also pay for the books immediately by using credit cards. This is not significantly different from any other retail operation except that the customers are doing the work of order entry.

Where the most significant change occurred was in Amazon's ability to process these orders in real time. The minute an order is entered into the Amazon Web site, the highly automated process of picking, shipping, and restocking the books begins. This is far different from the old batch world of gathering all the orders for a day to run an overnight process that would print warehouse picking lists or re-order reports. The per-transaction cost of completing a purchase at Amazon is a fraction of the cost of completing the transaction at a traditional retailer, and it does not require expensive retail space.

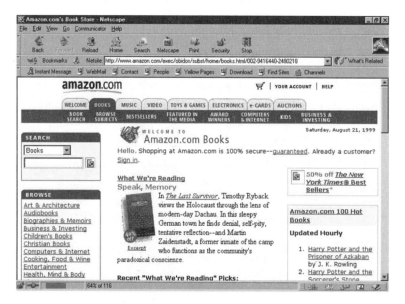

Figure 8.2

Amazon.com's home page is linked to its internal, real-time operating system.

The Near-Zero Transaction Cost

So what does all this have to do with e-commerce and you? Simply that e-commerce is the movement toward real-time and fully integrated systems and away from batch systems and batch-processing methodology. You must decide how your organization will do this if you have any hope of competing with the Amazon.coms of the world.

A real-time system processes a transaction instantaneously from start to finish. There are no information flow stoppages or holding of data or intermediate delays for human processing. This drives the per-transaction cost (the total cost to complete a transaction) to an extremely low level.

The following list includes traditional costs to complete a single order (a per-transaction cost can be calculated by dividing a total cost figure by the total number of orders received over a set time period such as a year):

➤ Monthly telephone expense	To receive orders
➤ Long distance or bulk expense	For 1-800 lines
➤ Staff wages customer service	Customer service clerks
➤ Rent/Utilities CS	Customer service center
➤ Desk/Supplies CS	Customer service center

123

➤ Desktop   PC CS hardware costs & software licenses

➤ Desktop maintenance costs   To keep customer service PCs running

➤ Staff benefits CS   The cost of benefits provided to the staff, such as health care

➤ Server & networking expense   Inclusive of hardware/software/maintenance/depreciation

➤ Payment handling charges   Staff costs, as opposed to automated payment systems

➤ Order printing   Paper, toner, printers, maintenance, physical order storage

➤ Staff wages and benefits WH   Warehouse staff for picking and packaging order and preparing shipping documents

➤ Shipping expense   Packaging and courier expense

➤ Rent/utilities WH   Customer service center

➤ Warehouse supplies   Racks, bins, etc.

➤ Other corporate overhead   Admin/accounting/mgmt staff, insurance, bank fees, etc.

➤ Inventory carry charge   Lost interest earned on the value of inventory

➤ Marketing & promotion   Expenses related to attracting customers

➤ Credit/fraud/loss   For fraudulent credit card usage

➤ Returns & damage   For damaged or returned goods

Just What Time Is It?

There is an extensive body of research related to real-time systems. Many of the universities in North America have dedicated their intellectual resources to the study of real-time systems, and most of this science studies machine and work processes. e-commerce, however, is more concerned with back-office functionality or how efficiently the internal systems process a transaction or perform a function. The goal is to reduce the resource expenditures on a per-transaction basis. For example, if a customer enters an order, there is no reason why the income statement should not reflect this transaction a few seconds after the order has been placed.

Obviously, the more costs that can be eliminated through the use of systems, the greater the advantage you will have over your competitors. Approaching zero cost is attainable, but only if your systems can process a transaction with very limited human involvement. To achieve a near-zero cost level will require the additional benefits and time savings provided by real-time systems. By making *all* your company's systems real-time, you will provide the business with a very solid foundation from which to grow.

Real-Time Systems in the Back Office

One of the easiest places to start the process of moving to real-time systems is the back office. The back office comprises all of the functions that support the "visible" or "production" operations of the organization. Production processes are actions, such as manufacturing or construction, and visible processes are external functions, such as sales and service. The vast majority of the back-office resources are dedicated to accounting and finance.

There are numerous accounting packages available that operate in a real-time mode. Navision Financials is an example of an accounting package that has the functionality to create an automatic sales journal entry when an order has been completed. However, the greatest difficulty with any of the existing accounting systems currently on the market is their legacy—old programming methodologies that have been given a fresh coat of paint, i-commerce capabilities that are ineffective or incomplete, and old batch methodologies that are fired up one transaction at a time. However, the consumer would not accept waiting for a batch process.

Bean Counting 101

Number of accountants

Approx 1.5 million

U.S. Census

Actual number of accountants including accounting clerks

A bazillion

Some guys who drink too much coffee

The Need for Speed and Storage

Operating a real-time system requires two important components, very high-speed processors and large storage capabilities. The whole purpose of the old batch processing strategy was to capture the speed and efficiency of a repetitive process, much like the efficiency of an assembly line. These concerns were very real issues in the 70s and 80s, but now those issues are not as prevalent due to the low cost of processors.

The ability to complete transactions one at a time requires a great deal of processing speed from the computers that will perform the tasks. Today, a 500Mghrtz chip set for

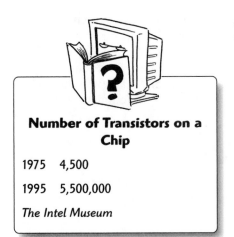

Number of Transistors on a Chip

1975   4,500

1995   5,500,000

The Intel Museum

a server is under a thousand dollars, and the introduction of programs and systems that can perform multiple tasks simultaneously (asynchronous processing) and distribute the workload over one or more processors in the same server has reduced the processing time required by these applications. The power of a Web server running true multithread operational software built with true object-oriented programming on a system that has multiple processors is more than adequate to start the creation of a virtual back office for your company.

The second important element is storage. As each customer enters data into your system, you will need to store this information for a variety of reasons. Data mining (see Chapter 13, "There's Gold in Them Thar Hills: Data Mining") is a concept that is based on the collection and storage of *all* transactions and information. This is particularly valuable when the information pertains to customers.

The Data Mine

Data mining is the process of using stored data to assist current operations for financial benefit. The most common of these is to analyze customer sales information to adjust product mixes (which products are carried). However, data mining can also be used to assist in creating sales promotions, manage inventory levels, cash flow requirements, etc. Capturing and storing all operational information is the key to the success of future data mining activities.

Storage

There are a number of storage methodologies and hardware available in the market today, and each method has different benefits and costs. When implementing a real-time, back-office system, the existing storage capabilities of the organization must be reviewed. This is especially true when an organization moves toward the storage of objects within a database (code and information together). A simple full-color graphic of an inventory item can take up a significant amount of space on a disk. Hundreds or thousands of these items can swamp it. In addition, new technologies, such as video (see Figure 8.3), are likely to play an increasingly important role in business and will require even greater amounts of storage.

Figure 8.3

You can get streaming video from the Internet by using a video player like Real Player.

When you research storage possibilities for your company and its e-commerce opportunities, here are some terms you'll need to be familiar with.

Storage Terminology

➤ IDE hard drive—A single storage mechanism, multiple IDE drives can be installed on a server

➤ SCSI (Small Computer System Interface)—Takes the concept of IDE one step further by allowing more drives and more functional sharing

➤ RAID—A storage architecture in which multiple disks operate as if they were one

➤ Optical—CDs are an example of an optical storage device.

➤ SAN (Storage Area Network)—Where data is stored over a distributed network in different locations

➤ Data Warehouse—A large centralized storage area such as a database

➤ Data Mart—Smaller, distributed data storage areas

➤ Online storage systems—Storage at another location, usually run by a third party

Understanding these concepts will help you start implementing the new systems that will provide the foundation of your e-commerce program.

The Least You Need To Know

➤ Define what a real-time system is.

➤ Know a very brief history of computing and the Internet.

➤ Review the concept of object-oriented software.

➤ Decide why we need real-time, back-office systems.

➤ Know something about the near-zero cost transaction.

➤ Comprehend the need for speed and storage.

King of the Jungle— The Automated Supply Chain

In This Chapter

➤ Defining the supply chain

➤ Automating the supply chain

➤ Getting vendor buy-in

➤ Automating warehouse and delivery systems

➤ Defining the customer-driven supply chain

Defining What a Supply Chain Is

A supply chain is simply the combination of tasks that a company performs to move services or products from suppliers to customers. This basic definition is simple, but becomes far more complex when we try to build a model of a generic supply chain that can be used by all companies. Your company may sell software, but that is a significantly different supply chain from a company that drills for oil. Or is it?

We need a model to assist us in defining standards that will drive the development of our e-commerce automation. Without these standards, we run the risk of developing inconsistent and incompatible systems or systems that won't work together. Microsoft Windows is successful because its software is a standard for operating systems. Microsoft originally pushed its way into delivering its software to users for what appeared to be no charge (it was bundled with the PCs), and because users could easily pirate the software, its use grew to critical mass.

Why It's Difficult To Define a Generic Supply Chain Model

Trying to define a generic supply chain that is applicable to all type of organizations is very difficult for a variety of reasons.

1. There are almost as many variations of supply chains as there are companies.

2. Each organization participates in the supply chain to varying degrees.

3. There are physical supply chains (actual physical product moves through an organization) and virtual supply chains (no physical product moves through the organization).

The Generic Supply Chain

At one end of the spectrum are companies that control the entire chain from the production of basic materials right through to the delivery of the end product to the customer. For example, a large energy company that explores and produces natural gas may also ship the product through its own pipeline to its own power generating station and deliver electricity over its own grid to its own customers. This is an example of a highly controlled supply chain.

On the opposite end of the spectrum are companies that open a Web site with some form of content to attract customers and then link to a sales organization such as Amazon.com. They provide their customers with the capability to order product through their Web site, but never manage the actual physical flow of the product, such as the mySimon Web site shown in Figure 9.1. This task is managed by the actual online sales company (we will discuss this e-commerce business model in a later chapter when we look at sales linking organizations).

Figure 9.1

mySimon Web site connects buyers and sellers only without carrying inventory.

A Generic Supply Chain Model

Vendors	Accept orders from company
	Supply inputs or final products
	May ship product direct to customer
Company	Send purchase order to vendors (purchasing)
	Manufacture final product if needed (operations)
	Present product to customers (marketing)
	Accept orders for product (sales/customer service)
	Ship product to customer (logistics)
	Receive payments/pay vendors (A/P—A/R)
Customer	Order product
	Receive product
	Pay for product

Note: When we discuss products, we are including both products and services.

This model is general enough to apply to all businesses, regardless of their products or services. If I run an escort agency, my product is the service of provisioning companionship, and my employees are essentially vendors that are supplying an input (labor). Microsoft supplies software, but it doesn't own the forestry company that makes the box or the plastic plant that supplies the CDs (at least, not yet). These products are considered inputs into the software production process so Microsoft both orders and manufactures products. Both these examples fit the model.

Why do we even need a generic model? Because it provides an easy starting point for understanding how to and why we would want to automate a supply chain. We have just defined the process in general, and now we can define how to automate the process. It's that simple.

Breaking the Chain—Automating Your Supply Chain

If we keep in mind the simple supply chain model cited previously, we can see there are two main flows to automate.

1. The flow between the vendor(s) and the company.
2. The flow between the customers and the company.

Step One: Automating the Vendor Flow

The vendor/company flow consists of sending an order to the vendor, receiving a product from the vendor, and paying for the product. The first thing to do is to automate the communication process that occurs between the company and the vendor. One of the easiest ways to automate this process is to email your orders direct from your purchasing system to the vendor. It is usually a relatively easy task to have a purchasing system dump purchase order information into a text file that can then be sent to a vendor inside of or attached to an e-mail (see Figure 9.2).

A more complex solution is for your vendor to design an ordering system that accepts order information directly from the Internet. Your company could establish an account with the vendor and sign onto a secure server on the vendor's Web site to complete orders. Another automation method would be for your company to send the data electronically in a file that can be processed by the vendor's system. This may involve a direct link to the vendor or the delivery of an encrypted order file over the Internet. The drawback to this particular scenario is that each vendor will probably have a different order/entry system, each with its own unique file format for processing the information. Building a different interpreter for each vendor would be very time-consuming and costly.

Figure 9.2

Email is one way for order information to be sent to a vendor.

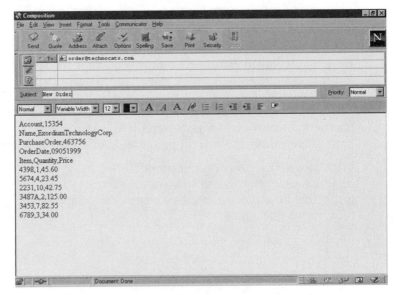

Electronic Data Interchange (EDI)

Electronic Data Interchange was developed to solve this exact problem. Using a set of standards (ANSIx12 or UN/EDIFACT), companies were able to send their information in standard formats that the vendor could then interpret by using the same standards. The problem is that most companies do not have the capability to interpret their own information into ANSIx12 so the services of an intermediary are required to act as a translator. This task earned companies like IBM and the major banks a healthy revenue and severely limited the growth of EDI.

A New Blend of EDI and HTML

In 1997, a W3 working group started work on the development of a set of standards that would combine EDI and XML. This combination is presented as a needed standard for electronic commerce transactions so that Net developers will be able to design e-commerce solutions that easily communicate with each other. The one drawback to this approach is that standards are by their nature inflexible, and e-commerce systems at this time require a great deal of flexibility. The risk is that any new attempt to tightly regulate format and content is likely to receive limited acceptance. For more information on this initiative, you can surf to http://www.w3c.org/ECommerce.

Vendor Buy-in

People resist change. People want control. These are two of the biggest roadblocks to successfully automating the vendor portion of the supply chain. Most of your vendors have systems and operations that are no doubt unparalleled in efficiency and effectiveness. Or at least that's what they believe. If you now tell them that you want them to change these processes, you will likely receive significant resistance to this effort. Simply put, people resist change and want to be in control so that unless your orders are of significant size, your ability to change your vendors' operations will be limited.

The best approach is to give them a dozen copies of this book, try to persuade them to your way of thinking, and provide them with options that are easy to implement or adjust. Some of the most successful vendor automation programs start with the vendor as a development team member, included in the process from the start. This assists in lowering vendor resistance and leads to the design of better systems.

Step Two: Automating the Receiving Process

Now that order information is being captured and processed automatically, the next step is to automate the receiving process. This step consists of two pieces:

1. Receiving the product into inventory
2. Confirming and tracking the shipping of products delivered direct to customers

The thing that will drive this process will be the receipt of goods at the warehouse or the confirmation of delivery to the customer.

A Standard Model for Receiving Inventory

➤ Order product.

➤ Set up a vendor information object.

➤ Set up an inventory information object.

➤ Create a purchase order using the vendor and inventory objects as inputs.

➤ Deliver the purchase order information to the vendor.

➤ When the product arrives or is delivered, add items to the inventory as received.

➤ Create the payment file (this can be automatic or based on an invoice).

➤ Create the final product (the new inventory item may include multiple old inventory items).

➤ Transfer items between types of inventories (raw material to finished goods).

If every input into an organization is treated in a similar fashion, including the application of labor and overhead as an instantaneous inventory (the costs flow into a pool and then get allocated to the final product cost), then the ability to create a real-time financial system is relatively easy.

To automate the receiving process, the information used to produce the purchase order as shown in Figure 9.3, will also be used to acknowledge receipt of the product. In older receiving models, a purchase order is printed and mailed, and the receiving information is keyed into the system when the product is received. You can automate this process by having re-order information posted to a secure server for pick-up by the vendor, allowing your vendor to view your inventory levels online to automatically ship the product, or by pushing re-order information to the vendor's Web site or system.

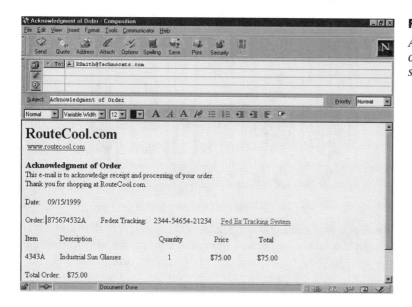

Figure 9.3

Acknowledgment of an online order is usually sent via email.

The Barcode

A barcode is a series of vertical black lines of varying width separated by white spaces, most commonly used on grocery products as shown in Figure 9.4. A barcode can be used to represent various alphanumeric information, such as inventory item numbers. This information can then be attached to a product and read by a scanning device that uses lasers to read the dark and light area of the bar code. A computer would interpret the data for use by an application. Organizations such as the UCC (Uniform Code Council) and ECCC (Electronic Code Council of Canada) set standards so that product manufacturers and vendors can read the codes on all products regardless of the hardware and software used. For more information on barcodes, try http://www.uc-council.org.

Figure 9.4

Barcodes allow computers to use scanning devices to read information from labels.

In our automated supply chain, barcodes could be attached to products that are shipped from the vendor if your vendor agrees or has standard codes already affixed to the product. However, having the vendor barcode such information as the PO number, product count item number, and even bin locations on packages would greatly aid in the automation of the receiving process. When the product arrives at the warehouse, the receiver can simply scan the code with a reader, and the system will match the receiving to an order, update the inventory level, release the PO for payment, or cause an automated warehouse to store the product on a shelf.

The Automated Warehouse—a Hypothetical Example

The automated warehouse works like this. A product is received on the loading dock, is read into inventory by a barcode reader, and then is placed in one of a series of standard plastic bins by the receiver. An automated placement system controls a series of belts that accept these standard plastic bins and pass them to a tagging system (larger products are stored on pallets and placed by forklift robots). The tagging system reads a barcode card that is attached to the bin, and the bin is then sent along a series of belts to narrow storage isles where a placement robot will store the bin and transmit the location to the inventory system. Multiples, or groupings, of product are placed in dynamic bins that are reset when the warehouse staff takes an item from the bin.

When a customer places an order for a product, the system knows exactly how much of the product is available and where the product is stored. It uses the reverse of the storage process to extract the items for shipping, automatically prints and attaches delivery information to the box, and then sends it to the loading dock.

Automating Delivery Systems

Another area that can be easily automated is the delivery of product. Many of today's largest courier companies are already a great distance down the e-commerce path, such as FedEx and their Internet Shipping Service. Their ability to track a package is unrivalled by other industries and relies heavily on real-time systems, extensive use of bar coding, and automation.

It is highly unlikely that these companies will change their systems for your company, but as a customer, they will provide you with a variety of alternatives such as Internet access, software, and if your company is large enough, they will build an interface to your logistics systems. Luckily, these couriers have made this quite easy for their customers by limiting the amount of information required for delivery through the use of customer account numbers and standardization of the dynamic information such as delivery addresses. By using these standards, you can easily mirror the information within your system to produce a delivery slip. Tracking packages through the Internet is an easy way to provide your customers with a low cost method for following their orders simply by including a tracking number from the courier in the order confirmation email and by providing a link to the courier's tracking system on your Web site.

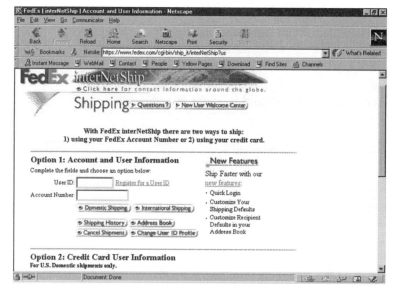

Figure 9.5

FedEx Internet shipping service allows companies to easily ship products.

If you choose to use your own delivery system, then you can automate the delivery process by using tablet PCs for your delivery staff (computers that resemble the screen portion of a laptop and use a stylus or electronic pen for entering data). A tablet PC allows you to load shipment delivery information, obtain a digital signature from customers with a stylus, and easily transmit delivery information back to your system for

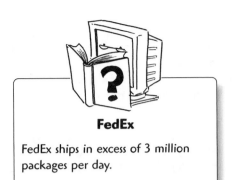

FedEx

FedEx ships in excess of 3 million packages per day.

FedEx

Web access by your customers. You can even incorporate GPS data into the mix by automatically tracking deliver truck positions against a database of GPS delivery locations.

At this point, automated systems should allow you to order product from a vendor, receive and store the product in an inventory, track product as it moves through different inventories, and ship the product and track the movement of the package through the delivery system.

GPS

Global Positioning Systems use a series of low-level satellites that transmit messages back to earth. Messages are comprised of the satellite's position and a special digital code used to calculate the message travel time. Three of these signals can be received and used to triangulate the position of the receiving unit, called a GPS Receiver. This information can then be transmitted by radio or cellular to a computer to track the delivery progress of a truck.

The Customer Flow

The second major type of flow in the process of automating the supply chain is the flow between the customer and the company. This flow is also known as the order/entry flow.

Customer-Powered

In the current world of order entry, customers are rarely required to enter order information. Call centers are staffed often with hundreds of operators who key in the details of customer orders and the information to establish customer accounts or payment details. Call center staff do provide an important link to the customer, and, in some instances, have been shown to add to the volume of sales. However, in most instances they only provide minimal incremental value to the organization and are simply high-level key entry clerks.

Standard Model of Order Entry

1. A customer chooses to purchase a product.
2. A sales order is created or derived from a quote.
3. Inventory is checked and reserved.
4. A back order is created if required.
5. Product is shipped.
6. An invoice is sent to the customer.
7. The payment is received and deposited.
8. The payment is applied to the invoice.

A better solution is to move the organization towards an automated environment where the customer enters the order and account information directly into your system, such as the Amazon order screen shown in Figure 9.6. This can be accomplished through the transmission of order information online for high-volume customers or through Internet order systems for low volume transactions. The key to the success of this type of migration is simplicity of use. If your customers find it complicated or time-consuming, they will not use your system.

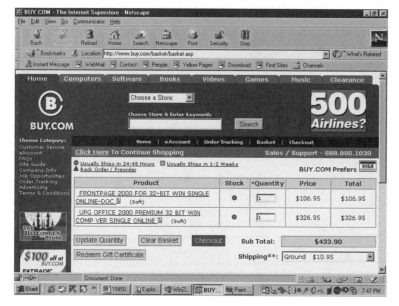

Figure 9.6

Buy.com order entry screen allows customers to enter order information that is used by internal systems to complete the order.

The major benefit of this type of program is that your call center key-entry staff can now be directed to perform value added functions, such as help desk, service, and sales or data mining. The downside is that you will still require some level of call center operation for those customers who refuse to deal with a machine or are not sophisticated enough to place their own orders. You will also have to dedicate staff to assist customers who want to transfer bulk information electronically (this should be easier when standards for e-commerce ordering are set and accepted).

i-Commerce Solutions

Businesses have created systems that customers can access directly through phones or dial-up software, but these are limited either to those customers who have the accessing hardware and software or by the limitations of phone systems. So the obvious choice for effective automated order entry is the Internet, and it is such a good option that it is the only one we will discuss. Almost everybody has access to it, and the standards used in the Internet, such as HTML and forms, make it an ideal automation solution.

We will discuss some aspects of marketing in later chapters, but for now let's assume that customers are interested in doing business with your company. The first step in the order/entry automation process is to create a method for allowing your customers to create new accounts or access existing account information. This is the personal information related to a customer, and it is essential in order to complete the order and to manage and mine the information related to that customer (we will discuss data mining in more detail later).

Another critical function is the presentation of decision-making information to the customer. This includes everything from a catalogue of items and prices to detailed company or product information like the mySimon Web site. Your Web site will provide the medium for data presentation, and it should be built in such a way that the data can be easily updated or automatically updated in real time by your internal systems.

Your customer must also be able to easily assemble an order. This is usually accomplished by purchasing either shopping cart software or by utilizing the services of an online shopping company.

The final piece is the capture of payment information, usually processed through a secure connection to a secure server so that others are unable to see your credit card information. All of these technologies are currently available and easy to implement.

The Simple Online Order System

Step 1: Create a Web page form that is comprised of the following information:

A series of check boxes beside a list of your product's description, prices, and an image.

A series of entry boxes for customer information.

A link to a secure credit card server or service like escrow.

Step 2: Wait for orders via email

The Least You Need To Know

➤ Define what a supply chain is.

➤ Understand how to automate the vendor process.

➤ Know how to automate the receiving process.

➤ What options are available to automate the delivery process.

➤ How to automate the customer order entry process.

➤ Identify i-commerce solutions to managing customer orders.

The Customer Is King

In This Chapter

➤ Defining on-demand customer service

➤ Different types of call centers

➤ The virtual call center

➤ The Web information model

➤ Outsourcing your customer service

On-Demand Customer Service

In the previous section, we briefly discussed some of the issues related to automating the call center, specifically the order entry functions. On the surface, the goal of automating the call center appears to be the reduction of staff levels, but, in reality, the goal is to reduce the cost of activities that provided little or no return on investment. Those costs are associated with employees whose primary task is to enter order information into an order entry system. Most organizations will still require some form of call center, depending on the size of the operation and the success of your Web site to provide easy and clear assistance to your customers.

Tasks Handled by a Call Center

There are a variety of tasks that are handled by a customer call center that all pertain to the interaction between a company and its customers. These include the following:

➤ Entering customer orders for callers unable to complete an order online

➤ Providing information about the company, products, or services

➤ Customer product assistance (help desk)

➤ Contact management (directing incoming calls)

➤ Investor relations

➤ Emergencies

Most of these tasks can be handled online over the Internet by an effectively designed Web site. However, larger organizations and those with critical support programs (emergency assistance) may still require a "live" call center. A visit to the Microsoft Web site, shown in Figure 10.1, will show that it provides an extensive amount of online information, but no two-way, online sales support for potential new customers. Support shortcomings such as this won't impact the Microsoft bottom line, but they will significantly impact the bottom line of other organizations that have stronger competition.

Figure 10.1

Microsoft home page provides online customer information through its Web site.

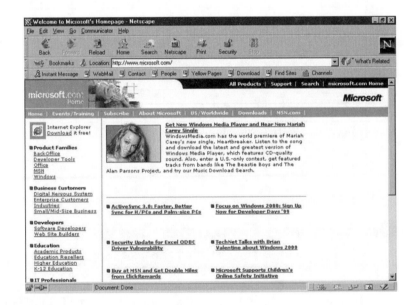

Why a Call Center

Should you have a call center at all? This is a difficult but essential decision for any organization. The trade-off is simple—a call center provides your customers with a human voice to talk to for service, support, and sales information, but the downside is the very high cost of staffing. Some of these costs can be reduced with the use of an online or virtual help center to handle some of the questions from customers.

The balance between the costs of the call center and financial rewards that are derived from customer satisfaction must be weighed carefully. Just to make the

144

decision a bit more complicated, consider that the larger and better known your organization becomes, the easier it will be for customers to get satisfaction from an online Web site. Smaller organizations may need a "live" voice to close sales and build trust with new customers.

The 24×7 Call Center

The term 24×7 refers to call center coverage that is provided 24 hours a day, seven days a week. This level of coverage is usually created by providing a fully staffed, 24-hour call center. It is essential to have a 24×7 service center if the assistance it provides is critical, such as emergency services, or if you are operating across international time zones. In most cases, however, the 24×7 call center is a luxury that returns minimal value in the middle of the night.

The Shifting Call Center

The shifting call center is a term used to describe the relationship between two locations in different time zones. For example, a call center on the East coast could handle the bulk of the call traffic from 6:00AM EST. Then gradually throughout the day the calls could shift west starting at 9:00 EST to a West coast call center or 11:00AM for one located in Hawaii. The West coast call center could close at 12:00 EST or 2:00AM for Hawaii. This could provide your North American customers with 18 to 20 hours of coverage using regular day shifts, and also provide double coverage for high traffic times in the middle of the day. The key to the success of shifting call centers is telephony management software that can distribute calls between all locations throughout the day based on the level of calls.

The CCJ

Some companies have a very high volume of customer service calls and others simply want to better manage the calls during peak times. To help in this task, these companies sometimes employ Call Center Jockeys. These individuals play music, provide queue information, and monitor the size of the queues to ease the stress level of customers who are waiting. The result is that during peak times, customers will wait on hold longer, resulting in fewer dropped calls, which translates into higher sales and lower overall costs.

The Online i-Center

The real focus of automating call center functions for e-commerce is the development of the online or Internet-based i-center. The greatest benefit of the i-center is a 24-hour-a-day virtual operation. The greatest problem is that the information is either static (unchanging) or delayed (online responses via e-mail). The structure that you use to build the virtual i-center will define its effectiveness and success. It is usually broken into a few main areas.

Information

The information section provides static information about the company, products, services, pricing, and delivery or contact information. It is simply a series of searchable Web pages of general or specific information (see Figure 10.2).

Figure 10.2

A Web site is usually made up of a series of Web pages.

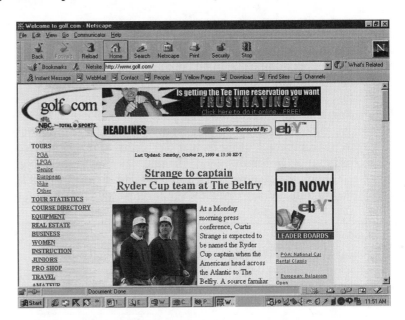

Frequently Asked Questions (FAQ)

The second piece is a Frequently Asked Questions (FAQ) section. This section is also a group of HTML documents or series of organized links that list the previous questions asked by other customers and the answers provided by the company (see Figure 10.3). This section should also be linked to a form that allows your customers to send their own questions. Most ISPs provide autoresponse software that will confirm that the form has been received.

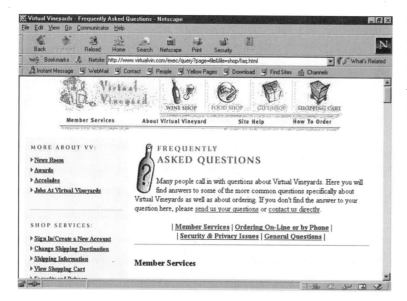

Figure 10.3

A Web page that lists frequently asked questions (FAQs) is a great way to provide your online visitors with information they may be looking for.

The Chat Room

Often, companies will provide an online chat facility to allow customers to meet to discuss issues or to meet online live technical support staff (see Figure 10.4). This is an excellent way to provide live assistance without the long distance telephone tolls. Some organizations are even supplying video links.

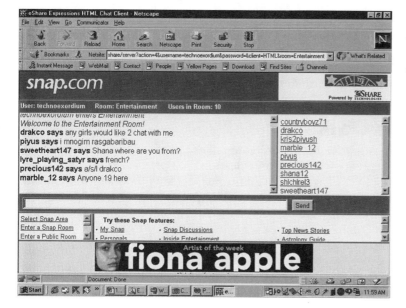

Figure 10.4

A chat room is an online facility where visitors can post and read electronic messages.

147

The Site Search Engine

Another important piece of an i-center is a document search engine for locating specific references to a word or phrase both in the company Web site and on the Internet (see Figure 10.5).

Figure 10.5

Many sites offer a search engine for searching the Web site.

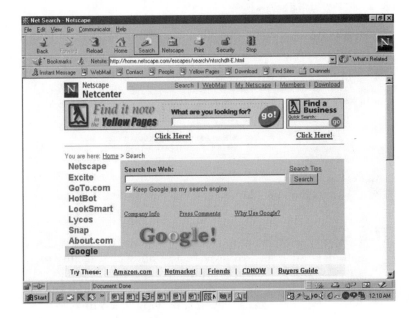

Customer Transactions

Customers should be given the opportunity to place orders, obtain downloads, or access functionality or online programs (for example, Web casts) easily and efficiently. You can see an example of a Web cast in Figure 10.6. The instructions should be logical and simple, and online wizards should be provided for more complex orders.

The Online Help Desk

When customers have a question about your company or products, they usually expect a direct point of contact with your organization. You provide this service either to encourage sales, in the case of those customers seeking product information, or to assist with product usage so that customers will be satisfied with your products or service. Dissatisfied customers have a direct negative impact on future sales in that they will be less likely to purchase new products from you.

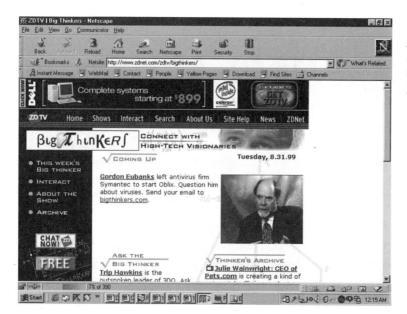

Figure 10.6

A Web cast is one way for a company to send information over the Internet for customers to access.

So the two key functions provided by the help desk are answers to questions and product use assistance. One easy way to do this is to provide a well organized series of online help tutorials that take a user through actions on a step-by-step basis. You can also link to online tutorials with online organizations. Answers to questions are most efficiently provided in a FAQ section with an associated FAQ search engine. Instead of answering the same question hundreds of times for individual customers, the FAQ provides one answer that all the customers can access.

When the Virtual Help Desk Fails

Believe us, nothing is more frustrating than having to spend an hour to solve a five-minute problem. Many of the online help functions available today are disorganized and use voluminous dumps of FAQs that can cause a user to spend hours searching for information. Even embedded search engines often return results that are not related to the question.

A Bad Search

We had a question about the registration wizard in Office2000. The registration wizard forces you to register the product with Microsoft every single time it is installed. Our question was "What would happen if a user has more than one PC, loses a PC, changes a hard drive or upgrades, etc.?"

1. We started by surfing to www.microsoft.com.

2. We went straight to the search option and typed "registering more than one copy of office2000." We got a "no results" message.

3. We narrowed the search to "registering Office2000." We got a "no results" message.

4. We returned to the main page and selected "support," "home customer," and "online support."

5. We chose "search personal" and entered "Office2000," "registration," and "go." We received five responses, none with any reference to registering Office2000.

6. We tried the Office2000 troubleshooter and, after reading 20 responses, found that there was no information on registration.

7. We returned to the main page and searched by product, selecting "office," "downloads & support," "support online," and "using Microsoft Office." The result was a blank page.

8. We backed up and tried "Installing Microsoft Office." The result was a blank page.

9. After a quick search, we found that there was no place to submit a FAQ.

10. We quit and decided to use Netscape Composer for word processing.

You can try this search by starting at www.microsoft.com to see whether they have changed anything.

A Good Search

However, you can also get good searches from search engines.

1. We started by surfing to www.microsoft.com.

2. We went straight to the search option and typed "digital nervous system."

3. We got 20 responses related to the "digital nervous system."

The only problem is that this isn't really a good search, just a lucky one.

Bad and Good FAQs

More often than not, long lists of FAQs force users to scroll through page after page of emails to find an answer to their question. Companies tend to dump information into a Web site, anticipating that its customers will magically find the answers to their questions, but the risk is that customer attention spans and tempers are very short. There is definitely a growing dissatisfaction with the ability to get good information from the Internet, and as companies heap more garbage into their Web sites, customers will look elsewhere for information.

Clearly organizing your data, providing a search engine that ranks responses, eliminating extraneous or old documents, and giving the customers an easy way to communicate a question and receive an answer are vital elements in building a successful virtual call center. This will result in good FAQ lists that are relevant and informative while reducing the amount of time for the majority of users.

A Simple Web Information Model

1. Design the information in an outline before placing it on the Internet and design it for use from the user's point of view. There are a number of Web site design programs available to assist in the task. You can obtain a Web site design program from http://www.investorsguru.com/freeso11.shtmlwww.

2. Use graphical images that imply their function or indicate what they are linking to.

3. Use different categories to sort links so that customers can access the same information from different paths (for example, by product, by type of information, and by type of problem).

4. Use the *three click rule*—in general, it should take no more than three clicks for a customer to access the information he needs.

5. Limit the total number of links per page while still trying to follow the "three click" rule because too many links can make it confusing for visitors.

6. FAQs should have a way for someone to submit a FAQ and should have a ranking search engine that ranks searches by the most popular related request or by number of references to the search phrase.

7. Search engines should be accessible from every page.

8. Search engines should only pull up information that is relevant to the type of search (sales information should be only sales information). Extraneous Web documents should be excluded.

9. Design the site so that the information has a logical flow. A customer should always know where she is in the site. http://www.netscape.com is an example of a Web site that moves logically and still provides an indication of where you are.

Customer-Driven Service

The primary goal of automating a call center is to have the customers do the work of order entry and searching for support information. They will perform these functions as long as the process is easy, fast, and efficient. If the process is cumbersome, difficult, and slow, you will get customer dissatisfaction and a reputation for poor service. This will ultimately lead to reduced sales.

One definite disadvantage to the Internet is that customer dissatisfaction on the Internet travels very fast and very far. Customers are becoming more savvy at using online information from other customers to select products and services, and some Web sites are even offering a place for shoppers to post their opinions of companies or products.

If you succeed in satisfying your customers' queries quickly and efficiently, you will have created a self-propelled, moneymaking machine.

Anticipating Your Customers' Needs

An important part of any i-center is the need to anticipate your customers' requests. For example, if you design a software package with a new security algorithm embedded in the code that will be frustrating to your customers, you can mitigate negative customer feelings by adding help information to your Web site in a visible and easy-to-access area. This will help answer your customers' questions and reduce the number of direct calls that have to be managed by your staff. If you do not anticipate your customers' information requirements, the cost will be additional resources and lost sales.

Data Mining Your Service Information

One process that will add immense value to the i-center is data mining your service information to change the actual product or service, assist in the design of new products or services, assist in the design of Web information, or to anticipate new problems. Some of the best research available to any company is available in the information requests by its own customers. For example, if customers continually ask whether your product can perform a new function, changing the product to add this functionality may increase sales.

Outsourcing Customer Service

Many organizations are currently wrestling with the concept of outsourcing. There are numerous horror stories of companies that have outsourced internal functions, only to be later held for ransom by the outsourcing company. Also, critical functions, such as customer service, directly impact future sales, and therefore have to be closely monitored and controlled. By passing these responsibilities to another company, you limit your control and flexibility over functions that may be essential to achieve excellent customer service. However, it is clear that there is great financial potential to be gained from the efficiencies of using an outsourced call center.

At this point your company has started to automate processes, defined how to process orders and ship product (supply chain), and now how to support those customers.

153

The Outsourcing Checklist

1. Carefully study your operations to determine any potential impact from out-sourcing. For example, if you outsource your accounting function, determine the impact on such areas as daily management, customer service, etc.

2. Review outsourcing options, verify company reputations and financial stability, and check references (nobody supplies a bad reference, so ask for a complete list of past customers and a reference list, and then cold call the customers not listed on the reference list).

3. Ensure that the terms of service are detailed in legally binding agreements that include clear and firm pricing, disaster recovery guarantees, the level of resources guaranteed by the outsourcing company, benchmarks and performance mea-sures, reporting, tasks and responsibilities, rewards for performance, etc.

4. Develop a contingency plan to reintroduce the function back into the orga-nization on short notice.

5. Carefully monitor the work performed by the outsourcing company and the results of this work, such as reports, programs, content creation, etc.

6. Make sure your customer and company information is secure at the outsourc-ing company by reviewing their security procedures and store backups of your company data and outsourcing systems at your site.

The Least You Need To Know

➤ How to define on-demand customer service.

➤ Learning the pros and cons of different types of call centers.

➤ The key is to understand FAQs, have a reliable help desk, and anticipate your customers' needs.

➤ Learn how to use the a Web information model.

➤ Learn how to use the outsourcing checklist.

Show Me the Money

In This Chapter

➤ What electronic funds transfers are and how they help your online business

➤ Making and receiving payments electronically

➤ What types of security concerns exist

➤ Security solutions available to businesses including SSL

➤ e-banks: The new online banking alternative

Electronic Funds Transfer—EFT

Value is the foundation of any economy and forms the basis of all trade. We measure the worth of something by its value even when we do not use currency. If value was to disappear from an economy so would the economy. For example, the Internet is successful because we perceive that it provides something of value (information), and we pay for the right to use it. When we conduct business on the Internet, we are looking to trade something of value (cash) for something else of value (product). But we will only do this if the value that we derive is greater than the cost. Even though the current primary use of the Internet is communications (email) and information gathering, shopping is growing rapidly as a favorite pastime of surfers, and as long as people continue to perceive a benefit to online shopping, this growth will continue.

So what's the point? The point is that we will shop as long as there is value in lower prices, satisfaction guarantees for products or services, and very low consumer risk. The failure of any of these could shake the foundation of i-commerce. So businesses have to be very careful about how they conduct business on the Internet, especially where payments are concerned.

Businesses such as Amazon.com learned very early that the real value in the Internet was not just to provide information, but also to provide access to products (see Figure 11.1). One of the greatest hurdles to overcome was convincing customers to send credit card information over the Internet and trust the company.

Figure 11.1

Outpost.com provides visitors with access to a variety of products.

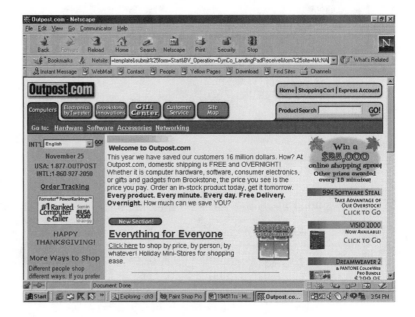

Internet Customers and Payments

People are afraid to send their credit card information over the Internet. What a surprise. With all the ways your information can be used against you, it is a wonder any business is done at all. Customers are far more wary about providing credit information than ever before. Originally, only computer software vendors that were well known in the tight-knit Internet community were able to succeed at getting credit card sales, but now every company that sells something is headed for a Net address, and they all store credit and sales data. The greatest threat to future Internet sales growth is the press story waiting in the wings about some company that has had its customer database hacked for credit card numbers, names, expiration dates, home addresses, email addresses, and even products recently purchased.

To reduce the threat of this potential disaster, a number of new companies are trying some innovative approaches. Companies that pay the vendor through the Internet without sending your personal credit information or banks that use electronic checks are two examples of new services that are reducing the risk of providing credit information.

Payments Types

There are two primary flows of funds inside corporations:

1. Payments received from your customers
2. Payments made to your suppliers (including employees that supply labor and governments that supply bureaucracy)

As an incoming payment becomes due to an organization, it is set up as a receivable in the books; as an outgoing payment becomes due, it is set up as a payable. When the actual payment is made, these accounts are reduced, and the offsetting entry becomes an outstanding item in the bank account. This simplified process is one of the largest contributors to overhead expenses in most modern organizations. The problem arises as a result of the differences between keeping track of the actual cash and reconciling this amount back to the general ledger bank accounts. As well, money has a time value that must be managed, and if you use different currencies, movements in these currencies can result in losses. Large and expensive treasury and accounting operations have grown to fill the roles of cash and risk management.

One goal of e-commerce is to reduce these expenses by streamlining the cash collection and payment operations. In the prior chapter on automating the supply chain, we saw that the receipt and payment processing functions could be automated along with the rest of the supply chain. The receipt of an actual product or confirmation of delivery to the customer could automatically produce vendor payment information, and customer payments could be automatically deposited when they are received through the use of credit card software.

Payments In—Receipt of Payments

Payments come from three sources:

1. Retail customers
2. Wholesale customers
3. Various miscellaneous payments (or everyone else)

Prior to the growth of online electronic payment methodologies, most of these payments were received in cash or checks and periodically the organization would make a physical deposit at a bank. Newer electronic methodologies allowed funds to flow faster through the use of wire transfers that did not require a physical deposit. Although the funds were electronically deposited to the bank account, the downside was the high cost to use the service. In the early 70s, major banks began a concerted effort to allow corporations to electronically transfer funds directly from one bank account to another. These transfers were primarily used for transferring funds between bank accounts inside the same bank, but this has since spread to interbank (between bank) transfers.

Modern Payment Systems

The introduction of PCs and modems resulted in the development of externally accessible bank systems known as PC banking (see Figure 11.2). Companies could sign directly onto the bank systems using PCs and transfer funds through EFTs or wire transfers. As well, EDI (electronic data interchange) usually incorporated an EFT component that allowed an organization to accept invoice documents and automatically generate payments after the documents were verified.

By the late 70s, payments could be made to companies by retail customers through direct debit (automatic withdrawals from the customer's bank account) or ATMs (automatic teller machines). Payments using these methods transfer funds from the customer bank account directly to the company account. Today, there are numerous payment options available, most with an EFT (electronic funds transfer component).

Figure 11.2

The figure shows an example of a PC banking Web site.

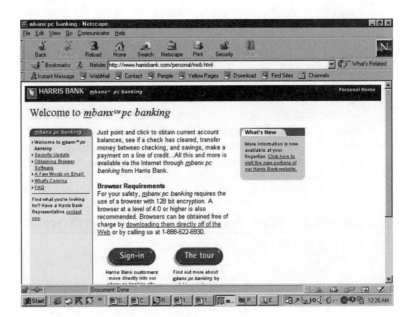

Credit Cards—a Brief (Very) History

In 1958, the Bank of America issued a blue, gold, and white BankAmericard in California that allowed a select group of users to pay for products at participating merchants without cash. The users would then pay the bank at a later date for the purchased items. In 1976, two banking associations that distributed BankAmericards changed their names to VISA USA and VISA International. However, the history of credit goes back as far as the beginning of trade. It is likely that promises of future payments were made early in the history of humankind and thus started the provision of credit and probably the first bad debt.

One of the advantages to using credit cards is that users no longer have to carry cash to pay for a product. In the early days, simply providing a credit card so that the number could be imprinted was enough to complete the transaction. Electronic processing was introduced later to provide online authorization and depositing functions. In the late 90s, the Internet provided an unlimited opportunity if businesses could get paid for product or services sold electronically. The inevitable marriage of the two technologies was a match made in virtual heaven.

At first, credit card numbers, user names, and expiration dates were provided over the Internet in insecure forms. This risky process has since been updated to include measures that ensure your credit data is not visible to other users (encryption) and a way to ensure that the party you are sending your information to is the only company receiving it (authentication).

To accept credit cards as a payment option, you simply have to sign on as a merchant with your bank or credit card organization. You will be required to pay a percentage fee from 1% to 3% depending on your size and the products sold. There are also a number of vendors on the Internet that will process the credit information for you once it has been entered into their Web site.

Credit Card Processing

After a customer has supplied you with her credit card number, name, and expiration date, two things must occur to complete the transaction:

1. The credit card must be authenticated with the credit card company so that you can receive an authorization number. This provides a limited guarantee that the funds will be made available to you when you complete your deposits by ensuring the user of the card is not over his credit limit and that the card has not been stolen.
2. The electronic credit card information must be turned into an actual deposit at your financial institution.

Some companies, such as Cybercash, provide Internet payment processing software that can accept and process credit card information to receive online authorizations. The cybercash home page is shown in Figure 11.3. They can also provide software for linking to your financial institution to create electronic credit card deposits.

Figure 11.3

Cybercash is an online company that provides software and services for processing electronic payments.

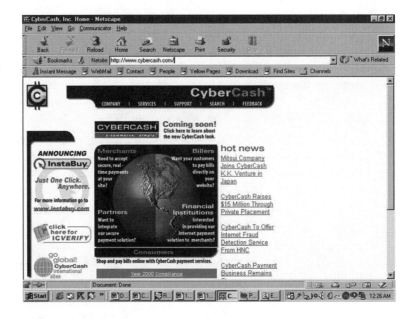

Electronic Checks (i-Checks)

Electronic checks or i-checks are used to make electronic payments between two parties through an intermediary. This is not much different than the current check processing system except that electronic checks are generated and exchanged online. The intermediary will debit the customer account and credit the merchant account.

Micropayments (Electronic Wallet)

Micropayments are cash payments that are made as a result of using a service on the Internet. They are also made between two or more Internet companies to help generate traffic through links. The way a micropayment works is that a company usually registers with an organization that verifies and reports on traffic levels between sites. Next, a very small payment per link or per click is calculated and when the total owing reaches a specified threshold, the payment is released from either the customer's actual or virtual bank account to the vendor's account. Micropayments are used to charge visitors to Web sites for using games, viewing pictures, and so on (see Figure 11.4). They are also used between Internet companies to pass payments from one company to another for the generation of traffic to the Web site through the use of links.

Figure 11.4
Microsoft Wallet is a micropayment, which is one electronic payment option.

The Traffic/Micropayment Model

Company A offers Company B a fee for each user they send to Company A's Web site. The users will link to the A site from a link on B's home page. Company A can manage the process, or they can register with an organization that will track incoming messages for them. When the number of visits reaches a certain threshold that makes economic sense, a payment is made from Company A to Company B. The main reason for using a third party to track pay-per-click micropayments is to reduce the potential of fraud. These organizations will manage the security aspects of these programs to ensure that the traffic generated is not repeat traffic or that it has not been artificially created by Company B.

Payment Security

There are a number of ways that criminals will attempt to steal or alter payment information. The intent is to capture personal financial information such as credit card numbers, the name on the card, and the expiration date. This information can then be used to purchase other goods online for delivery to a temporary address. By the time the fraud is detected, the perpetrators have disappeared. These techniques include spoofing, sniffing, content alteration, and denial.

Spoofing

Spoofing is the act of mimicking a legitimate Web site including layout, colors, and function to obtain credit card information or steal business. The technique involves registering a domain name that is very similar to a legitimate sales site, but is perhaps different by a single letter such as Amazin.com.

The illegal Web site then copies the text and graphics of the legitimate site and builds some functionality to mimic the feel of the links contained in the site. The next step is to offer a popular product at a ridiculous price to entice people to send their credit information. Of course, not all sites that mimic using the misspelling technique are bad, some are just creatively diverting business to their legitimate site. Others are simply capitalizing on famous phrases. For example, at the time of this writing, www.whitehouse.com was a pornography site. Figure 11.5 shows an example of a legitimate spoof site.

Figure 11.5

This company legitimately owns the domain name that resembles a U.S. government Web site, and have placed a notice indicating that it is not the government Web site.

Sniffing

Sniffing is a term used to describe the act of reading unprotected packet information as it travels over a network. The act of sniffing packets is relatively simple with the use of various network sniffing software programs that were originally designed to assist in network error detection. Sophisticated hackers lurk or watch for messages to and from certain IP addresses, and if they find something, sell the information to criminals or competitors.

Content Alteration

One method of diverting payments would be to intercept a bank account number and change it to another. This is called content alteration, and is used by sniffers who capture the packets, alter the content, and then send the new packet to its intended recipient. Another piece of information that could be altered is the shipping address for an order.

Denial

This illegal technique involves conducting business with an organization electronically and then denying that the transaction occurred, or denying it was ever initiated. An Internet user may order product on a credit line and have it drop shipped to another location. Then, when the bill is received, the user denies that he ever ordered the product (which is, obviously, now at a vacant warehouse).

Security over Networks

There are a number of ways to combat these fraud techniques by using existing products and technology available in the market. The goal is to implement enough security on your network so that it is protected without limiting the users so much that they are ineffective at completing tasks. Another concern is the high cost of managing the security function or the high cost of outsourcing. If you sell 100 T-shirts a year and lose one to a bogus order or fraud during the same time frame, it is unlikely that using an Internet security service will be cost justified.

Secure Socket Layer (SSL)

SSL stands for Secure Socket Layer and is a technology that encrypts or codes the packets of information sent over the Internet so that only the sending and receiving computers can reassemble and read the information. Encryption is used along with registered certificates that use a third-party registration service (or your own registration site) to confirm that your customers are actually connected to your site. The combination of SSL and certificates make transactions very secure.

When you establish a connection to a secure server, the two computers will agree on an encryption algorithm and cryptographic keys that are used by SSL to scramble and reassemble packets of information (see Figure 11.6). Keys (or codes) are provided to users in pairs with one key kept private and the other made public. When secure communication is required, an external party will use the public key to communicate with you. Only the matching private key can decode a message that is coded by a public key, and a message coded with a private key can only be decoded with the matching public key.

Figure 11.6

SSL connections provide online users with a secure connection to a Web site as indicated by the "https" in the URL and the locked padlock in the lower left corner of the browser.

Padlock———

An Example of Keys

Let's say that two people each have a set of cryptographic keys, and they want to send each other a very secure message. Party A would encode the message using her private key and then re-encode the message using the public key of Party B. The result is that when Party B receives the multi-encoded message, he will first decode it using his private key (so only he will be able to decode it) and then use Party A's public key to complete the decoding process. If a sniffer gets the packet, his ability to decode the message will be virtually impossible.

Certificates

Certificates (see Figure 11.7) are encrypted files that are stored on your Web server and usually registered with a third party. The files then communicate with your customer's browser to confirm that the site they are accessing is in fact yours. These can also be used to authenticate users that access your networks from both outside and inside the office. In this instance, you would provide a certificate to a specific individual who would then store the file on her computer. When she signed onto your system, the server would search for the certificate before allowing access.

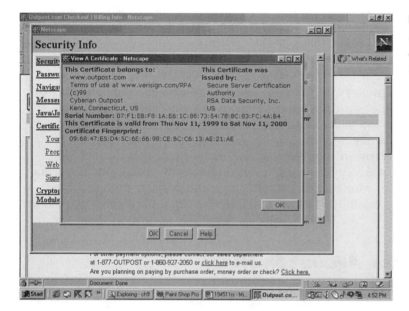

Figure 11.7

Outpost.com provides an online certificate for viewing by visitors.

PKI (Public Key Infrastructure)

Public Key Infrastructure is the engine that drives certificates. It is essentially a mechanism for the storage of public keys along with a certificate that identifies the owner. Certificate Authorities perform the PKI management function by registering end-users, validating their identity, revoking certificates, and distributing the CA's certificate widely through software such as browsers. For intranets, this task is sometimes performed by owner organizations, but for the Internet, the task is usually outsourced to an existing CA, such as Verisign.

Verisign Web Site

Verisign is one organization that provides online certificates. You can get more information at http://www.verisign.com.

By implementing SSL on your servers and using certificates, you can provide a secure method for your customers to communicate with your Web site to exchange information, make payments, order product, and so on.

How It All Hangs Together

All of the preceding security measures can be used to tighten the security for electronic payments as well as all types of transactions and information distributed over intranets, extranets, and internetworks. Maintaining security helps customers and Web site visitors feel more secure and this helps encourage them to buy products. It also helps keep your business information and transactions private.

Authentication (Protection Against Spoofing)

SSL and encryption technology will allow a user to obtain a registered public key to decipher messages from a particular source. The certificate authority will provide a certificate electronically when you initiate a secure transaction with a registered company. Most companies will post a link to a secure server, and the connection will cause a certificate to be sent to your browser. The certificate verifies the identity of the company that you are connecting to. In this instance, a spoofing site would not have the capability to provide the same information, and as the use of certificates grows, the ability to successfully spoof sites will decline. That is until they find a way to spoof certificates.

Privacy (Protection Against Sniffing)

To ensure that information cannot be read, encryption will provide a method for sending information without any risk, as long as the dual key, multikey encryption technique described here is used. After you have obtained a public cryptographic key from the party you are communicating with and have stored it, you can encrypt a message using your browser's security function. Remember that in order to encrypt the message, the receiver must possess a corresponding key to decode it. Any public certificates will be automatically remembered by your system for later use.

Content Integrity (Protection Against Altered Content)

The use of encryption provides one of the easiest methods for determining whether the content of a transmission has been altered. In the first place, the only key that can decode a message is the public key of the sender. If another party alters the message, it will be decoded as garbage because he does not have the ability to code it (private key) or if he did encode it using the public key, you could not read it (you don't have the private key). Any attempt to decode an altered packet would result in garbage.

Non-Repudiation (Protection Against Denial)

If an encoded message is sent to you and you use a public key and certificate to decode it, it must come from the registered owner of the certificate. In fact, the certificate authority will guarantee its authenticity. That way he said, she said, we said will never be an issue...as long as you understand the language of the message.

Payments Out

The second type of payment that flows through an organization is payments made to your suppliers. For many years, organizations have had the capability to make direct deposit payments to employee bank accounts. Usually, all this required was a voided check from the employee's checking account and the use of the bank's direct payment services. Because the organization created and controlled the payment information file, it was unlikely that there would be any of the difficulties usually associated with dynamic external payments (such as supplies). Payments for supplies require more work to verify the accuracy of the transaction, review invoices and shipments, and verify the total price. Employee information, on the other hand, is relatively static.

Electronic Data Interchange (EDI)

EDI allowed some organizations to streamline the payment process by making the invoice review task more automated. A supplier would send the invoice to your bank, and the bank would then interpret the invoice into an EDI standard. This file could then be sent to your data processing department for processing by your internal procurement system. Once approval was received to pay the vendor, the bank would initiate an electronic funds transfer. Some banks even provided a matching service that would match vendor invoices to preapproved purchase orders and then automatically pay the invoice through an EFT if a match was found.

Even though this process reduced the significant expense of processing checks at the bank, very little of these savings ever reached the companies. Remittance forms still had to be printed and mailed, and the cost of implementing EDI interpreters or using the bank networks and services was very high. Usually, only the largest organizations had the resources to implement such a program.

The Newest Arrivals on the Payment Scene

Payments can now easily be made through online banking programs that provide the company with the ability to send e-checks over the Internet. Using this model, the company could transfer funds to another company's bank account using a method similar to wire transfer. The process would include the registration of the payee (vendor) and the transmission of payment instructions using the security measures defined above. Remittance information would be emailed to the payee company at the same time.

A modification to this model could be for a company to establish an e-bank distribution account that disperses a deposit of funds to other registered e-bank accounts. Each vendor would sign up for a free account that would then automatically transfer funds to their main bank account or hold the funds in the e-bank for investment, etc. This allows larger organizations and trading groups a legal way to become banks without the usual regulatory approval (as they are simply managing internal payable accounts).

e-Banks

E-banks are electronic banking organizations that provide banking services without branches like the one shown Figure 11.8. Accounts are usually created for users when they sign up. For payments to be sent, the account holder must transfer actual funds from her regular bank into her e-bank account. Those same funds can be transferred out of the account at any time (at a high cost). The implication is that the user must also maintain a regular bank account for day-to-day transactions. The goal is to reduce the transactional costs of traditional banking by eliminating the overhead of branches and cash handling. Lately, many variations on the e-bank model have started to crop up including the following:

➤ Traditional banks that still charge the same fees

➤ Entirely new electronic e-banks that charge no fees

➤ Brokerage houses that manage electronic investment accounts

➤ Credit card companies that provide online credit facilities

➤ Insurance companies that provide account operations

➤ Crooks, con men, and those guys at big retail stores who guarantee the lowest price

➤ All kinds of variations on the preceding

An e-Bank Warning

Be very careful of online e-banks. Some e-banks are fronts for organized crime, often from other countries. We suggest that you carefully check out any e-bank by doing the following:

➤ Researching the company through traditional methods (rating agencies)

➤ Verifying its existence by visiting or calling the bank

➤ Verifying their claims with listed participants, such as federal regulators and deposit insurers

➤ Reading published articles from respected news agencies (if you can find a respected news agency)

➤ Reviewing associations

➤ Ensuring that the site is not a spoof

Figure 11.8

Security First e-bank is an online bank or e-bank.

The Least You Need to Know

➤ Define various electronic payments types.

➤ Identify customer concerns regarding security.

➤ Be able to identify security risks.

➤ Understand SSL, encryption, certificates, and PKI.

➤ Identify solutions to security threats.

➤ Understand what e-banks are.

The Virtual Workforce

In This Chapter

➤ Defining what is a virtual workforce

➤ Understanding the benefits of a virtual workforce

➤ What are virtual employees

➤ Building virtual workspaces for virtual employees

➤ How outsourcing can help your company

➤ Building a staffless organization

➤ The pitfalls of virtual workers

➤ Solutions to avoiding these pitfalls

What Is a Virtual Workforce?

A virtual workforce is the human resources of the organization. They are no different from any other HR group, except that they do not work on company premises. Being "virtual" would imply that they are almost employees, but that is not the interpretation we apply to a virtual workforce. A virtual workforce is one that performs functions without a physical presence, or with only a partial physical presence, at the company workplace. They are sort of like ghosts. They can be working offsite, or they can be working offsite occasionally and onsite occasionally. Sales or service staff who travel extensively can be considered virtual employees because they do not really perform tasks in a company-owned location unless you call their car a company-owned location.

That is the real distinction between a virtual staff and a regular offsite staff. The virtual staff does not have a physical location that they can call "their" office. Instead, they work permanently or part-time away from the office in locations not paid for by the company. This can be a home office, an employee-owned shop, a car, or even their bed. There are three types of employees: those on company property, those who are not, and those who are a little of both—and this is the trend that is rapidly growing (see Figure 12.1).

Figure 12.1

The Telecommuting Jobs Web site offers helpful information for telecommuters.

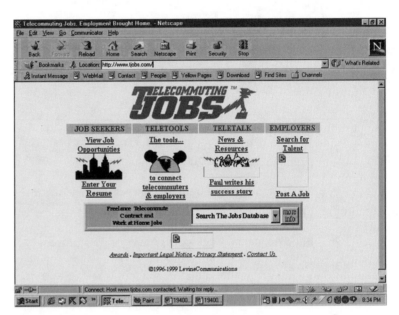

Beating the Traffic by Telecommuting

This concept of working away from the office is often called telecommuting. It is called that because the employees actually commute to work using telephone communications for computer connections and voice communication. Essentially, they are commuting through the phone to their place of work. Well, not physically commuting unless someone has found a way to fax himself to work.

Telecommuting requires a number of basic requirements from the company point of view. The employee must be able to communicate with the company through readily available public phone networks. The second requirement is that employees must have the capability to send and receive data such as e-mails and files, as well as access centralized applications. Essentially, this requires that the company have a network configuration capable of handling employee access whether by dial-up connection, dedicated line, or Web access. It also implies that there must be a way to contact the employees if they are using the phone line, such as through email, Internet, and intranet telephony or a separate phone line. The goal is to allow the employee to work at a cheaper location than the rest of the organization, whether that location is a satellite office or a home office.

Home Office/Satellite Office

A home office is just that—an office in your home. Not the kitchen table, but an actual office or workspace off the beaten path and preferably away from the fridge and TV. Way, way, away from the fridge and TV. No Oprah while you work. OK, a little Oprah, Rosie's fine, but no Springer unless it's a real tough project. Satellite offices are smaller offices away from the main office, which have meeting rooms, equipment, and all the facilities of the larger offices without all the cost.

Examples of the Virtual Workforce

Examples of virtual workforces are growing more and more prevalent. IBM, Hewlett, Apple, and AT&T are some of the organization benefiting from the move to virtual workforces. These organizations have had to overcome a series of problems associated with virtual workforces, such as the networking and communications logistics, the choice of employee candidates, changes to the way managers evaluate and review employees, and even the difficulty in convincing shareholders that their investment was not being misspent. In each case, the company took on the task and realized both benefits and pitfalls, but recognized that, in general, the overall results would be favorable.

SmartValley Telecommuting Guide

To see an online telecommuting guide, surf to www.svi.org/resources.html and select the Telecommuting Guide Link.

The positive impact on society of a move to a virtual work force is relatively easy to measure. Some of these benefits include the following:

➤ Lower stress levels, leading to lower health costs

➤ More efficient productivity, resulting in more free time for employees

➤ Proximity to home, leading to more mothers with valuable skills staying in the workforce (unfortunately, women are still leaving the workforce in far greater numbers than men after their children are born)

➤ A greater understanding of technology and communications by the virtual employees

There is no doubt that employees have to interact in order to conduct business. Some organizations have tackled this problem through the use of meeting technologies like Microsoft Netmeeting (see Figure 12.2), while others have approached the task by having employees come to work periodically for "meeting days." The fact is that face-to-face communication, while important, is not necessarily vital to the organization. In fact, many meetings result in extremely low levels of productivity (if you don't believe us, read a Dilbert book). However, the sharing of ideas is an important concept toward managing and ensuring the correct mix of offsite work and onsite work, (video conferencing can be useful in this regard). Plus, employees have particular personalities that may require interaction with other employees on a regular basis to make them content with their position.

Figure 12.2

Microsoft Netmeeting provides an easy way for virtual employees to conduct video meetings.

The Benefits of a Virtual Workforce

There are a number of benefits from a virtual workforce for both the employee and the company. Employees who work offsite tend to appreciate the ability to focus on their tasks without interruption. This leads to a higher level of productivity without more time or greater effort. In fact, employees who have the correct environment often work in what are microbursts of productivity. During these microbursts of productivity, the employee is able to complete a significant amount of work in a short period of time. This is very similar to the effect of closing the door to your office and forwarding the phone to voice mail for a set period of time. Virtual employees also tend to be more relaxed and can produce more creative content when they are relaxed. For the right employee, working virtually can result in the same or greater levels of work at a significantly reduced stress level. This results in a more happy and content employee.

Offsite employees provide a great cost saving to the organization. Because the cost to the employee of commuting, car insurance, and clothing is significantly reduced, the move to an offsite work location is usually considered a significant cost benefit to the employee. However, even greater savings accrue to the organization in the form of reduced office overhead. In some locations, this overhead can run as high as $110 per square foot per month when costs such as business phone lines, electricity, heating, rent, common area, supplies, coffee, and parking are factored into the equation.

Savings for the Community from Telecommuting

Another saving is the cost of health care and benefits associated with telecommuters. For example, companies that allow employees to work from their homes and promoted dental care on a regular basis found that insurance costs were significantly reduced because the employees had fewer inhibitions about brushing their teeth at home, as opposed to in the office. Other benefits include the following:

➤ Reduced gas emissions from commuting vehicles
➤ Less use of public transportation
➤ Lower overall corporate insurance costs
➤ Reduced taxes
➤ Reduced communications expense (fewer phones)
➤ Reduced office furniture and moving expenses
➤ Reduced maintenance and cleaning expenses

Savings for the Employee from Telecommuting

The employee also significantly benefits from the "virtualization" of the workforce. A virtual employee can save on gas and insurance on vehicles including wear and tear, parking or public transport fees, fewer expensive business clothes, reduced expenses from buying restaurant or convenience lunches and drinks, and reduced costs in after school daycare (big expense for parents). Society also benefits from telecommuting through less strain on the public infrastructure, such as roads, transport, and emergency service (as a result of less accidents). Society also benefits from having parents available for their children after school, lower stress levels in the population, and associated benefits on the health system. The benefits from "virtualizing" the workforce are clear and measurable.

How To Assess Who Can Be Made Virtual

Not every employee can be "virtualized." Some employees have functions that require close coordination with other employees or the operation of equipment that cannot be moved. Other tasks have to be situated close to customers, such as retail staff. More importantly, not all employees can be "virtualized" because of their personalities. Some individuals are wired in such a way that they crave the interaction with co-workers, while other employees have a limited ability to focus on tasks well enough to be unsupervised.

A Mobile Computing Support Site

There are a number of Web sites that support mobile workforces and mobile workforce management. One is

http://planetit.com/techcenters/
indexes/mobile_computing/
support/17

You will also get employees who feel that if they are offsite they will not get recognition for their work and often have managers who confirm this pattern by favoring nonvirtual employees. You must carefully evaluate whether an employee is capable of working effectively outside the home, and you must also evaluate his or her offsite work environment. The best scenario is a self-motivated employee who can work in a quiet, sequestered home environment. You must also ensure that the employee is willing to become a virtual employee by discussing the concept and eliminating his concerns.

The next step in the process is to evaluate what the employee does on a daily basis to decide whether the tasks can be "virtualized." Don't be too surprised if the first response from your managers is that the tasks cannot be "virtualized." Managers who are afraid of losing control will meet the concept of managing employees who function outside the work environment with resistance. They will also fear that if you find out the employees can work by themselves, you will think the managers are redundant. Addressing these concerns prior to establishing a virtual workforce will smooth the transition to that state. In fact, the first people who should learn to telecommute are the managers.

When evaluating the tasks of an employee, try to decide how and when the employee will need to communicate and with whom. If these are face-to-face communications, ascertain whether they can be scheduled for onsite time periods without any impact on the performance of the task. Also search for the impact on other job-related functions that will occur because these tasks are "virtualized."

The most important questions that must be answered are can the work be done offsite? and, if yes, can the work be effectively measured? If it can be measured, how will your managers set performance goals and ensure that they are being met? Measurement of the completion of tasks and work is critical. In the current world, your boss will likely call you in and give you some vague description of a task with no timeline for completion. In the virtual world, employees are considered suppliers, and, as such, require a clear definition of what needs to be done, when the tasks must be completed, and what priority is assigned to the task. The implication is that your managers will have to be trained in how to make their expectations clear. One of the best ways to do this is to have those managers start emailing project directives to employees. Once the employee is comfortable with complying with these email orders, he can start the process of becoming a "virtualized" employee.

One of the most critical factors is the workspace that the employee will use to work offsite. In most cases, simply letting the employee set up his worksite will be sufficient. However, to reduce the risk of working in bad environments, you can supply the employees with corporate guidelines along with a one-time bonus for equipment. Depending on the level of the work required, the environment will have a direct impact on performance.

Quiet, sequestered workspaces are the best for virtual employees to allow them to focus on their tasks. They should also be clean, uncluttered, and comfortable. If the environment is set up to foster productivity, then the employee will likely deliver that productivity. However, you will have to encourage some development of the offsite workspaces by providing information that helps your employees create the most productive workspace for them.

Information on Designing Home Offices

There is a variety of information on how to design home offices at `http://realtimes.com/rtnews/rtcpages/19980304_homeoffice.htm`.

How To Manage a Virtual Employee

Managing a virtual employee is nothing like managing an on-site employee. For the vast majority of their time, you, as a manager, will have no contact with your employee. This is often a very difficult concept for a manager to accept, but the task need not be difficult. Training managers on how to set task goals and priorities, how to clearly communicate their expectations to the employees, and how to follow up with performance measures and personal discussions will reduce the problems associated with managing these employees. As long as everyone clearly understands the game plan, the team will perform up to expectations.

If the game plan is not clearly communicated, the managers should not expect goals to be met. The whole approach to managing virtual employees will require more work on the part of your managers. They will have to maintain better information on schedules and expectations. However, they can make this process easier by maintaining electronic performance templates that track the employee's incomplete tasks to a task schedule. The manager can add the tasks and the employees can maintain the information in the file.

Communicate Goals and Objectives

The key to successfully managing virtual employees is to clearly communicate goals and objectives for each employee and then identify milestones toward the completion of these goals. Setting goals is a difficult task, but can be made simple if these goals are identified and agreed to by both the virtual employee and the manager. The goals should be both attainable and measurable. If you are unable to measure the goal, you will be unable to tell how close you are to completing the goal.

The second piece of information that you will need is an estimate of the amount of time that will be needed to complete the task. This is called a milestone or benchmark, and there can be one milestone per task or a number of milestones for larger tasks. Periodically, the manager of virtual employees should meet with those employees to evaluate their position in relation to these benchmarks. If the employee is "off track," then assistance should be provided to get the employee "on track." If missing benchmarks is a consistent behavior and is not attributable to poor goal setting, then that employee may not be suited to "virtualization."

Measuring Your Virtual Employee's Performance

Performance measurement is an integral part of goal setting. Virtual employees are given tasks and goals, and their performance is measured against these goals. However, it is also important that employees are motivated to complete these tasks by linking rewards to either individual performance or corporate performance. The obvious method for rewarding employees for corporate performance is stock or options. The most effective way for rewarding employees for personal performance is a bonus. Examples of goals for employees might be to successfully complete the development of a part of an application by a specific date. If the milestone is met, the employee can be rewarded with credits toward a project completion bonus, shares, etc.

Obviously, if an employee is incapable of completing assigned tasks away from the office, the best thing is to reverse the virtual agreement and bring that employee back into a controlled environment. However, arbitrarily pulling an employee from a virtual assignment will likely cause bad feelings. To avoid these situations, the employee's manager should outline a virtual working agreement that explicitly describes what constitutes a breech of the agreement and then clearly inform the employee that any breech will result in the cancellation of the virtual work agreement. Prior to an agreement being cancelled, the manager must make every effort to communicate and remedy any perceived problems. If the problem still persists, the virtualization agreement should be reversed or cancelled.

Partially Virtual Employees

Not all staff or functions can be made totally virtual. The vast majority of tasks in a corporation that are performed by employees will have to be completed on company property. In these scenarios, the employee and manager may opt for a part-time virtual agreement.

A part-time virtual agreement allows the employee to block hours or days that are spent off-site. Travelling back and forth between off-site and on-site offices is highly inefficient and should be avoided at all costs. Managers should also be made aware of this fact and held accountable for the impact they have on employee travelling time. Part-time virtual employees will save less in resources than fully virtual employees will simply because they will spend more resources on travel to and from the office and create higher overhead expenses while working in the office. However, they will tend to use less overall resources than the full-time employee does.

Reviewing Tasks for Part-Time Virtual Work

All tasks performed by the employee must be carefully reviewed for how critical they are to the organization. Each one should be evaluated by simulating the impact of the task on the company as a result of an inability to communicate with the employee for two days. For example, if you have a part-time virtual employee, and she manages entry and reconciliation of miscellaneous journal entries in the general ledger, and you are unable to communicate with that employee for two days, what would be the impact on your operations? The likely answer is not much impact at all. However, if a network administrator is unavailable for two days, the impact may be devastating. This employee can still be made virtual, but contingency plans will have to be developed in the event that the employee is unable to communicate for a couple of days.

Be Flexible on Hours and Schedules

The key to a successful transition from traditional work environments to virtual work environments will be the ability to be flexible on hours and scheduling. The implication is that your systems and employees must have the capability to effectively and easily manage scheduling. If they can't schedule or prioritize tasks very well, then any attempts to "virtualize" the function will likely fail. It is also imperative that the corporation and manager learn to be flexible with their work hours while still meeting hard deadlines.

An existing example of this type of scenario is the construction industry, which has one of the highest levels of virtual employees because most of them are subcontractors and most work offsite, usually out of their trucks. Contractors learned a long time ago that hiring employees was a costly experience, especially during the economic downturns in the

Subcontractors or Employees

Subcontractors are individuals who incorporate a company to do business, but usually only have themselves as employees. The advantage for companies that hire contractors is that the organization can shed workers without having to pay severance packages. The benefit for the subcontractor is greater autonomy and usually higher wages.

80s. The construction industry quickly adopted the concept of hiring individuals as subcontractors. This allowed these virtual employees to decide when they would show up for work, choose what work would be done, and provide input into the timetable for completion of the work. When a house is constructed, work is scheduled to begin and end at certain times, and the contractor is rewarded with payment and future work for completing milestones. But if a drywaller, for example, wants to hang drywall in the middle of the night, that's up to the subcontractor. All the contractor is concerned about are the project deadlines. These same concepts can easily be applied to the workplace as long as the communication infrastructure that the corporation relies on is working. In fact, virtual workforces can keep a company up and running even if disaster, such as a storm, strikes the company offices.

When Can an Employee Be Virtual

If we look carefully at what employees do in their day-to-day work, we can start to analyze what tasks they have to be physically present for. Someone who deals with customers on a daily basis at a centralized premise such as a retail store may have to conduct the bulk of his tasks at that location. Therefore, part-time virtual work may be a solution, or part-time virtual work may be entirely inefficient. In most scenarios, scheduling the workload of part-time workers so that tasks that require their physical presence are performed on a single day will help provide some mix of virtual and onsite work. Some examples of tasks that will require nonvirtual or onsite employees include the following:

➤ Direct face-to-face contact with customers at a company facility such as a retail store

➤ Work with specialized equipment that cannot be installed remotely

➤ Manufacturing processes that must be maintained together

➤ Work that requires a controlled environment, such as a call center or systems operation center

➤ Work that will benefit from daily personal contact with coworkers, such as financial trading rooms

The difficult part will be to admit that a person's function need not be onsite at all times. An administrative assistant (or secretary) can work just as quickly on a project from his home on a computer connected to the company network and can even forward his office phone to the offsite location. However, in most cases few executives would admit that their assistants could do this effectively. They would claim that the individual was an integral part of their own daily function and that they couldn't get the same level of responsiveness that they would get at work. The question that has to be answered is does this "level of responsiveness" justify the additional cost that the company must bear for this position? If you look carefully, the answer will usually be "no."

The Virtual Work Zone

At some point, the company must make some serious decisions about its environment and location. Historically, companies centrally locate near each other. This was to facilitate interaction with suppliers, competitors, and customers. But, today, with the rapid advancement in communications technology, this is no longer the case. Now, suppliers, competitors, and customers are so widely dispersed that the idea of locating in close physical proximity to them is proving less and less feasible. Also, rents in locations that were traditionally part of this philosophy, such as city centers, are extremely expensive. An organization that moves to a business park in the suburbs can greatly reduce its operating costs and pass these savings to either their customers or shareholders. Suburban locations can greatly reduce the cost to its employees by providing shorter commutes, parking, more facilities, etc. The company can still maintain a presence in a centralized area with a satellite office.

Workplace Design

For information on workplace design, surf to: http://www. workplaceforum.com/, but be forewarned you will have to sign in.

One of the most important items that must be addressed when designing a work environment is communications. Employees must be able to access communications equipment as easily as if they are in their own home office. Therefore, networks have to be designed in such a way that employees can access their own files quickly and easily from any location.

One of the best techniques is to issue laptop computers to your virtual employees and provide every office with a docking station. There must also be a way for phone communication to travel with the employee either through the use of cell phones, local digital wireless networks, or call forwarding systems that are managed by a central check-in point. Security must also consider the flow of virtual employees in and out of the organization with environments built so that security sensitive areas are kept out of the general traffic flow. Finally, employees should have a way of booking meeting rooms and checking the availability of workspace, which will require a centralized booking application capable of managing this aspect.

Occasionally, companies will place remote worksites throughout a city. This further alleviates commuting costs while providing someplace for the virtual employee to go. Linking these remote sites through sophisticated communications will be critical to its success. Technology, such as linked video conference rooms, individual video conferencing capabilities, and a high-speed wide area network between sites will become necessary in building the virtual work environment. The goal should be to construct a convenient meeting place that provides fast and effective communication with other places for meetings that cannot otherwise be conducted using technologies such as the Internet.

Docking Station

That's where Sulu parks the Enterprise, but it is also a platform that sits on top of a desk and is connected to a monitor and a network. The docking station allows a computer user an easy and fast way to connect a laptop to the corporate network by simply sliding in the laptop. The downside is that laptops are a hot commodity among thieves and leaving one in the open will surely lead to its disappearance.

The Virtual Workspace

The company must also consider the individual workspaces of the virtual employees both on and offsite. Most virtual workspace offices utilize a sharing concept in allocating workspace. The employees will check in when they arrive at the site and be assigned a workspace, phone link, and keys. In that workspace, there should be a docking station for their laptop computer and a phone. Individual and personal items can be either brought by the employee or stored in baskets. At the end of their workday, they can check out of the office by taking all their personal belongings from the workspace and returning the keys. In this type of environment, it is important to have a set of ground rules about acceptable and nonacceptable behavior. Territorialism must be frowned upon, over use of the workspace must also be discouraged, and workspaces must be vacated.

Online meetings are a mainstay of any virtual work environment. Video meeting packages like Netmeeting allow the virtual workers to actually see their coworkers (see Figure 12.3). This visual communication is an important part of the virtual office because it provides offsite workers with the ability to connect with their coworkers in a manner that provides them all with the benefits that we get from face-to-face conversation. Body language and gestures often provide signals and clues as to the reception that our ideas are receiving. A phone call is a one-sided communication mechanism where we are trying to judge the response of the other person based on vocal intonation and tone. Video allows us to focus on many more clues and responses from eyes, gestures, body language, etc. To conduct online video conferencing can be done as simply as using NetMeeting and the Internet, although more sophisticated technology is available.

One thing that will make the transition to the work environment easier is uniformity. If everybody has the same desk, workstation, and supplies, it will be difficult for status levels to develop, and this will in turn reduce internal politics. However, if you make a differentiation between workspaces, employees are likely to develop negative

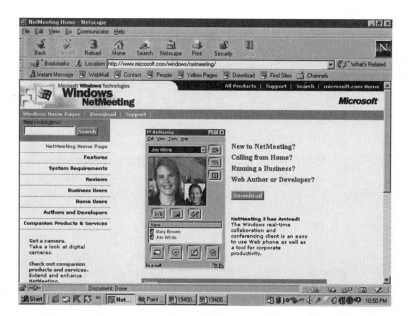

Figure 12.3

You can download Netmeeting for free from Microsoft.

opinions of working virtually if their co-workers are perceived to be consistently getting "the good" offices. Gaining consistency will be difficult because current buildings are not designed to be virtual offices, they are designed for corporations with executives in large corner offices, managers in the rest of the window offices, department managers and senior clerks in the inside offices, and line workers in the cubicles. Converting these spaces and achieving consistency will be very difficult given that someone is bound to get the sunny side of the building, and someone else is bound to get the office by the coffee machine.

The offsite office is just as critical as the onsite office. If the virtual employee works in another location, this factor may be beyond the control of the company and its employees. If they work from their cars, again the aspect of "offices" may not be as vital. But if they are planning to work from their homes, some effort should be invested by the corporation to assist the employees to develop a quiet, sequestered workspace and timetables that permit them to complete tasks. Sending a task to an individual late at night and expecting her to complete a response by 9:00 is unreasonable if that individual also has the responsibility of sending his or her children to school at 8:30. The workspace should also be comfortable and bright, not buried in a sub-basement (unless your worker happens to be a troll).

Outsourcing Staff

One definite strategy to "virtualize" your workforce is to outsource your work to subcontractors or companies. In this scenario, tasks performed by the company are given to another company or individual to do. This is especially beneficial when the tasks

183

Outsourcing References

You can get some references by surfing to http://www.brint.com/EmergOrg.htm.

are routine and simple, and the outsource company or contractor can perform the task cheaper than the company. For example, many data entry tasks have been "farmed-out" to companies specializing in this type of work. Their staff is usually faster, more focused, and less costly than in-house staff, and they get economies of scale by doing the same tasks from multiple companies.

Which staff can be outsourced is a very difficult question. The downside of outsourcing is that the company will lose direct control over the function. Subcontractors answer only to themselves and will likely endeavor to do a good job, but on their own terms. You may feel that the way they conduct their business affairs is highly risky, but as long as they deliver a finished product or service on time, you will be unable to exercise any authority or control. So when it comes to deciding if an employee's tasks can be outsourced, remember to consider all the costs associated with your decision.

Two methods for outsourcing staff functions are to hire outside companies that will build some sort of interface to your organization and bear all the costs of employees. The second method is to hire a subcontractor. The first method allows an organization to know with a relative degree of certainty the costs related to the completion of the outsourced tasks. The problems are that you will lose control of the work once it is sent to the other company and costs may fluctuate, depending on your outsourcing company. The second method allows you greater control over the work, but still only limited control over the employee. Subcontracting also comes with a higher cost since the risks of employment are borne by the subcontractor.

In both cases, the first step will be to define the tasks that are to be completed and a timetable for completion. The next step is to identify the required skill sets needed to complete the task, and the third is to identify the costs that you are willing to bear for outsourcing. The next step will be to decide if it will be better to outsource the function to a company or an individual.

In either case, the next step in the process is to search for that particular organization or company and have your lawyers prepare any necessary contracts. It would be best to lock in a price over the terms of the agreement so that cost surprises would be minimal. Also, always check the references provided to ensure that the company has the capability to support your organization. Finally, ensure the employee's functions have been documented, and a contingency plan built.

Outsourced Functions

There is a difference between outsourcing an individual staff function and outsourcing department functions. Entry of data into systems, application development, and accounting are all functions that can be entirely outsourced to another company. The question is whether they should be and what it will cost. Evaluating whether functions should be outsourced boils down to a couple of key decisions. The first decision is to decide if the function is critical to the operations of the company. If the answer is "no," then this task is a good candidate for outsourcing.

The next decision should be if the task is a core competency. The decision that the company has to make in this scenario is if the function performed by the staff or department requires an expertise that brings a high return to the organization. If it is not a core competency, then the tasks could be outsourced.

Another deciding factor is whether the costs of running the function are greater than the outsourcing fee. In general, outsourcing should cost your company no more than if the company performed the task in-house. The outsourcers make their money by lowering the staffing costs, using more costly but more efficient systems, and by gaining greater productivity from its workforce by focusing a particular group of tasks, such as accounting.

The benefits for the company are that they can shift high-priced managerial and business development resources from these tasks to high-return tasks, such as marketing or sales. An example is a company that designs office interiors. It may use a design software to assist in the task. It will also likely have back-office functions such as accounting, sales, information technology, business development, and human resources. If the company evaluates these tasks, it may find that sales and business development are critical, but accounting and information technology are not core competencies. It may now evaluate outsourcing organizations to see if this type of outsourcing is financially feasible. If the company chooses to outsource the IT and the accounting, then fewer resources will be required in the human resources area. This is the entire philosophy of outsourcing corporate functions, and in the world of e-commerce, it opens thousands of doors for companies that can deliver non-competency services, such as accounting, over the Internet.

The Staffless Organization

One of the newest "holy grails" of the business world is whether an entirely staffless organization can be built. In fact, it can if the company sets up a Web site on the Internet to conduct business with affiliates as a linking site only. Companies that are highly automated and involved in outsourcing those functions that are considered non-competencies may succeed in getting close to the goal of the staffless office.

The reality, however, is that a staffless organization is not likely to grow and prosper, and is likely only to succeed with small i-commerce companies. One concept that is

Learnlots.com

Learnlots is an example of a company that is composed of individuals who have decided to join together their specialized skills and competencies in exchange for equity ownership.

attainable is a company with a virtual staff. Grouping of contractors will likely become more commonplace as individuals become more dissatisfied with their lives and seek to leave established organizations for their own companies. Thousands of employees do this every year so this concept is not new. However, what is new is that these employees will decide that they can fund their own organization in a similar manner to the one they work in for their own benefit.

Pitfalls

There are a number of serious pitfalls that await unsuspecting companies that are trying to create a virtual staff. Some employees will take advantage of the situation to the detriment of the organization. Even if you hire staff in a non-virtual environment, you will still occasionally get bad staff. However, it can be proven that the staff that chooses to work "virtually" will likely be the ones who are most responsible. To reduce the risks even further, simply "virtualize" those employees who have a track record for self-management and discipline.

The second problem that can arise is poor communications. If someone is located in the office next to you or just down the hall, it will be easier to communicate with him in person, rather than if he is working offsite. As well, even if communications are working, the virtual employee may choose to "go dormant" or stop communicating through e-mail or phones for a period of time. The problem is that poor communication can cause costly delays since tasks may be duplicated, performed incorrectly, or not performed at all.

Another problem is that the employees will need a low noise workspace. The problem is that most of these workspaces are not quiet at all. Kids, phones, and other factors can directly impact the performance of employees if they are unwilling to try and sequester themselves away from a noisy environment. The ability to focus on tasks will be lower, which, in turn, will result in work of a lower quality.

Virtual employees will have limited interaction. The phrase "you can't operate in a vacuum" is very pertinent here because virtual employees will have significantly less interaction with their coworkers. The problem with this is that if you are trying to come up with innovations, the last person you want to provide input is an individual who operates in a vacuum. For this reason, it is important to ensure that the virtual employees have the ability to communicate by using the technology, and that this factor is considered before they are made virtual.

Solutions

The first technique for eliminating these problems is to use a "results-based" performance review and compensation strategy. The goal is to weed out the bad employees and reward those employees who are working the hardest. This task is primarily accomplished through the use of periodic performance reviews that determine the quantity of tasks completed by the employee and, if they met, the timetable for these tasks.

Another thing that helps is to send managers offsite. They are usually good candidates for "virtualization" and can lead the way for other employees. Their example sends a powerful message to the rest of the employees that "virtualization" is both acceptable and is a favorable business task. If the managers are "virtualized," they are less likely to have objections to the virtualization of their staff.

Virtual employees should be treated with the same dignity and professionalism as regular employees. They should also be expected to return the same level of respect back to the corporation. They should be made to feel welcome at the central office, and managers should go out of their way to reinforce the equality of all workers. Continuously maintaining this professionalism will lead to employees who feel obligated to complete assigned tasks.

The Least You Need To Know

➤ Define what is a virtual workforce and how it can be used in your company.

➤ Understand the benefits of a virtual workforce.

➤ Understand how to identify tasks that can be made virtual.

➤ Understand how to identify entire corporate functions that can be made virtual.

➤ Know how to build a virtual work environment in the office and how to assist your employees to do the same at home.

➤ Understand how to manage virtual employees.

I GOTS SOME!

There's Gold in Them Thar Hills: Data Mining

> ### In This Chapter
>
> ➤ Valuing your information
>
> ➤ Automating the supply chain
>
> ➤ Getting vendor buy-in
>
> ➤ Automating warehouse and delivery systems
>
> ➤ The customer driven supply chain

The Value of Information

There is no doubt about it. The most valuable thing that a company will ever own is its information. Information is the single most vital input into the decision making process, and if the decisions made are good decisions, the company will succeed. One of the most important aspects of a company's information portfolio is the effectiveness of its ability to capture, store, and analyze this information. The output of this analysis provides a valuable tool for everyone in the company from marketers and statisticians to traffic consultants. This valuable information has been captured by companies for many years, and is often stored in large databases; however, companies rarely capitalize on this value. As long as the data site is untouched, it provides no benefit to the organization. It is the same thing that would occur if a mining company purchased land, built roads, imported mining equipment, and then never touched the ore in the ground.

Data Mining Defined

Data mining is the use of software tools or applications to gather, report, and analyze operational information, such as sales, in order to instigate an action by other systems or employees that directly impacts the operation of the company.

Companies have a very valuable asset in the information they store, but it is an asset that will produce nothing unless it is "mined." The process of data mining simply involves the use of data mining tools and applications to extract and report on information contained in long term databases. We say "long term" because short term or near term information should be managed and reported on a daily basis to help run the operations of the company. An example of near term information is current day sales statistics. However, data mining can be combined with regular reporting and modeling tools to use both longer term and near term information to initiate other processes, like coupon mailings. Long-term data mining by itself is used to spot changes in customer tastes or operational efficiency.

The Data Mining Process

The first question that should follow this definition is how is data mined? The entire process of data mining involves capturing, storing, gathering, and analyzing the information of the company, and the very first step involves capturing information. Valuable information can be as simple as the name of a customer or as complex as operational performance measures like rates of return on investments.

There are two viewpoints on this. The first is that all information has or may have some value in the future so that all information should be captured and stored. The second view concludes that information is costly to capture and store so that only strategically required information should be captured.

The second method places the organization at risk of missing or losing some valuable data. For example, a company that sells computers may find that information about peripheral use is valuable to future development, but the company may ignore other information, such as customer opinions on how they found out about the organization. If the company then decides to release a new product through a print advertising campaign, they may find that the success of the campaign is less than it would have been if the bulk of the resources were allocated to an Internet promotional campaign. Data mining could have provided information that indicated most customers located the company through the Internet, as opposed to print ads.

To Mine Data, It Must First Be Stored

However, this data would only be available if it had originally been captured and stored. The best technique for capturing data is to have the customer enter this data directly into a capturing application such as online product registration forms.

Another technique is to have the information captured by staff during a customer account set-up process. A third option is to have the information loaded from other databases sold by other companies, including your competitors.

Some companies go so far as to run contests and promotions simply as a way to get people to enter information. This happens because there is a negative attitude beginning to grow in the Internet surfing community that entering personal information is both time consuming and invasive. This attitude is less prevalent with contest entry forms; however, individuals who enter information into these forms may not be representative of a normal population. This means that getting information that 90 percent of all respondents like contests may not be a good representation of the general population and may result in bad decisions.

Data Mining Resources

To find resources on data mining, surf to http://www.kdnuggets.com/.

The second piece of the data mining puzzle is the storage of captured data. All data that is captured should be stored for future data mining opportunities. This storage has traditionally taken the form of relational databases, and, in fact, most data extraction tools are based on standard relational data base formats such as Microsoft SQL. It is important that the storage mechanism be fast and efficient since extracting information is a complex process that can often take a great amount of resources. If the database chosen is inefficient in its design, then the ability to get information out of it will take an excessive amount of resources.

Mining Databases

The key is a database structure that can store and analyze large volumes of information. Some newer databases store objects that include pieces of code that manage the information. In this case, analyzing volumes of data may prove less efficient than a standard relational structure. Random customer data should be stored with some idea of how it will be extracted for mining in the future. Information that is immediately pertinent, such as sales data, can run though object code that analyzes it prior to its storage. Long-term data can run through code objects that append other information that will be useful later on, such as a code that indicates the links a customer has taken from your Web site to an affiliate's Web site. Also critical to data storage are backup and recovery resources and strategies.

There are a wide array of extraction applications that will analyze the data in a database for trends. Historical data, such as the age of a consumer and their purchasing habits, is very valuable for such functions as developing future product mixes or promotions. For example, a store that has a general consumer population in its mid thirties can analyze what those people buy. If 60 percent purchased a baby pacifier in the

ODBC

Open Database Connectivity is a set of standards that have been created so that software developers can build interfaces to different databases. This allows them to say that they are ODBC compliant.

last six months, then a mailing promotion on baby supplies to those individuals may increase the overall sales of baby products in the store. Extraction tools are often closely related to the type of database being mined; however, some sophisticated extraction tools are ODBC compliant and can interface with a variety of databases.

Extracting and Analyzing Data

The function of extraction software is to either search for set information that indicates a trend, such as the example above, or allows users to search for specific types of data that match parameters they enter. In this latter extraction process, the application may locate customer information in a piece of a database, mine operational data with the same key, and statistically report on such items as sales volume by product category or dollars spent per trip. The goal is always to try to provide information that decision makers can use to plan new programs that, in turn, will add more revenue. It is important to note that data mining does not have to apply to sales and marketing campaigns only; it can also apply to a variety of functions and tasks such as the following:

➤ Customer service volume

➤ Service and repairs response times

➤ Customer satisfaction

➤ Advertising results

➤ Delivery times

➤ Product quality

➤ Employee satisfaction

➤ Employee Internet usage

Another important piece of the data mining process is the analysis of mined information. Data analysis is usually handled by individuals who study the statistical results from the data extraction section and then report or make decisions based on the results. However, more and more sophisticated systems are starting to provide analysis tools that cause some action to occur automatically. An example would be a tool that analyzes sales to determine which type of automatic coupon should be sent to the consumer. This can be an automated process that counts the number of purchases of a type of product by a particular consumer and then causes another application to begin based on the results.

Making Better Decisions through Mining

The end result of data mining is the finished product, which in this case is information that identifies current and future trends or provides base information like addresses or different ways of quantifying information. Where data mining can have a direct application to i-commerce is in the creation of communities of value. If you are a retailer with an extensive collection of stored customer purchasing behaviors, then you can probably use the data to design the Web site based on the results of a data analysis. As a retailer, you may find that your customers who surf the Internet are primarily in an age band from 18 to 35. However, you may find that the bulk of your sales are made to high-income individuals between the ages of 30 to 35. This information can then be used to either attract more of the younger component of your bulk market or to market direct to the older component through the design of the Web site.

More Data Mining Resources

Surf hyperlink `http://www.info-goal.com/dmc/dmcdwh.htm` get more information about data mining resources such as data warehousing and Neural Nets.

How Is Data Mined?

One of the most important pieces of data mining is the software available to perform the task. Data mining software comes in two varieties: statistical modeling software that uses advanced mathematics and theories to provide information that predicts future events, and reporting software that produces reports on the number of customers in a geographic area. Companies such as IBM, Silicon Graphics, and Thinking Machines all offer software that can mine a file of data and apply statistical modeling tools to assist in the analysis.

Many of these software packages incorporate concepts such as Neural Networks or artificial intelligence. Neural nets are applications that mimic learning by adjusting the software parameters. Other concepts include decision trees, which use a set of predetermined decisions to predict future outcomes and a variety of other advanced mathematical concepts. The overall theory of data mining is still quite simple. The

Neural Network

A neural network is a storage and application that operates very similarly to the human mind. The idea is to take a dumb computer and get it to start analyzing data for trends, etc., by using advanced math and statistical models. For example, a neural network may have historical foreign exchange rates, and it may use this data to run a mathematical model to predict the future FX level. What makes a neural net different is that it would then analyze the outcome and adjust its level accordingly.

basic premise of the concept is this: input a file of data, define which extractions parameters are important, and then allow the software to produce a result.

Decision Support Software (DSS)

Some of the software noted above costs as much as $1 million per installation. The whole purpose is to provide the people who make decisions with the information they need to make better decisions. This type of software is called decision support software or DSS. The fundamental problem with all decision support software that predicts future occurrence is that no one person or computer can predict the future. That is where real analysis of information plays a role. For example, it is highly unlikely that decision support systems would have predicted that Amazon.com would open its virtual doors on the Internet. However, decision support systems could have reported the number of book purchasing customers that were in a technological position to use the Internet for purchasing. Any old Wall Street analyst could have then figured out the rest. When analyzing data, it is important to remember that machines cannot understand all the subtle interactions of the world well enough to make decisions. They can, however, provide base information to make more effective educated guesses.

It is important that decisions made through the use of data mining techniques consider the corporate strategy. This strategy is the map for the corporate operations, and if it is not considered when other decisions are made, then the company may go toward the wrong goal. For example, if a company were to receive data that 35-year-old customers were the most likely to respond to the development of a new product, but the corporate strategy was to target 30-year-olds, then a decision based on the mined data would take the company away from its strategic direction. It is better to use data mining to help determine the overall strategic direction of the organization, and then use it to fine-tune operations such as promotional campaigns.

The Benefits of Data Mining

One of the most usable areas of mined data is the marketing department of the organization. Customer purchasing information can be used to design new marketing and promotional campaigns to assist in the growth of the organization. Marketing strategy is based on the identification of customer groups so that campaigns can be directed toward a certain audience. Originally, marketing companies and departments subdivided the population based on demographic principles such as income or gender. Later theories further developed the concept of promoting to cross-sections of these markets such as individuals with a certain income and genders. Newer theories now discuss concepts such as "psychographic" marketing techniques that are based on perceptions and feelings or cross-niche marketing that is designed to develop a program for a variety of groups who have a common perception.

Using Mined Information To Target Customers

Data mining can greatly aid in these newer marketing concepts by providing information that crosses the old demographic lines and redefines groups by communities. Now companies can target a select group of consumers with products and promotions that emulate the concepts of the community. For i-commerce companies that are developing an identity, this information can be infinitely valuable.

Advertising and Mined Data

The world of advertising is a world of images and vague concepts, and for these types of tasks, data mining has a direct role. That role has two unique characteristics. First, an analysis of mined data can indicate groupings and concepts that can be used to design advertisements. Second, more advanced data mining software can predict potential outcomes based on past information, and this information can be used to test images or the media mix used to distribute the advertising.

An example of the first type of data mining is a technology company that mined the data in an online Internet database of the age group 18 to 23. The information indicated that the group was not purchasing mainstream software, but did have a strong interest to search for free software as well as online music information sites. Combining the free release of the sound software along with the promotion of free music on those information sites started the rapid growth of their Internet concept. The second type of data mining predicted that the growth would next occur in the immediate age groups on either side of the original group, and that further directed cross promotion through sites like Amazon and the search engines and hard ads in magazines like *Wired* would provide the greatest growth for the organization.

Banner Ads

Banner ads are those thin ads that you usually see at the top and bottom of Web sites. They are easy to create and easy to place at sites like Amazon.com, but the fees charged are based on coverage. The best coverage will occur if you can place the ad to come up for certain people. To do this, you will have to mine or capture the data to have an indication of where to place the ad.

Promotion and Mined Data

In the same way that data mining assists in developing and delivering advertising, it can also assist promotional campaigns. Promotional campaigns, as opposed to advertising, require significantly more planning. That planning depends on the promotional activity. Manipulation of the press can often be achieved with just a good idea. However, most promotional campaigns will require an understanding of the market they are designed for. To this end, data mining can still assist the development and direction of promotional activities from traditional campaigns like press releases and sponsorships to unconventional campaigns like live Webcasts of controversial content.

The same concepts apply to the analysis of mined data for promotion as for advertising. Some mining software will assist in defining opportunities and other mining software will assist in predicting the outcome of promotional campaigns. An example of the use of mined data in the formation of a promotional campaign would be if the software were able to find a link between young males in their mid twenties who surf to no more than four new sites per week at night and an attitude that new software will only be accepted if it has been identified by hot new sites and newsgroups. This might encourage a new sports analysis tool to be promoted on the newsgroups and by banner ads on "cool sites."

Data mining also assists in defining targeted sales promotions. For example, an advertising or promotional campaign can be created for an existing set of customers. In this scenario, the mined data may or may not assist in the initial development. The marketing manager can then use the data mining tools to produce a list of customers who have the highest potential to favorably respond to the advertising or promotion. This will produce a "target" list for the campaign and provide a higher level of return for the level of money expended. Target lists can also be used to reward loyal customers, direct sales efforts, and tailor giveaways and direct sponsorships.

Using Mined Data for Designing

Another place where data mining can provide a significant benefit is in the area of design. In this case, Internet information or customer service information can indicate design changes that are necessary. Data mining software can assist by providing report data on such factors as consistent complaints, requested changes from customers, and inquiries by potential customers. Old data designs can also be mined for components test results and probable outcomes of design changes. The most common example of this is using existing wind tunnel data to design products.

Looking Ahead: Using Statistical Modeling

Another common use of mined data are the sophisticated financial and trading programs that use historical information to apply statistical modeling concepts to identify future potential risk. These results are then used by traders to place hedges that protect against these future risks. The goal is to give the data miner a way to predict the future.

However, there are a number of people who do not agree with these techniques, believing that historical data has no relation to the future outcome. These individuals try to predict the future by using current information. An example is currency traders who adjust their currency positions based on the latest releases of information. Data mining for this type of philosophy is more interested in producing data that predicts a trend. Another example is a report that indicates a decrease in hits to body piercing Web sites and a corresponding increase in hits to branding Web sites. This information can be used by the body alteration shop to predict trends and adjust its mix of product offerings.

Better Customer Service through Data Mining

One of the immediate uses of data mining software is to allow customer service staff to access customer information while they are talking to the customer. Two types of information can be provided, such as historical data about the products that customers have purchased and software predictions about what other products the customer might like. With this type of information, customer service clerks can better assist individual customers to make decisions based on information about their preferences. This type of information is becoming more prevalent on Web sites in order to provide suggestions to customers.

The better the information available to the customer service function, the better the service to the customer. The better the customer service, the higher the sales. But the information must be readily available, easily analyzed, and presented in a format that is easy to understand. In this way, if a customer calls a call center, the call center system can analyze the phone number and present a page of information to the center clerk, including:

MP3

The MP3 Web site at www.mp3.com sends an email to customers about new MP3 releases and recommends specific new music releases based on your preferences.

➤ A list of items purchased

➤ Total sales to date

➤ Outstanding amounts

➤ Suggested new products

➤ Customer's contact with the service center

➤ Links used by the customer from the company's Web site

➤ Miscellaneous personal information gathered from previous calls

In one particular company, a customer called in about an order and mentioned that her daughter was going to college, and the customer service clerk entered the information into a personal notes area. When the customer called back the following week to place an order, the customer service clerk could see the reference to the daughter and asked how things were going. A positive and personal rapport with customers has been proven to increase the level of sales, and a key ingredient of this formula is information mined from the corporate database.

Data mining also provides management with valuable information. Managers can mine basic information, such as how long employees spend on particular functions on the network or where they surf to on the Internet. They can also mine data for forecast purposes, such as the average volume of sales from customers by customer service clerks. Decreases in this measure may indicate an employee who has stopped encouraging sales. Managers can also use data mining to forecast future financial performance for use in budgeting and forecasts.

Better Customer Information

Data mining also greatly contributes to the information available to the customer through Web sites. Personalized Web site access provides customers with personalized information. Data mining software can assist in loading information into a personalized Web page, such as product offerings or newly released data that may be of interest to the customer. The predicting type of software can also be used as a search engine initiated by the customer. Most of the "find other similar products" links are simply data mining tools that search company databases or the Internet, including those used by Amazon.com (see Figure 13.1).

Figure 13.1

The "if you like this book link" provides a suggestion based on other customers' purchases.

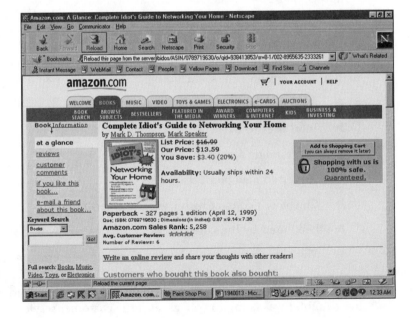

The goals of providing information directly to customers are the same as the goals to provide managers with information: to assist in making better decisions and thereby encourage sales. Data mining software can also provide search capabilities for past customer information and one day may result in a personal data storage killer app where people store and analyze a variety of personal information to improve their lives.

Customer Created Data

The vast majority of data mined is entered by the organization into vast database storage systems known as data warehouses. Mining this data produces a valuable resource for decision making, but the cost of this data capture is current very high. E-commerce provides the model that significantly changes that equation by having the customer enter the information or by having real-time integrated systems store the data automatically.

However, customers will only enter minimal amounts of information before they find the experience distasteful. Therefore, data capture systems must be very fast and efficient with the customer's time. How the customer enters data into the system will dictate the quality of the data received. For example, if you are blocking access to your site to try and obtain customer address information through a form, then you will likely find that less and less of the data being entered is valuable. However, if you run a contest where the winners are notified by mail, then the quality of the data will be higher.

Special Considerations for Web Site Design

The design of the Web site is also important. Certain Web sites provide forms with look-up lists of cities and states to assist in data entry (see Figure 13.2). This makes the task of data entry easier, and will likely result in better entry information. Other Web sites use cookies, which are bits of information and code that are exchanged by browsers and stored on the customer's computer. The next time the customer enters the site, an exchange occurs between the two machines that causes the customer's profile to be accessed. This is why when you re-enter Web sites like www.shockrave.com, the Web site greets you with your own name (see Figure 13.3). Some browsers provide you the option to not accept cookies.

Information that is entered by customers or captured by internal systems is usually stored in relational databases.

Figure 13.2

This figure shows a form with a selection box for the country.

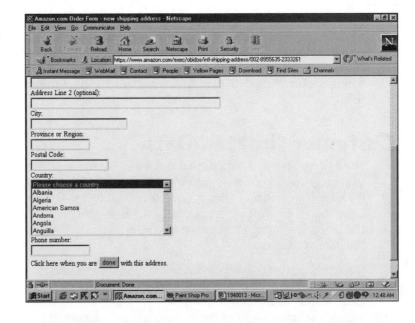

Figure 13.3

This figure shows the personalized entry screen for the Shockwave Web site.

Relational Databases

Relational databases are storage areas for information that is organized into tables. Each table pertains to a particular grouping of data, such as customer information, and is indexed with one or more keys. Keys are unique identifiers for each line in the table. For example, a customer will have a unique number that differentiates him from other customers. This customer number can be used as a key in a customer information table so that if you have a customer number, you will only get the information related to that customer. Later, when the customer calls for an order, you can use this customer number to quickly and easily complete the customer information section.

As a customer enters information, a customer number can be applied to that information so that it can be easily retrieved for later use by mining technology. The next time the customer signs onto the system, that information can be retrieved very efficiently from the database. Currently, most Web sites have the customer create a sign-on ID and password. This gives the customer the opportunity to create a familiar logon without having to remember a customer number. The problem is that a common ID like RSmith might already be used, so customers are finding that they have to create variations on the ID such as SmithR.

Warehousing Data

When an organization centralizes the storage of data, it is said to be putting the data into a data warehouse. These warehouses contain millions of pieces of information about customer behavior and demographics, and they are starting to contain information about our other personal traits and behaviors. Even though the phrase "warehouse" implies that the data is shelved, in fact the storage spaces are often nothing more than servers that contain large arrays of disk for storing information.

The Storage Area Network (SAN)

Another growing concept is the notion of SANs or storage area networks, which are numerous independent databases connected together through a network. This type of structure provides an organization with the same fail-safe structure that currently powers the Internet, which means that if a part of the SAN goes down, the balance of the information can still be retrieved using other routes. The downside of SANs is that they require an exceptionally good data administrator who can identify where the fragmented information is. Data marts are simply a lighter version of the data warehouse with some of the functionality of a SAN.

The final step in the capturing of data is to provide a way to access the data for use in mining applications. Accessing data in data warehouses can be complicated if you do not understand the structure of the warehouse. However, accessing data in a SAN will require both an understanding of the structure of the individual data storage areas, as well as an understanding where the data storage area is on the SAN. Many larger organizations have a team of specialists who do nothing else but analyze the relationship between how the data is stored and how it is accessed. Their goal is to make the process more efficient by using software to anticipate what data will be required.

Pulling Out the Data

The standard method for pulling data from a warehouse is through a data query language such as SQL. However, there is more sophisticated software available, such as that used by Ask Jeeves, to analyze regular grammatical phrasing in questions to identify information. The question "What is a dog?" is broken by the software into the phrases "What is" and "a dog." The software then knows that it is looking primarily for "definitional hits" on the phrase "a dog," and it will evaluate those sites that have the highest ratio of references to the selection criteria.

If the question had been "Where is." then the site would have ranked "location" hits higher than definitional hits. This is an example of how this type of software mines for data in large data warehouses. The more unstructured the data storage, the easier it will be for the mining software to locate the information you are seeking. Creating a query that selects precisely the information you are seeking may be essential to internal operations, but presentation of general information, such as responses to a Web site search, will require less rigidity. For this reason, it is vital that business consider a variety of storage and mining applications from relational and object databases, to query reporting tools to advanced analytical modeling programs.

Sophisticated Mining and Analytical Tools

Most data mining software will have a mathematical or statistical modeling tool built in. These tools use complex algorithms, historical data, or both to predict future events.

The easiest way to explain these tools is to take a trip to Vegas. Picture that you are sitting at a blackjack table with your IT expert at your side. You are holding a 10 and a 6, and you are not sure how much to bet or whether you should take another card. You turn to you IT guy and say "What do you think?" He's sweating a little because they took his laptop at the door, but he turns to you and firmly says, "Go for the next card and bet high." You are not too sure how many free drinks he has had, but you bet high, take another card, and receive a 3. The dealer turns over a queen and proceeds to take a 2 and a 10. You win your hand and leave the table. On the way out the door you ask the IT guy how he was so sure. He responds by telling you that there were three decks in play, and he counted that 47 out of 65 cards, eight or greater had already passed, but that only 25 cards, five or fewer had passed by. He reasoned that the odds of you receiving a five or less were quite high and worthy of a higher investment. The same principles apply in the sophisticated math and statistics tools employed by more expensive data mining software.

The idea is to use past information that has happened to predict the probability of an outcome in the future. Advanced mathematics based on population distribution theory, random simulations based chaos theory, and a variety of other methods are included in various types of data mining software currently available on the market.

Data Mining Software

For a information on data mining, surf to
`http://www.data-miners.com/`.

To Sell or Not to Sell—a Future View

The big question that is a topic of extreme controversy on the Internet is whether companies should sell the information they have collected in data stores. These huge repositories of data have an extremely valuable collection of information about what we have purchased, what we like in terms of entertainment, what we eat for dinner, how much we spend per month, and even what our income is. However, there is growing resentment on the Internet toward companies that demand our personal information, and slowly these databases are growing full of inaccurate data as people answer the questions with any answer, as opposed to the correct one. This has caused companies that purchase information to be far more selective about whose information they are buying. It has also caused some companies to give up the concept of selling information because customers are becoming irritated, and because competitors are using the data against the company that sold it.

Yahoo.com is one of the leaders in the movement toward a new model of sharing customer information. Their concept is based on the fundamental principal that customers should approve the information that they receive. That means that if a customer of Yahoo does not want her information freely distributed, then she will not provide it. If a customer authorizes Yahoo to allow certain types of promotional literature through, then this information will be presented to the customer. This philosophy places the ownership of information back into the hands of the consumer, as opposed to the current philosophy that the company owns the information and can sell it to whomever it wants to for any purpose.

Consumers inherently seek information regarding new products; however, they want to choose the categories and have control of when to stop receiving this information. Many Web sites have tried to solve this problem by providing links to the information; however, given the volume of information available, surfers are having a more difficult time trying to locate usable information. This is where personalized Web sites can ease that problem by allowing the user to set parameters about what kinds of information they will receive. This makes online consumers more responsive to promotions from online companies that are using this controlled technique because the customers are getting information that they have already approved.

This technique also allows companies like Yahoo to gather more information from the customer since the adversarial environment of providing information is going to be less of a concern for these individuals.

What Do You Do with the Information?

After you have captured, stored, extracted, and analyzed your customer data, then what do you do? As a business owner or manager, you have to decide what to do with the results. Decision making is truly an art, and the best business people in the world know that information is essential to good decision making, but that some level of intuition is essential for success. Many of the most successful Internet companies today would have been hard pressed to find data mining software that indicated that they should start up on the Internet. Even more unlikely would be any recommendations related to Downes and Mui's concepts in Chapter 6 about building the killer app. Intuition, however, had a big role to play in decisions of people like Bill Gates and Jeff Bezos of Amazon.

Gut instinct, intuition, insight, experience—whatever you call it, that little subjective piece of decision making can be made better with information. This is particularly true of decisions that pertain to existing ongoing operations. The business owners still need some information to fire their imagination, but the hard decisions about strategic planning and operations can be made more effective with mined data. This is also true for smaller organizations with smaller client bases. In order to grow the company, the decision makers must have the best information they can obtain from what they already have. However, don't dwell on it. More than a few large companies have gone bankrupt as a result of spending too much time studying operating results and not enough time looking into the future.

The Least You Need To Know

➤ What data mining is and how is it used.

➤ Understand how to store and capture data in a data mine.

➤ Know some of the techniques for extracting or mining data.

➤ Understand how to analyze data once it has been mined.

➤ Know how to use the output from data mining to make better decisions.

Part 3
e-Marketing

It's an entirely new world out there, and it requires a comprehensive understanding of an entirely new way to market your new e-commerce company. New advertising, new promotion, and even the way you build your Web site all depend on your understanding of this new e-commerce landscape.

In the first chapters, we'll talk about how marketing on the Internet has changed the traditional marketing world and the ramifications it will have on your existing or new company. Then we'll look at Internet advertising and the opportunities to use this powerful medium to deliver your message.

You'll get detailed information about the most current types of marketing models that will help drive customers to your e-business. Finally, we will cross over to the off-Net world and explain how you can use some traditional techniques to build your e-business using traditional mediums like TV.

Finally, we will revisit the data mine and show you how to use the data to develop your marketing strategy, as well as how to get mined information from the Internet.

Knowing how to promote in the world of e-commerce is not the same as it used to be, and you will advance from this section with a clear idea of what you should do and what pitfalls you should avoid.

Spinning a Web— Internet Marketing

Marketing your Web site on the Internet is different than marketing a product or a service. The number of people who surf the Internet, the volumes of information and Web sites available, banner ads, promotion, public relations, online surveys, and new media all blend together into an ever-changing model of Internet marketing. In the old days, the choices were far simpler—you selected a target market, an image, and a message; a media outlet then implemented your marketing strategy and evaluated results.

Now the models mix traditional advertising and promotion with some new concepts about how to attract attention and a wide array of new media. Gone are the days of static images in printed magazines or audio clips on radio stations. Now you can target millions of people with audio and moving images that have the impact of a national TV ad, but at a very low cost. Newer technologies even go further by offering the opportunity for users to interact with the ads. Savvy PR firms as well are starting to develop promotions that don't follow any of the old rules of public relations, but instead create interest through shock or innovative promotions that draw visitors to

Web sites designed specifically to distribute advertising (ad site). However, some of the old strategic marketing principles still apply, and the results of combining strategy and technology can be phenomenal.

Who Are Your Customers?

Advertising and promotion cost money. That's the bottom line. The success of your e-commerce marketing program will depend on the level of resources that you are willing to throw at it. However, more resources will not always equal more success. There is a long list of companies that spent money advertising only to wind up with very little to show for their efforts. Some misguided campaigns with poor imaging and a failure to understand the market have even cost some companies their lives. Planning your attack on a market cannot be underestimated, but there is a great deal of intelligence that must be gathered prior to the assault, such as information about the terrain, the enemy, the tools available, and what is coming over the horizon. One of the most important pieces of the puzzle is knowing who your e-customers are.

Way, way back in the deep history of the Internet, like three years ago, the primary users of the Internet were the high tech gurus of new technology. University students, hackers, scientists, and large institutional information departments primarily used the Internet to send data between computers. Very early in the development of the network, form-based technologies allowed these individuals to exchange messages, and it was during these early years that people started to understand the huge potential of a world connected by computers. It was the concept of critical mass that gave life to these theories and opened the Internet to everybody.

It was entrepreneurs who captured the first major beachhead in the war to attract mid-level computer users to the Internet. Millions of computers had been installed in homes and offices thanks to the push of companies like Apple and IBM. Early local Internet Service Providers or ISPs and the larger national ISPs like America Online started the move to critical mass by making Internet access affordable for the masses. Now anyone with a PC and a telephone could get on the Net and start performing simple functions like surfing to text-based Web sites and sending e-mail. Companies started to provide e-mail access links to their internal e-mail systems, which further added to the growing user familiarity with the world of the Internet.

Today, the explosive growth of the Internet has created the critical mass of Metcalf's law, and has opened unlimited opportunity for growth. It has also created the largest advertising pool in the world. Internet users number in the hundreds of millions and will likely reach billions in the next decade. The size of the Internet audience is so large and so varied that companies have a difficult time trying to understand how to allocate their limited advertising and promotional resources. Targeting customers who are most likely to purchase your service or product will become more essential as global advertising possibilities become expensive for small and mid-sized organizations. The Cokes and Microsofts of the world will be the only players with the reach capable of justifying large expenditures on the global advertising level, while companies with fewer resources will have to be content with trying to attract the interest of market leaders to their Web site. They will have to be more selective about who they are going to target in order to ensure an adequate return on their advertising and promotional investment. They will essentially have to know who their customers are.

Where Are Your Customers?

After you have defined who your customers are, the next question will be where on the Net are they? You can be pretty certain that specific demographic groups can be easily located on the Internet by using the expertise developed over years of marketing research. If you want to know where a group of sports-loving males in their 30s hang out, then the Internet will provide you with that information. This results from the electronic nature of the Net, and its ability to capture and store information about users and their transactions.

For example, www.espn.com, the sports network's Web site, will have the target market defined previously, but it will also have a large number of visitors from outside this market, such as males over 40 or under 30 and now a growing contingent of women. If you place an ad on this Web site, you will have to pay for the impressions or the number of times your ad is shown, regardless of who views it. A better use of resources might be to advertise on a feeder Web site that targets your demographics by offering links to the larger site. The cost would be cheaper, and the probability of a "good hit" would be higher.

Finding your market is critical at this point in the history of the Internet, and will become more critical as traffic builds at the major sites and the return to impression ratio gets lower. Other options may be more financially sound, such as paying micropayments for traffic or contact information; however, the same problem of identifying your market to increase your buy ratio will still remain intact. The good news is that the level of statistics pertaining to network traffic is growing and more and more companies like Yahoo are starting to use customer provided demographic information to build targeting packages for Net advertisers. This allows advertisers to have their banner ads shown only to specific individuals, as opposed to a random group of users. This way a company can tightly define which users they are going to target by their interests and not just by their basic demographic information. For example, when you sign up for a personal My Yahoo customized Web page, the form will ask you to choose your interests. This information can then be used to deliver targeted advertising specifically designed for users with similar interests (see Figure 14.1).

Another way to locate customers on the Internet is to place your ads with Internet companies that maintain transactional information on users. Some companies, such as My Simon, track user purchases by account, and this information can be a valuable marketing tool for ad placement. For example, let's say I sold fountain pumps for backyard ponds. I could use the stored buying information to identify which users have recently purchased garden products and then have a banner ad shown when those users re-access the Web site for other shopping.

211

Figure 14.1

When you sign up with Yahoo you will be asked to enter your personal preferences.

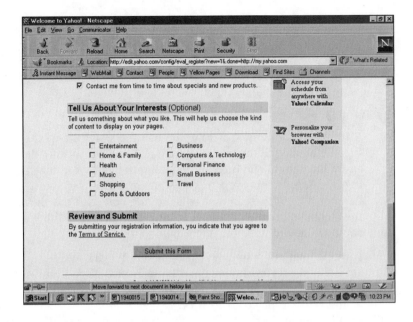

There are also companies that are starting to analyze the data contained in Web sites for correlation opportunities. This information will provide a way to define what products or services will be required by a group of people that gather at a specific site. For instance, a group that surfs to a Web location that contains negative information about Microsoft may be the perfect place to advertise snowboards if a correlation has been identified between the user groups and its tastes. Analysis of tastes and preferences are the realm of psychographic or behavior analysis.

Psychographic Analysis

Psychographic analysis is the study of behavior usually in relation to utilizing the data for defining marketing user groups or communities of value. For more info, surf to `www.knowthis.com/research/companies/psychographic.htm`.

The benefit of identifying your customers on the Internet is that your resources, namely cash and marketing staff, will be more focused and will produce better results, namely profits.

Promotion on the Net

Want to get traffic real fast? How about a good scam? We are serious. One of the best ways to get traffic to your site is to pull the equivalent of a Blair Witch (see Figure 14.2). Create the equivalent of an Internet urban legend and then let it loose on the world and capitalize on the traffic. This has included everything from people selling vital organs on an online auction site to stars having stomach surgery live to reduce their weight. First, your most creative staff geniuses will have to concoct a story that is likely to attract visitors either to your site or to a location where your banner ad will be viewed.

Let's say I started an online auction site and then decided that I needed to draw enough traffic to create a traffic jam and thereby raise the profile of the site with a series of corresponding news releases. Let's say I put a product up for sale that would cause a stir, such as a body part. Then as the price is bid up by a few mysterious friends, I send out worldwide news releases about our organization's position not to interfere with our customer's strange actions. Why would I do this? It's simple, I get traffic, and if I get enough hits, I can release a second news release to identify the trouble we are having handling the volume. Now, all of a sudden, I have instantaneous press coverage just as long as the story is weird enough.

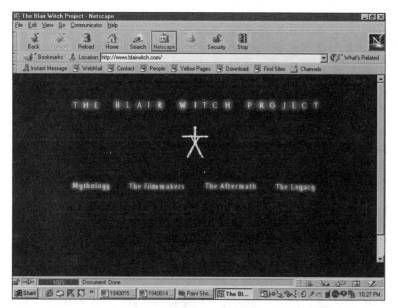

Figure 14.2

A Blair Witch Web site is part of a movie promotion which originally gave the impression that the film was a true story.

Some would argue with the ethics of creating false stories to generate traffic, and there are a number of pitfalls in this concept. However, if your team is really creative, they will be able to dream up concepts that are not false, yet still generate traffic and interest. The obvious benefit is that you can start to create a following or community if your team is effective at getting its message out. It is also important to remember that information sites that depend on traffic levels will have to continuously attract traffic to their site as more and more comparable or new "cool" sites compete on the Net.

One of the best promotional tools available is the newsgroup. Newsgroups are a way for individuals to discuss relevant topics such as the latest cool site, technology, or entertainment. The users of this technology are not particularly friendly to direct promotion from organizations or even corporate "plants" that pretend they are just regular newsgroup users. These corporate plants are usually hired by large technology companies to do nothing else but argue and promote their company in the newsgroups. However, the best way to promote your company is to generate buzz from outside the newsgroup and let it filter in by itself. A little careful crafting of images and messages and some good "ex-Net" (outside the Internet) promotion and advertising will go a long way toward getting lots of buzz about your site. There was a lot of buzz about the "Blair Witch Project" movie in the newsgroups prior to its release, and this helped spread the word without the benefit of a large "ex-Net" promotional budget.

Of course, there are a variety of other ways to promote on and off the Net. You can sponsor Net events like Webcasts (see Figure 14.3), do give-a-ways and contests, or promote the site "ex-Net." Often, sponsoring events at trade shows such as Comdex can start the process of generating buzz on the Internet, especially if the product or service you are selling is very unique or a killer app. Obviously, discussing your Web site with affiliates, suppliers, and potential customers will also help to generate a buzz.

Figure 14.3

Zdnet Webcast page provides links to Webcasts.

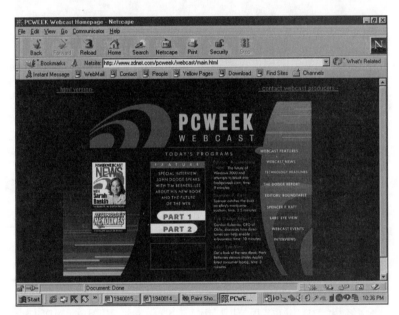

On–Net Advertising

The primary forms of "on-Net" advertising available today are banner ads. They are the long thin ads that you see at the top of most Web sites, and are comprised of an image, which is usually an animated Graphic Interchange Format (GIF) or one that has some motion to it and a linking mechanism so that if Net surfers click on the ad, they are instantaneously sent to the advertiser's Web site. Simple animated GIFs are multiple images that give the impression of motion when run together. These ads are usually placed by larger organizations, and are often run in a rotation, meaning that each time you access the site you may only see the same ad every third time.

Sometimes, the ad placements are traded and sometime the company running the ad pays a commission on sales or a micropayment on traffic. Most often, the ads are paid based on the number of impressions or the number of times the ad is seen. The payment is made on the basis of a cost per thousands of impressions or CPM. These prices range from $20 to $100 per thousand.

Ads, however, can sometime be placed for free. In these instances, companies are providing links to services for their online community.

On-Net advertising can also take the form of link ads that are smaller than banner ads and often only show the logo of the Web site. These take up significantly less room, and are considered less intrusive than the banner ads.

Learnlots.com

`Learnlots.com` provides information in the form of "how to" tutorials on a wide variety of topics. Since they offer their service free of charge, this encourages companies to link to the site for free, in exchange for providing the service to their community.

These ads are often used on the main Web page of companies and search engines (see Figure 14.4), usually to link to services or sites that pay a commission, like Amazon.

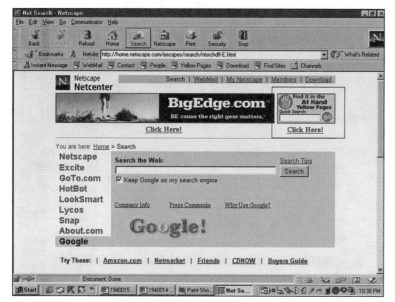

Figure 14.4

Small link ads link to other Web sites, such as the Yellow Pages service

The greatest benefit of online advertising is the ability for advertisers who have a product or service with a wide appeal to market to a large number of people or for advertisers whose products have a narrow appeal to target ads at a more select audience. The combination of data mining from Web sites and the careful placement of

215

Internet Advertising Information

For more information on Internet advertising costs, you can surf to adres.internet.com for a variety of helpful links

an ad can be a very successful combination for organizations that are sophisticated enough to have clearly defined their customers. The ads themselves are also becoming more sophisticated with the inclusion of sound and interactive functionality.

Off-Net Advertising

If a company has on-Net advertising, why would it need off-Net or ex-Net advertising? The answer is speed. When Snap.com entered the search engine war zone, they became one of a number of search engines (see Figure 14.5). They needed fast growth in their traffic levels to start generating ad revenue and to give them the critical mass so essential to survival. The viability of the investment in Snap was dependent on fast success. This success was dependent on critical mass, and that made it essential that traffic develop quickly. The answer was to use traditional advertising mediums, like widely dispersed national TV and print ads, to generate the kinds of traffic numbers needed to position Snap as a serious contender with Yahoo.

Figure 14.5

There are many successful search engines that compete for visitors, as shown in the figure.

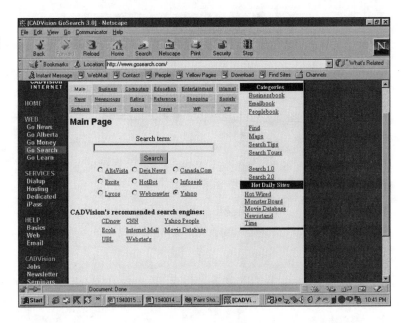

The approach is to first generate a curiosity about the brand by running ads that introduce the brand name of the company and the image. Short messages and interesting imagery or dark humor are the hallmarks of an Internet hard ad campaign and the more memorable the ad, the better. The acronym KISS or "keep it simple stupid" is the rule of the day in designing the first ads. The goal should be to have people remember the brand name such as ebay.com and thereby remember the location on the Internet. Try to avoid lofty messages with complex ideas since people will tend to find them confusing and will tune out the message. The goal is to have as many people as possible remember the name of the Web site.

The Personal Approach

Advertising and promotion are an excellent way to gain attention for your organization, but the personal face-to-face meeting is a more powerful method for raising awareness. The problem is that you cannot spend the entire travel budget on meeting your potential Internet customers (unless you're selling rare art). However, it is an excellent way to generate industry buzz through face-to-face meetings with your affiliates or partners. It also provides you with a chance to understand the strength of their business.

Outpost.com Advertising

One of the most effective advertisements to raise the profile of an existing brand was the TV ad campaign for Outpost.com in which a high school marching band is attacked by wolves. Dark, savvy, and cynical, yet highly effective in the eyes of a savvy and cynical target market that it was designed for. The great strength of the ad was to position the company as being one with the consumers by sharing their cynicism. Outpost was creating a community of value.

The process is simple: Locate the phone number for the organization that you would like to partner with and then phone the company and ask for the person in charge of channel marketing or partnerships and affiliates. Next, discuss your new Web site or concept, how they might fit in with the plan, what benefit you will provide, and what you would like in return. Finally, ask for a face-to-face meeting to discuss partnering opportunities. Remember that the partnership has to provide a matching value. You can't ask Amazon to put up a banner ad in exchange for a banner ad on your site and expect them to be ecstatic. However, if you have a concept that requires the involvement of an equal partner, then this approach should work.

Learnlots may not have had as favorable a response if they had simply tried to establish the partnership over the phone. In the first place, seeing your partner puts a face to the concept, and provides your partner with a comfort level. Secondly, as most salesmen know, it's hard to say no to a face-to-face close; it is far easier to say we'll think about it over a phone. Of course, the downside is the cost of this approach including airfare, hotels, transport, meals, etc. You will have to make sure that the partner you are going to meet is able to provide you with real value, such as an operational advantage (i.e., e-commerce shopping site), traffic (i.e., major link site), or exposure (i.e., an online zine compiling a story).

Learnlot's Shopping Connection

`Learnlots.com` is a Web site that provides free tutorials to the Internet community. They generate revenue through traffic and commissions; however, to round out their concept, they required a link to a shopping service so that their community users could link to this partner. For that they turned to `mySimon.com` and visited face-to-face with the San Francisco-based shopping service to promote the concept. MySimon signed on to the Learnlots concept as a result of this meeting. It also provided significant information to Learnlots about its new partner.

One of the best ways to get your message out to the world is to take your application to the trade shows. Comdex in Las Vegas attracts ten of thousands of visitors annually, and can provide a lot of coverage as long as your presence at the conference is noted. This implies that you would have to create some mechanism for getting your name out since there are hundreds of other companies represented. So how do you do that? It's simple, send two teams to the show. One team should work your trade booth with cool promotional give-aways, and the other should work the trade floor gathering information and talking to partners. Also, consider sponsoring some of the side events that will attract attention.

Backing Up Marketing with a Good, Working Web Site

One of the most critical pieces of any Internet marketing campaign is a good and working Web site. Although most people seem to understand this concept, they are often in a rush to get to market and many different aspects are overlooked. The first is how the Web site functions from a visitor's perspective. Are the pieces in place that will allow the customer to fully evaluate the benefit of belonging to this online community? If you have only some of the functionality up and running, then the problem will be that new visitors may feel the site does not offer them enough. The painful lesson here is that these first visitors are the bread and butter of any marketing campaign; they are the market leaders.

The second piece that is essential, but often overlooked, is the look and feel of the site. This goes back to all those design and image lessons you likely never learned, but that are an integral part of the graphics and advertising programs in the art colleges. If the image doesn't match the community, the visitors you attract may not stay. Cowboy hats are not going to excite the boarders, just as suits are not going to excite the tech world. Image counts.

Another important aspect is the technical readiness of the site or application. Nothing turns off visitors faster than a site they cannot access or a slow-loading application. Many companies have run advertisements and anticipated a specific number of hits on the site only to find that their pipe was overloaded.

An overloaded pipe simply returns a "cannot access the domain" message back to the visitor.

A Pipe Is a Pipe

The term pipe is used to refer to an Internet connection. Borrowed from the telecommunications world, it was originally taken from the fiber optic installers. Now, it is used to refer to any Internet connection as in "My pipe is down."

They will, on average, try to reload twice and then quit. Moreover, their attention spans last an average of 10 seconds so an application that is slow to respond will cause these initial users to lose interest very quickly. Once again, they are likely leaders in their market and therefore critical to generate significant future traffic. The moral here is to ensure that you clearly understand the capabilities of your network and then schedule your promotion accordingly.

How To Choose a Good PR Firm

So, you want to market your new Internet firm, and you're a little short of resources? Well, we suggest that you use the services of a professional PR firm. Let's face it, you probably don't have near the level of contacts that they do, the experience, or the time. So, unless your available resources do not include money, it is best to let the pros do their work. What they will do is build a plan to take your organization to the world through a mix of promotions and advertising and through the tangled world of publications both online and offline. In order to succeed, you will have to ensure that the firm you hire has the right mix of talents, experience, and cost.

First, ensure that they have the capability to understand your business and the world of the Internet. There are a wide variety of PR firms in the market and some have specialties; if they have a track record for Internet start-ups, then you've won half of the PR battle. However, some good younger firms without a track record may not only understand the Internet world better, but also have an exceptionally talented and savvy staff that will produce better results. Some older firms may not have the Internet concept understood, but may have a better grip on the marketing image relationship and may also have an extensive contacts list. The choice of a firm depends a great deal on the correct mix of experience, size, talent, and understanding of the public relations process.

Secondly, ensure that they are within your budget. Going to a successful PR firm may open a lot of doors, but may also cost too much for the return. Their focus should be to start the process of generating market buzz by working to ensure that the most beneficial PR tasks are complete at the same time that the site is launched. Their cost will be a reflection of the level of impact that you require, but ensure that you decide how deep you want the PR to go. International as opposed to national, national as opposed to local, online as opposed to offline, technical as opposed to general public, all these decisions will result in various levels of return and will have different levels of cost. Remember that Coke generated its critical mass by hiring low cost artists to paint its logos on the sides of every old building they could find. They still hire graffiti artists to legally paint the sides of stores.

Media Mix

A media mix usually refers to the mix of media that you will use in your advertising and promotions. On the Internet this mix will consist of ads, promotions, and media such as sound, video, or graphics.

Using Mined Customer Data

You may have to buy some data. Many organizations sell data on demographics and psychographics, mined from their own databases. In order to effectively target your advertising and promotion, you will require some indication of where the target is. This raw data provides the information that becomes the starting point for trying to decide a media mix.

A media mix is the mix of advertising and promotion that you develop based on the marketing plan of the organization. The marketing plan should specify real hard targets such as the following information:

➤ Number of hits on the Web site by a certain date
➤ The demographics of the market
➤ The psychographics of the market
➤ A definition of the community
➤ How the images are to be interpreted
➤ The actual images to be used
➤ Locations of the target audience
➤ Number of visits to the site per target population (i.e., an ad will be read by 20,000 of my target audience, and I expect 2,000 hits), etc.

Mined data provides a very valuable resource as to where the target market is located. You will likely receive data that will indicate the demographic mix of a particular site. Placing an ad on this site should generate a relatively predictable response if your market's demographics happen to match. Some search engines can provide more detailed information pertaining to the interests of users. Delivering ads to these users will also result in higher returns on your expenditure if the "interest" profiles match your expected market.

The data can also help to adjust your market definition if you find that volumes of a slightly different market are significantly higher. For example, let's say that your site is designed to attract grandmothers over 80 who skateboard, but on analyzing mined data you find that the hits from this target market on the skateboard sites is only 10% of grandmothers who skateboard. The implication is that by changing the Web site to a nice floral background and including a link to the www.grandmas-shop.com, you will generate a higher hit ratio. Mined data can help you fine-tune the images on the Web site and locate choice advertising sites.

Working with Affiliates

Affiliates are the organizations or Web sites that you will partner with to generate traffic. This relationship is usually mutually beneficial to both parties, although it is often not equal. Smaller start-ups can provide traffic through links to larger sites; however, the larger sites will be hard pressed to add a link back to the smaller site. This is because the larger sites are inundated with requests for links while the smaller sites have lots of available free space. In fact, many of the more popular Web sites do not provide direct links back to the smaller sites, but will sell the smaller site banner space. In return, they offer either micropayments for "click-throughs" from the smaller sites or commissions for sales. Amazon.com has built most of its traffic through these payment techniques. This, of course, does not help to generate traffic back to the smaller site, and traffic is the name of the game.

Another type of affiliate is the cross-promotional affiliate. This is an organization similar to yours that is offering a complimentary product. Let's say that you sell toothbrushes on the Internet to dentists. You can partner with a Web site that provides online information to dentists to provide a link to your organization in exchange for a commission. This payment will encourage the other Web site to partner with your organization. As you continue to add partners, your traffic will grow and more potential affiliates will become interested. Eventually, you may get to the size where other smaller organizations seek to partner with your site, and you will have to evaluate the benefits of each new partnership. In general, the more partners you can add, the more benefit will accrue as a result of the critical mass theory.

The Customer-Driven Model

Many online organizations are no longer providing direct access to their customer database to outside companies. This means that they will not provide e-mail addresses, but will provide a different type of access. Outside companies can advertise on the Web site to specific types of customers based on criteria that the customer has provided, such as their interests. Other companies ask customers if they would be interested in receiving information from partners. In this scenario, these partner companies would then send e-mail information to the online customer. These are called customer driven models because the customer or visitor to the Web site provides the approval to receive this information. Without this expressed approval, no information is sent. In the case of the online banner ads, the entry of "interest" information simply allows the online company to offer a more directed delivery method to its advertisers.

Traffic Jams

Traffic is simply the number of visitors who go to your Web site. The goal of advertising and promotion is to attract these visitors to your site. If you are too effective at your promotion you may cause a traffic jam. A traffic jam is when your advertising or promotion is run to an audience who all try to access your site at the same time. If you have a single connection to the Internet and a single Web server, the result may be that your customers cannot get through. When this Internet busy signal occurs, a message pops up in the user's browser that indicates that the connection cannot be made. Most ISPs provide demographic applications that will track the number of hits to your Web site, where they came from, when they were visited, volume of traffic, etc.

When an ISP connects to the Internet, it often uses T1 lines or direct fiber links that carry a large number of calls. A traffic jam occurs when everyone tries to access your Web site at the same time after an ad has been run. It is therefore vital that you discuss with your ISP the capability of their network to handle the volumes of traffic to your Web site that you anticipate and plan with them for your marketing campaign so that they are not overwhelmed. Occasionally, you will be required to change providers to someone who is capable of handling the traffic.

The second aspect that can cause traffic jams is the capacity of your server. Companies that have their own T1 line have the added worry of ensuring that their server is capable of handling numerous simultaneous hits. Options include using the ISP's server and hoteling or installing your own server in the ISP's location. A big consideration in this regard is the power of your server to manage the hits.

The i-Marketing Plan

Business development is the term usually reserved for the development of a business. This often includes marketing, planning, and strategy. Developing a business plan for your e-commerce company should follow the basic principles of planning including the following:

➤ Planning the company concept and image
➤ Developing a strategic or business plan including establishing goals for the organization and milestones for completion

➤ Developing a marketing strategy that identifies the target customer and media/promotion mix

➤ Obtaining the necessary funding to complete the company and building the applications or Web site that you will distribute

➤ Ensuring your technology is ready, complete, and capable of handling the traffic

➤ Identifying your partners and establishing agreements

➤ Preparing your public relations campaign for your launch

➤ Ensuring that your organization is up and running, including traditional areas such as back-office functionality, manufacturing, and logistics

---

The Least You Need To Know

➤ Who your customers are.

➤ How to promote your business on the Net.

➤ What to consider when building an advertising program.

➤ Why face-to-face promotion is important.

➤ The basis of an affiliate relationship and how it affects your plans.

➤ How to build an i-marketing plan.

WE'LL BE RIGHT BACK AFTER THESE MESSAGES...

Internet Advertising

In This Chapter

➤ Finding the ad customers

➤ The pros and cons of banner ads

➤ The future of rich media

➤ Animation

➤ Push technologies

➤ Linking

➤ Cross promotion

Advertising on the Net Is a Whole New Game

Internet advertising is rapidly become a subset of the larger world of commercial advertising simply because many of the concepts, principles, and media used in traditional advertising do not apply to the new world of the Internet. Of course, some of the basic principles of image and strategy still apply, but creating Internet ads requires a different focus or understanding of the mechanics of the Net. Advertisers who are familiar with producing print and video ads now have to develop banner ads consisting of short messages, cramped images, and motion. There are links to affiliates' sites, micropayments, cross-promotional ads, rich media, push technologies, sound bites, and a growing global perspective. This is different enough from the traditional advertising disciplines that art colleges and universities are starting to add Internet advertising courses to the curriculum.

But all of these technologies are still based on a fundamental design principle that it is more efficient to target a select group for your product than to target the entire world. Your "target," however, may appear to be as broad as the whole world—for example, people who want fast access to information or to purchase a book, which seems to include most of the Internet population. Unfortunately, if you have a limited advertising budget, you will have to select where to place your ad to get the biggest bang for your buck.

Another fundamental principle is that the design of your ads and Web site will have to use images that are consistent with the message of your site. The difficulty will be in imaging a message designed to build a "community of values" (see Chapter 6). You will also have to understand the dynamics of your market—the rules have changed, and the freedom of expression and individuality that is part of the Internet will have to be considered when you design new ads.

Where's the Ad Customers?

The Internet population numbers in the hundreds of millions and the ability to tap into that market through a Web site is incredible. If you sell books, the population of book readers is vast. If you sell stock, the pool of investors is immense. If you sell surgical-grade steel, your customers may be a little tougher to find. Amazon can sell books just about anywhere on the Internet, and if they place an ad somewhere, there is a good chance that they will hit some part of their market. But if the surgical steel guy tries that trick, he may spend hundreds of dollars for an ad and get zero responses. These people will have to be more selective about where they place their ads, searching possibly on Web sites related to surgical and hospital supplies. They also have to decide whether their market is "on-Net." Finally, they will have to decide whether they will get enough response to warrant the ad, or whether they are better off to change the focus of their effort. Perhaps putting an ad on a punk site will encourage direct sales from the body-modification community.

Traffic Stats

You can get an excellent selection of statistics at http://cyberatlas. internet.com.

The key to not pouring money down the Internet advertising drain will be to identify where your market is located in the vast expanse of cyberspace. The best way to do that is to study information about Web sites published by companies as well as e-zines (online information services also known as zines), as well as the traffic levels associated with these sites from tracking companies like Media Metrix.

You can also obtain demographic information or targeting statistics from Web sites themselves. The next step is to identify which sites have the most relevance to your market. How many of your customers will visit the site out of the total number of visitors; how many of them will see the rotation of your ad; how many will click through to your Web site; and how many will purchase something? This last item has caused Internet companies to start moving away from a "micropayment for click" model to a "micropayment for solid contact information" model. This ensures that click-throughs actually benefit the company before a payment is made by ensuring that micropayments occur only for customers who leave valid contact information. The other technique is to pay commissions on sales.

Ad Intelligence

A good link site for information about Internet advertising is www.adrelevance.com.

Creative organizations will find their customers in the most unusual places. Women searching for information about the Viagra impotence pill at viagra.com, men searching for lingerie at victoriassecret.com, politicians looking for one-liners at jokes.com. Often the market you are trying to reach is based on a psychographic division, such as people who think UFOs exist and that the government is covering it up. For these type of breakdowns, you will have to study other sources of information until the volume of stored Internet information about individual users grows enough to provide this level of detail. The best way to understand where the customers are who fit unusual psychographic profiles is to read information about the users who surf specific sites or to read the newsgroups that relate to the specific profile you are looking for and research any mentioned Web sites. The whole benefit of knowing where the customers are is to ensure that every dollar spent on ads generates the highest return.

Banner Ads

Banner ads are the long thin ads at the tops and bottoms of most Web sites (see Figure 15.1). Called banner ads because of their banner-like shape, these ads were originally made of a special layered graphic interchange format (GIF). Anyone can create a gif by using one of a number of graphics programs, such as Paintshop Pro or the Corel suite of graphics products.

A gif animator is a special software package that can be obtained for free on the Internet. It allows users to copy a series of GIF images into a program and save them as a single image that rotates through the series. By making slight alterations to the GIFs in the series, you will create the effect of animation or movement.

Figure 15.1

Here is an example of a banner ad.

Banner ad ———

Free GIF Animators

You can get free gif animation and graphic software by surfing to www.tucows.com, www.cnet.com, or www.zdnet.com or hundreds of other sites. You can also surf to sites that allow you to create and save banner ads online.

The second important piece of a banner ad is the ability for the user to click on the banner ad to go to the advertiser's Web site. This doesn't require any special software because your Web site software will be able to create a hyperlink from the GIF. However, you can also create banner ads using programming languages such as Java. Java allows you to include applets or small pieces of code that can perform tasks in a browser to provide the same effect as an animated GIF.

The problem with banners is that they provide a very limited amount of space to work in, usually only an inch tall by five inches wide. If you include an animated image to catch a surfer's attention, there is almost no space for a message. So the message that you deliver will have to be very concise, very clear, very short, and very creative.

The other issue that your advertising team will have to be aware of is that surfers are becoming immune to certain types of messages. Win Big, Make Money, Lowest Prices are all messages that are starting to lose their impact with Net surfers. They are being replaced with Elvis Nude, Free Computer, and Eat Flies/Save Big. (No, Elvis is not nude; it's just a line to get you to the site.) Other sites use interesting animated images and colors to catch your eye. Working in a four-inch square requires a different design philosophy of quick impact in a short time frame.

Rich Media

Rich media is another term for the latest type of banner ads. They are designed using software such as Java and have the added capability that the software provides to perform some form of interaction with the Internet user. Surfers to these sites can interact with the banner ad to open drop-down lists, perform actions with the mouse inside the ad, or select buttons. One example is a banner ad that shows a plane and a series of smoke lines, like you would find in a wind tunnel drifting over the plane in an animation. If you place the mouse over the plane and hold down the button, you can drag the plane inside the banner, and the smoke lines will adjust accordingly. This level of interactive banner ad is becoming more commonplace on the Internet, and it is forcing organizations that use the old style animated GIF to retool their existing banner ad.

Rich media ads are also beginning to deliver sound bites. In this case, a particular snippet of sound is saved in a file, and when the user clicks on the ad, the sound file plays. Again the messages are very short for efficiency reasons, and will have to be carefully crafted to present the correct image. Another type of rich media banner ad allows you to expand the banner size to present more information. One downside is that these types of ads can be incompatible with certain browsers and platforms.

Click Sensitive

You can see a number of expanding ads and information about rich media at www.bluestreak.com. The greatest benefit of this type of ad is the ability to present more information to customers after they have clicked the ad.

Animation

The intent of animation is to catch the eye of Net surfers so that they are intrigued enough to follow the link. The limitation of banner ads means that the image changes will have to occur in a small space, and this has caused some companies to start returning to a nonanimated approach to advertising. This serves a twofold purpose: first, certain demographic

Flash Technology

Flash technology by Macromedia provides a variety of new animation applications for Web sites and can be found at www.macromedia.com.

populations do not care for animation and often find it annoying and confusing; the second problem is that loading and running an animated gif can slow the Web site down. If you have a lot of information to load, this can be a significant problem. However, in general, the benefits outweigh the costs, and some animation will still be a significant part of most Web pages.

The image that is contained in an animated GIF requires different design principles from that of a standard two-dimensional advertising image. First, there will be numerous graphics in a single animated GIF. Each image must be designed to portray the specific marketing image of the company, and then the total animation image must be reviewed to ensure this same consistent image is ultimately portrayed. This is different from designing a standard, one-dimensional print ad simply because other factors, such as what the animation portrays, what the speed and message of the animation should be, what style of animation should be chosen, and how the users feel about the choices made, are all essential elements that will have to be carefully studied.

Rich media presents even more problems with designing sound bites, evaluating how users will interact with the software, how this impact will affect the image being delivered, and what can be done to improve the overall delivery of the ad. It also creates problems related to the type of rich media mix that should be used whether it is an application, sound, video, or animation.

Push Technologies

Push technologies primarily relate to information that is pushed to your Web page, as opposed to your computer going to get the information from the Web. The primary application driving this type of technology is the Webcast in which a stream of data is sent to numerous users and represents the more recent innovation to the static push technologies used by pointcast (see Figure 15.2) in which a file is sent periodically. This provides users with real-time information similar to the way a television network works. The advantage for the advertiser is that these technologies are starting to deliver a rich media format including sound and video. Push technologies currently require the user to sign up for the service, and this provides a registered viewer base to the advertiser, which can then be used to target messages. However, to use this technology will require Webcasting software and an ISP that can host your Webcast server. Another downside is that the "push" aspect of these technologies takes a lot of bandwidth to deliver a stream of content. In corporate networks this has proved to be such a problem that these services are being banned, which has been a serious detriment to push-based Web companies.

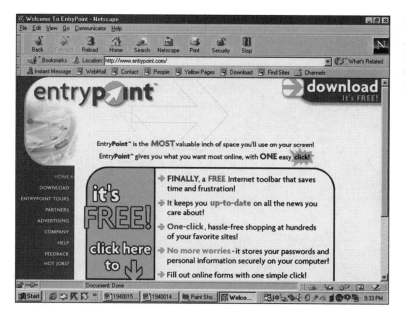

Figure 15.2

EntryPoint (pointcast) uses push technology to deliver news and information.

Pop-up Windows

An offshoot of push technology is the loading of special Web pages or multiple Web pages. These are essentially nothing more than linked pages that load six or seven other pages when you open the first page. Primarily used to drive up traffic stats, these multipage loads are annoying to the visitors who enter one of these sites. This technology is, however, being used more effectively by some Web sites, such as snap.com, to load a single pop-up window to access new software downloads (see Figure 15.3). The careful use of the pop-up screen can provide an excellent delivery mechanism to make announcements. The problem is that people will find it annoying if the information provided is not of some interest to them. Upgrading a browser plug-in is an acceptable use of a pop-up window, but providing a link to another site is not. Pop-up windows are easily programmed into a Web site using Java applications already available on the Internet. On the downside for the advertiser is a freeware program available called Pop-up Killer that can stop these windows from showing.

Pop-up Killer

You can download a copy of Pop-up Killer at `http://software.xfx.net/utilities/popupkiller/index.html` in the browser's utilities link.

Figure 15.3

GeoCities pop-up windows deliver advertising when a GeoCities Web site is opened.

Linking to Other Sites

Linking to another site is an effective way to both sell and buy advertising (see Figure 15.4). These smaller link boxes provide the same functionality as the banner ads. When a GIF or other type of image is loaded on a Web page, a hyperlink is added so that if the user clicks inside the boundaries of the image, he will be sent to the linked Web site. For companies that sell space on their Web pages, this linking provides ads, micropayments, or commission revenue. For the advertiser, it provides a direct link that can generate traffic.

Affiliate linking is usually an agreement between two organizations to link to each other's Web site for mutual benefit. This is the type of relationship between Learnlots, which supplies "how to" information and My Simon, which supplies an online shopping facility. The second type of link is related to adding a nonaffiliated organization on your Web page. These links are often encouraged, but rarely paid for. In this case, the Web page owner adds the link in order to attract visitors to his site with or without the knowledge of the linked page. This could include links to stock quote pages, news services, etc.

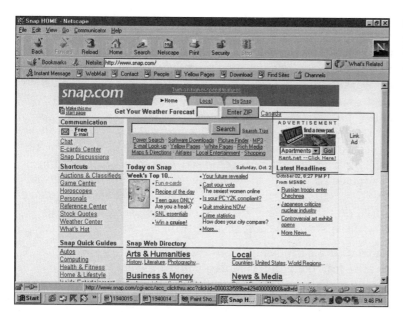

Figure 15.4

Link ads in the snap.com *Web page link to other Web sites.*

The process of getting others to link to your site can be as simple as offering the link graphics free for downloading, or it can be as complex as an agreement to establish a formal linking relationship. However, the one thing that must be present for both companies is a value for the applications that are being offered. If your Web site does not provide any value to the other site, then the chances of obtaining a link are unlikely. Amazon was a site that did not provide a significant value to other sites because it did not provide main page links. Although the traffic at Amazon was growing, it was difficult for Web masters to understand the value of a link to a site that sold books. Amazon solved this problem by creating a value through the payment of commissions for links to the site. Now the Web masters could see a value in adding a link to their sites. Yahoo didn't face the same problems because they did provide a valuable service, which was a way to search the Internet for information. It was easier for Web masters to justify adding this type of link because it provided a real value.

Adding Advertising to Your Site

Adforce is an online company that will assist you in managing your banner ads, including ad inventory management, reporting, and advertiser management. Surf to www.adforce.com.

233

Cross-Promotional Ads

The traditional advertising world has long understood the benefits of cross promotion. Co-op advertising, where two companies with a similar vested interest link their promotional activities to get the same coverage for less money, is a common practice in grocery advertising. This same concept is becoming more prevalent on the Internet as companies link together to reach the volumes needed to attain critical mass. Sometimes, these associations occur between companies that sell compatible products, but often these associations occur between companies that are direct competitors. For example, a company that manufactures chip sets may form an association with a company that manufactures communications devices to create a new technology or device. They may form a mutual partnership under a single banner and image that can then be advertised on the Internet. This way, both manufacturers can effectively sell their product while splitting the cost of advertising.

Some companies form advertising partnerships even though they compete directly. A simple example of this is the search engines that frequently show up in browser search pages all listed together. Although they compete directly with a search engine like Netscape, the Netscape search page lists them anyway. This is a similar concept to the idea of placing stores in a mall and advertising the mall. Centralizing stores in one location will not only save each store money on its advertising budget, it will draw people to the location to reduce the time that shoppers spend driving around. The same concept applies on the Internet. Saving time by locating a series of choices in one location is the future lifeblood of the Internet. Amazon doesn't sell a few books; they sell thousands from competing publishers. My Simon online shopping service doesn't search a few locations; they search hundreds of online stores. Often, the best way to add value to your site is to save Net surfers time by combining similar sites into a single location.

The Web Site as an Advertisement

Let's not forget the most important advertisement that will be on the Internet—your Web site. It is the place where visitors will travel to learn about your company, products, or applications. It must be carefully crafted using images that are designed specifically for the Internet. There are a number of issues that must be considered when constructing your Web page as an advertisement. First, the imagery must be appealing to the majority of your target market. Dark Web pages are less attractive to women than men, too many moving animations make the page difficult to look at, unprofessional designs fail to instill confidence, and too much information is cluttered and confusing. In fact, designing a Web page incorporates an entirely different design philosophy than that used in print advertising.

The second concern in building a Web page is the speed of the page in loading and operation. Visitors to Web sites on average have an extremely short attention span, and Web pages that load slowly are often abandoned in favor of other sites. It is critical that the technical aspects of Web pages, such as the depth of the color in the graphic, the speed with which an application loads, or the order in which the page loads are all carefully considered before the page is ever designed or built. As well, the way the page works should be tested from different locations and using different browsers to ensure that the page is functioning correctly. The speed of access will also depend on many factors that may be outside your control, such as the level of Internet traffic.

The content of information and flow through the Web site are also key elements in the design of Web sites. Flow is concerned with where information is located on the site and the structure of that information. Usually, the most used information is placed at the "front" of the site or on the home page, while least used information, such as investor relations, is put at the "back" of the site. The content is also important to ensure that the proper message is relayed to your customers. Web sites that are highly technical in nature will produce little in the way of sales to the general public. The content of a Web site should be designed as if you had created a print brochure and should reflect the tastes and images of your customer's world. All content should be carefully proofread.

Special Offers

A number of businesses on the Internet make special offers to attract traffic to their Web sites. The most common are contests that offer visitors the chance to win a prize. Online coupons are also becoming more popular as a means for enticing customers to particular Web sites. Other offers include

➤ Free games

➤ Free software

➤ Free products

➤ Free information

➤ Free help

➤ Free email

➤ Free Web sites

➤ Free advertising

➤ Free pictures

➤ Free graphics

➤ Free GIFs & Jpegs

➤ Free e-books

➤ Free e-zines

➤ Free music

➤ Free messages

➤ And so on

Are you starting to see a pattern? Yes, free, and the content of some of the offerings is excellent, such as a free computer after rebate offered by Outpost.com. The choice of quality freeware available on the Internet is outstanding at sites such as tucows.com and cnet.com. Animated graphics, free books, zines, and information on almost every subject are available by using the search engines. A free e-mail account awaits you at Yahoo, and most other major sites and messaging software is downloadable at AOL or ICQ.

Free "How To" Information

The Learnlots model is based on the provision of free "how to" information on the Internet. Anyone can access the information for free, and revenue is generated through click-throughs, micropayments, and commissions.

The entire Web offers a huge collection of free stuff and although most is funded through the sale of advertisements on the sites, a vast majority of the information is put on the Net for free.

The idea of distributing information or applications for a fee is rapidly disappearing as more and more e-commerce companies try to build critical mass through the provisioning of free stuff. It is highly unlikely that a company would succeed today on the Internet by trying to charge a fee for access unless the information was extremely valuable and, here's the key, not available anywhere else. The problem with believing too much in this last concept is that right now there are hundreds of thousands of individuals bringing their free content to the Net each year, and eventually no information will be sacred.

The best defense is to get there first and make a name for your Web site and its own free content.

Banner Surveys

Banner surveys are a market information-gathering tool available to anyone. Companies offer support and services for the creation of these custom banner ads that draw in Internet users often through the use of give-a-ways or contests (see Figure 15.5). The survey's links are then distributed through the placement of banner ads, and the data is collected and reported. This is one way to gather information about a population with very little effort; however, selecting a specific population (Internet users) who are gathered at a particular location (a Web site) and enticing them with an offer (contest) will undoubtedly skew the results of any survey. However, depending on the placement of the ad and the questions in the survey, the information should, in general, provide helpful insight into the market.

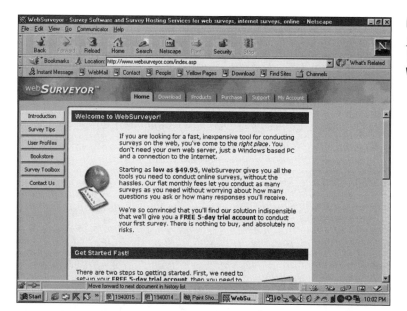

Figure 15.5

Here is a banner survey Web page for Websurveyor.com.

The Micropayment

A micropayment is a very small fee paid for each visitor who is sent to your site from another Web site. The payment is usually tracked by a third party and when a specific amount has accumulated, usually twenty dollars, the fee is paid to the Web site that sent the traffic. This payment mechanism provides a way for you to encourage other companies to add your links into their Web site. As customers visit the other Web site and click the link, the click-through to your Web site will be recorded. When enough visitors click-throughs have been accumulated, a payment will be made to the company that sent the traffic.

The problem with payments based on click-throughs is that some Web masters have found ways to defraud the system. The extensive use of pop-up technology to create the appearance of large traffic volume is one area of concern. Surfing to a Web site that loads numerous pop-up windows is recording a click-through at those Web sites. This way one visitor can generate instant traffic click-throughs to as many Web sites as there are pop-up windows. Another technique involves hiring rings of users to contin-uously surf through linked Web sites to generate click-through data. Companies have since moved away from the click-through model by only paying affiliate partners for the click-through traffic or by moving to different payment models, such as commis-sion on sales or contacts, or traffic trades where one company trades links to another company.

The Future of Internet Advertising

The future of Internet advertising involves greater use of Rich Format ads that allow a user to receive other types of media, such as sound bites or interactive functionality. As the delivery mechanisms for the Internet become faster and faster, eventually streaming video will be sent to each visitor to a Web site (see Figure 15.6). Imagine going to a Web page and being greeted with a true video message that is clear and fast. The technology currently exists to send and load both video and sound files, but its use has not been widespread due to bandwidth constraints.

Figure 15.6

Video delivery is available through the Internet as shown.

Bluestreak.com

Bluestreak provides services for creating interactive banner ads. You can see their Web site at www.bluestreak.com.

Interactive ads are primarily created through the use of languages like Java, and the cost to create a single ad can be quite high because it will require the effort of both designers and programmers. The advantage, however, is that the user can interact with the ad by entering information, selecting choices from a drop-down list, performing interesting actions on the ad like moving a plane or firing at a target, or by selecting a button. As these ads become more sophisticated, more functionality will be built into them, and customers will be able to do more interesting things like play sound bites of music or video clips in pop-up windows.

Personalized Ads

As data mining and content delivery become more sophisticated, ads that are customized and delivered to Internet users will become the standard on the Internet. These ads will use data-mining techniques extensively to deliver to those particular users, ads that are custom designed for them including using personal information, such as the user's name in the content, or designing images based on personal psychographic profiles. In the near future, users will surf to Web sites and be greeted with personal Webskins, or customized Web sites, that matches their personal profile. It may include darker graphics for men or lighter graphics for women. Messages will incorporate the visitor's name and purchasing behavior and will give the impression that the Web site is actually interacting with the user. All choices and selections will be logged for future mining. Sound a bit too much like big brother? All of this technology is available and either already in use on the Internet or nearing a launch date.

Advertising on the Internet may incorporate many of the design principles that have been identified over the years through print, radio, and television advertising. But they provide only the foundation to this new medium that will incorporate new delivery mechanisms such as direct customer interaction. This entirely new world will require that organizations, designers, marketers, programmers, artists, and sales staff rethink the way they use the technology of the Internet to advertise. A new understanding of advertising image, color, content, message, strategy, and execution is starting to develop, and the success of your e-commerce program will depend on your level of knowledge in this regard.

The Least You Need To Know

➤ How to locate ad customers.

➤ How and when to include animation on your Web site.

➤ How linking and click-throughs work.

➤ What the future direction of Internet advertising is.

➤ How micropayments work.

Internet Marketing Models

In This Chapter

➤ Affiliate marketing

➤ Free knowledge model

➤ Creative buzz model

➤ External drive-in model

➤ Repetitive one-hit–wonder model

➤ User group model

Affiliate Marketing

An affiliate is a business that you want to partner with in order to gain a benefit for your own business. This benefit can be traffic sent to your Web site, or it can be less obvious, like the bringing together of similar organizations into an association to form a critical mass. Companies like Amazon could not exist without the publishers, and MySimon shopping site would have difficulty without its online shopping affiliates. Affiliates are a standard method of doing business on the Internet, and although your e-commerce company will survive without affiliates, it will do much better with them.

In traditional business, the concept of affiliates came with a mountain of legal documents trying to protect the interests of both parties. These associations were just as essential as today's i-commerce affiliations, but the level of investment and counterparty risk tied to today's i-businesses is far lower. For this reason, many i-commerce affiliate agreements are less complex documents that do not require extensive negotiation or the involvement of teams of lawyers. To become an affiliate with Amazon.com requires that you complete a form and review a three-page agreement that clearly specifies the terms of the affiliation (see Figure 16.1). This, of course, places a great deal of trust that Amazon will live up to its commitments contained in the agreement.

Figure 16.1

Amazon.com provides an online affiliate agreement that lists the terms of the partnership.

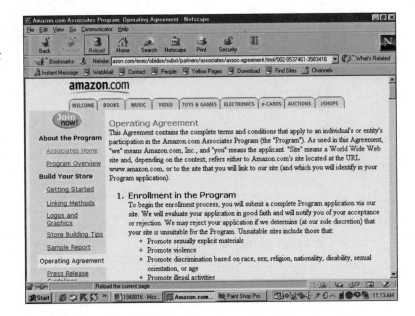

The Click-Through

It is in Amazon's best interest to ensure that the affiliate program functions within terms of the agreement. If the e-commerce community were to find out that click-throughs were not being compensated, Amazon could be embroiled in lawsuits that would keep it mired in battles well into the next millennium. Who would know that they hadn't lived up to the agreement? You, that's who. First, any click-through to Amazon can easily be recorded from your site by using standard demographic data (see Figure 16.2). Secondly, companies can use a third-party click-through tracking service to ensure the integrity of the agreement. Finally, even if you have been ripped off, it is unlikely that you have lost much as long as you haven't been recording click-through traffic as a receivable and borrowed heavily against it. The nature of the Internet involves an unprecedented level of trust between organizations, and any company that is unwilling to move fast in favor of extensive legal agreements will be left in the dust.

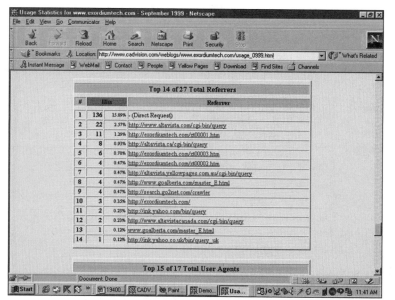

Figure 16.2

Most Web hosting packages at ISPs come with "demographic" reporting that indicates who has accessed your Web site and from where.

Strength in Numbers

Why even have affiliates? Well, you can go it alone; there is no reason why you can't. Many successful Web sites started with a good idea and had no support from the online world. But that has significantly changed in recent years. Savvy on-Net companies realize that they are far stronger by affiliating with partner companies that offer a compatible product than they are by themselves. The Metcalf theory of critical mass is more relevant today than ever before because of the level of competition that exists on the Internet. Affiliate marketing models provide benefits to both parties, and although some organizations are being inundated with offers to partner, they will in general be receptive to partnering in order to attain Melcalf's critical mass.

Learnlots Agreements

In order for Learnlots to develop the traffic that it required to create critical mass, it needed online organizations to add a Learnlot's link to their Web sites. Learnlots is doing this by encouraging these businesses to add a link as a service for their community. As an added bonus, online organizations will earn commission revenue on sales as a result of the click-through.

Click-Through Management

Adforce at www.adforce.com provides advertising and click-through
management and reporting for
third-party integrity.

How Critical Are Your Affiliates?

Developing an online affiliate program is an essential part of any online business that wants to grow
significantly. Most e-commerce start-ups dedicate a
great deal of time, effort, and resources trying to
establish an affiliate program. In general, they first
approach organizations that are critical to their
company's development and to the operation of the
online application. In traditional businesses, establishing your suppliers is an essential element to
starting up. In an i-commerce Web company, the
affiliate may not be supplying critical parts for your
manufacturing process, but it may still provide a
critical piece of your building traffic pattern, and therefore deserve just as much
attention as you would give to a major supplier of parts.

The next level of affiliate that you will add to your marketing program will be those
online organizations that are not considered critical to the early development and
growth of your e-commerce company, but are very essential to your long term
growth. These companies may be organizations that will carry a link to your application as an additional service to their own online community. Learnlots offers "how
to" information to organizations as an additional benefit to its own Web site. They
have also gone the additional step of utilizing a technology called a Webskin that will
make the link to the Learnlot's site look and feel like the originating Web site. This
allows a linking Web site to keep a consistent image while still utilizing the services of
Learnlots.

The third level of affiliate will be those organizations that will generate traffic by linking directly to your site purely for the benefit of their community. These affiliations
are usually registered through an online form when micropayments or commissions
are involved or simply by encouragement through a "benefits of affiliation" Web
page. Never underestimate the value of this type of program. Amazon owes its size to
these types of affiliations and the informal process that was used to sign these companies up. Of course, the more informal the affiliation, the more likely it is to cause
problems, so a couple of issues should be resolved prior to creating or joining an
informal affiliate program. First, the affiliate agreement should be clear, concise, and
enforceable in a court. Ambiguity should be avoided at all cost. Also, a dispute resolu-
tion mechanism should be outlined. Secondly, your organization should not consider
any income or traffic flows for the purpose of raising capital until those flows can be
ensured.

Partnering with affiliates is a key component of any e-commerce marketing program, and provides the most effective way to grow your traffic. Although there are some security and legal issues, in general, affiliate relationships will be beneficial to both parties and should be encouraged as much as possible. Maintaining these relationships will be an important piece of any ongoing growth.

Free Content Model

Content is the stuff that makes up a Web site, but it is also the stuff that makes up an e-company. A print news organization that now wants to deliver its news over the Internet is supplying content. But content doesn't just include information; for example, your Web

Cybercash

Some organizations are creating online banks to facilitate the flow of commissions and micropayments from affiliates.

Cybercash is one organization at the forefront of Internet payment technologies used by online banks. Surf to http://www.cybercash.com.

site may include gaming software in which the content is an application. Content is anything that is put on your Web site for access by others. It is extremely valuable to the organization, and almost every company would be unwilling to give that content away for free, right? Wrong. The Internet is a world that was built on the free flow of information and the hoarding of information is doomed to fail (see Chapter 6).

Hoarding information, by trying to keep it to yourself or by charging a fee for access, is a short term narrow view that is doomed to fail. It is doomed because your advanced expertise that is contained in your top secret database has already been gathered from the Internet by the "technokid" down the street, and he is ready to release it to the world in his new free information database. This was the case of online brokerages that thought their analysis should only be shared with paying customers. Along comes E*Trade and the traditional brokerage world was unprepared for the onslaught (see Figure 16.3). Most information that is available currently in the world will eventually make it to the Internet for free at some point in the future. Given this scenario, it is far better to provide your information for free than to force users to pay a fee to subscribe. If the quality of the information is exceptional, your users will come to rely on it, and will revisit your site. This now provides you with the opportunity to expand your information offering and grow your online organization.

Figure 16.3

E*Trade is an online brokerage that supplies stock-trading information for free.

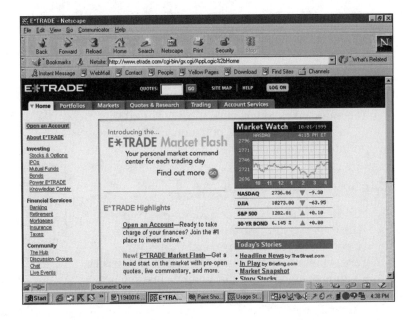

Free Applications

Applications are even more difficult to distribute for free. Companies and individuals invest a great deal of money and personal capital to develop an application. To release it on the Internet for free would seem to be a ludicrous waste of resources, or is it? Shockwave provides downloadable player software for free from its Web site. This technology allows visitors to the Web site to play games created using the Shockwave software. So what is the point of investing so much time in development if the software is going to be released for free? Traffic is the answer. By releasing the software for free, you will generate traffic to your game-playing Web site, and this will provide a number of benefits. The first benefit is advertising revenue for banner ads, the second is income from the sale of the development software needed to create similar games, the third is the ability to advertise your own e-commerce products such as Shockwave's new Shockmachine game system, and lastly it encourages more users to visit, which can make your software the standard of the market. We all know what being a standard can do for your company every time we fire up Windows.

Shockwave

You can download the Shockwave Player software at
www.shockwave.com.

However, to generate large volumes of interest, the kind necessary to create critical mass and make your i-business the standard, will often require more than just great information. In order for your concept to get enough traffic to become a standard, it will require some level of support from affiliates or partners, or some level of advertising and promotion. This isn't necessary if your expertise is not transferable to the Web. For example, a surgeon in Beverly Hills can't very well do surgery over the Net, but she will be able to attract visitors to her practice through free information offerings on her Web site. But is it necessary for her to generate huge volumes of traffic? No, she will only need a specific type of individual located in her home market. In this scenario, affiliate-marketing models are not appropriate for the site (see Figure 16.4).

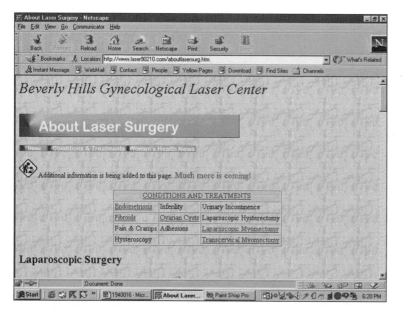

Figure 16.4

Beverly Hills Surgery Web site offers information to prospective patients.

How To Generate Revenue

If your e-business is designed to generate revenue from online sales, then the greater the number of visitors to your site, the greater the potential for revenue from sales. However, this is not the only way to generate revenue based on traffic. The most common form is advertising through the use of banner or link ads. Like most advertising programs, the more visitors to the Web site, the more revenue can be charged for the ad. Click-throughs that generate payments as a result of visitors who use a link are another form of revenue maker. The more visitors who visit your site, the greater the chance they will use a link that pays a click-through or commission.

Revenue that is generated as a result of comparable product offers, like the Shockwave example, is another form of revenue. After critical mass is attained and your application is the standard, there will be numerous opportunities to capitalize on it. The billions of dollars of wealth Microsoft created occurred because DOS became the standard operating system, and the step to Windows was their license to print money.

Being the choice of millions of online users is the goal behind the free content marketing model. This model is also the most prevalent in the world since it is used by almost everyone who has a Web site. Almost everyone who builds a Web site starts out by adding free content to the Web site that they think will be beneficial to Web surfers. It can be as simple as a recipe for salsa or as complex as an application that performs some beneficial function.

Creative Buzz Model

Often, Web organizations do not have the ability, resources, or compatible benefits necessary to grow through the use of affiliates. An organization like the Swank Movie Productions has interesting information available on its Web site, but provides little in the way of benefits to another Web site (with the exception of a movie link Web site). An affiliate-linking model would probably produce limited benefit for the volume created. The content provided by Swank is not only interesting, but the delivery mechanism technology for things such as video is very current. However, since the content has a relatively narrow range of interest, just supplying it for free will not guarantee good coverage.

In this case, it may be better to try to generate traffic by creating a buzz. A buzz is the conversation that occurs between people about a particular topic, for example, your Web site. Creating buzz in the correct manner can generate an extensive amount of traffic, and if your company continues to create buzz, the Web site will grow. This concept is used extensively by Hollywood stars and their PR firms to ensure the star is kept in the press spotlight. Keeping the stars in the spotlight encourages their popularity and that leads to continued roles in movies. Creating a buzz about your Web site and then periodically generating new buzz will drive traffic to your site on an ongoing basis just like the stars keeping their names in the press.

How To Generate Buzz

Buzz is generated in a variety of ways—face-to-face meetings, phone conversations, advertising, promotion, trade shows, media announcements, sponsorships, etc. Getting people to remember the name of your e-business is the first step.

It solves all kinds of problems if your market can remember your name. Amazon is easy, CNET is easy, but www.uwannawhat.com might cause some problems as you can see in the Figure 16.5.

So how is buzz generated? You can generate it by talking about your Web site to other people. Just before you do talk, however, set up a quick Web site just for people to go to. Even if it is not functional, having someplace to go that has some information will make it easy for you to say "visit my site" and start generating a buzz. It can take quite a while to generate a significant level of buzz, and it will depend on your resources and your tactics.

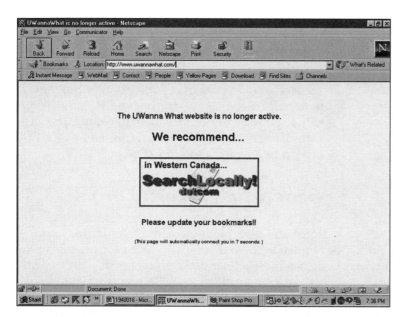

Figure 16.5

The Uwanna What Web site has changed to make it easier for people to find and remember.

Some companies generate buzz by using an affiliate model to start the process. Face-to-face meetings with partners and suppliers are a good first starting point, but may not generate the chatter necessary to grow significantly if your application is not interesting enough. The real win will come when the buzz crosses over from the industry side to the general population side of the market. If you create buzz inside an industry about an application, it will generate a lot less traffic to the site initially than if you can create buzz with the general population. Let's face it, a bunch of technical gurus getting excited about a cool Web site isn't the same as 100 million users wanting to know more about a new application.

Shock Promotion

Some companies go to great expense and great lengths to create a buzz by using shock promotions that gain attention—for example, live births on a Webcast, hosting an extreme sports demonstration, even using quirky ads during the Super Bowl. In creating these unusual sponsorships or promotions, it is vital to ensure that the name of the Web site is prominently displayed. If give-a-ways are handed out, make sure they are associated with the Web site. An example might be giving out free hot chocolate at an outdoor line-up or hockey game in reusable cups with the Web site name on the side. The main goal of these promotions should be to generate the buzz needed to attract visitors to the site and not necessarily huge volumes of traffic. If the curiosity of market leaders is captured during these events, they will generate the buzz that will eventually lead to the traffic.

CNET

CNET is an online zine among other things and publishes news stories about new sites. Surf to www.cnet.com.

Industry or affiliate buzz is a very essential element to getting a good response from the media. A good response from the media is the way that the general public starts to hear about new Web sites. It is this "general public" buzz that leads to larger and long-term traffic flows. However, the press is inundated with press releases from a variety of companies, and each day thousands of new start-ups send out information hoping for a spot on ZDNet or CNET.

Generating Industry Buzz

One of the best ways to have your information noted and recognized by media organizations is to have the organization already be familiar with your company. One of the best ways to do this is to generate industry buzz that crosses their desks or to partner with an organization that counts. For example, if we form an alliance with a small start-up and send out a press announcement under a company banner, it will likely get filed. If, however, we form an association with Cybercash and release the partnership under the Cybercash banner, the media will not only be more receptive to the information, but they will also take note of our name.

Generating buzz is a process of creating chatter first at the industry level, then through the media level, and into the general population. The benefits are that industry buzz opens the door to the media, which creates buzz in the general population. This is what translates into growing traffic volumes. It will help to stage some spectacular sponsorships or in-your-face promotions to further push the buzz. Also, you will have to continually create and issue information to keep the chatter alive. The results from this model should be a steady and growing traffic level.

External Drive-in Model

Traffic is the name of the game, and sometimes it is easier to go directly to the general public and "drive-em in." Using this model, e-companies will go directly to the market to promote their Web sites, with the goal being to create instantaneous traffic. The most visible example of this was the AOL and Snap.com national advertising campaign designed to generate traffic directly to the site. No affiliates and no generating buzz. Of course, both of these companies rely extensively on affiliates and buzz, but if you have the resources and an excellent content offering, you can go directly to the general public to create traffic.

Advertising is usually the fastest way to generate traffic, and the number one place to put an ad has to be the Super Bowl. Millions of viewers watch the ads during halftime, and they can easily generate significant traffic if they remember the ad. The problem is the cost. If your Web site is not up to handling the traffic load, and is not capable of capturing the attention of a bunch of football fans, then the money you spend will be wasted. On the other hand, if you're Doritos and you're running a contest to win tickets to next year's Super Bowl and for some reason want to generate traffic, show the Web site with a picture of Ali Landry (Doritos Chip Girl), and you will get lots of traffic (see Figure 16.6) from those very Super Bowl fans. That's called direct traffic generation, and is what an e-business does when it goes right to the source of traffic. However, if your product offering has a narrow interest, spending millions on a Super Bowl ad may not pay for itself. One of the best direct-to-source promotional campaigns involved billboards that were chosen on the traffic routes leading into some high-tech office buildings. Black with white lettering and a Web site address was all that was on the billboard. After a week of running the ads, the number of hits to the site from their target audience, those high tech employees, more than justified the expense of the billboards.

Figure 16.6

The Doritos Web site includes content from the advertising run during the Super Bowl.

Sponsorships

Another way to drive-in traffic directly to your Web site is through sponsorships of events that attract your audience. Pets.com (see Figure 16.7) could easily sponsor dog and cat shows around the country or touring events such as the Superdogs' show. If they place their pets.com name throughout the events, they would likely generate significant direct hits on their sales Web site. Other sponsorship ideas include having teams of people hand out dog treats in parks that simply have the Web site domain name imprinted on them. Promotional ideas have ranged from shining massive lights on large monuments to threatening to place a large floating billboard permanently in the sky. Success is always measured in hits, and traffic will translate into revenue either now or in the future.

Figure 16.7

Pets.com Web site could generate traffic to their Web site by sponsoring pet events.

Repetitive One-Hit Wonder Model

What is a repetitive, one-hit wonder model? It's a way of generating repeat, large volume traffic through a Web site by changing the content. This is essentially the model behind some of the most popular offbeat Web sites today, and is fundamentally what underlies most of the news sites. We read the newspaper to get information about the world around us. We rarely buy newspapers to get old news or stock information we could get elsewhere. In fact, we buy newspapers to get information about those odd events that just happened, the newsworthy events. We turn the TV on, and are glued to CNN not because we needed information about diaper rash, but because of the weird event that is unfolding. Disasters, politics, war, and the weird event of the day all make their way into the newspapers, and the circulation volumes drift with the story. The repetitive nature of these new stories is what keeps people buying and providing a steady circulation. If the story never changed, the traffic would decrease. This is the fundamental principle behind the repetitive, one-hit wonder model.

E-commerce companies that are trying to attract visitors to their Web site can implement this model to change their content frequently to keep visitors interested. When the hurricanes roll in off the Atlantic, CNN is deluged with hits on its storm watch pages; when a tech business makes a big announcement, ZDTV.com gets the hits; and when the markets drop, www.nasdaq.com or www.nyse.com gets the traffic (see Figure 16.8). One-hit wonders are all those little stories that drive up the traffic—for example, people getting live surgery, Webcasts of rock concerts, and breaking news stories.

Figure 16.8

The New York Stock Exchange home page is used to get information on market movements and stock.

Examples of the Repetitive One-Hit Wonder

Repetitive, one-hit wonders occur all the time in the world, and some i-commerce companies have taken full advantage of this to generate traffic. CNET runs breaking tech news stories on a continuous basis, CNN updates its online newscast regularly, and Webcasts.com shows new Webcasts as they are available.

So how is this even remotely about your e-commerce company? Simple. Even regular e-commerce companies can create direct traffic by frequently changing content. Just because

Webcast Software

Wanna create a Webcast? Then surf to http://www.real.com and follow the DevZone link and the Tools/SDK link for software to create your own Web casting company.

your site sells something doesn't mean it can't capture those one-hit wonder benefits. By recreating yourself or your company occasionally, you will keep the content of your site fresh, and your visitors will continue to return, especially if the one-hit wonders that you are using are relevant to your group. For example, let's say that you want to start an online travel agency with all the usual trappings, holiday planning, travel information, ticketing, hotels, cars, etc. Now let's say that you also want to generate traffic. You can start offering other services that will be compatible with your existing product but will enhance it on a regular basis. Travel advisories, travel destination weather, special last minute offers, chat, e-mail and wide variety of other information can all be provided at a relatively low cost or no cost with banner ads.

I, as a traveler, might become very used to traveling to your Web site, and if the information is good, I might even make it my home page. Now that's traffic building. As long as the information is fresh and contains those one-hit wonder items, visitors will return to your site seeking more information and may bring their friends as well.

User Group Model

The last model we will talk about is the User Group Model. In Chapter 6 we discussed Downes and Mui's 12 rules of building a killer app, and one of those rules discussed the concept of building a community of value. This is essentially a Web site or i-commerce company that is built around a community of like-minded individuals. They can be traditional demographic groups, or they can be a group that simply has the same opinions about a subject, shares an interest, or belongs together out of some sense of inner self-worth.

Ivillage.com

Ivillage.com or the women's network is one of the most successful i-commerce organizations to create a community of value for like-minded individuals. Those like-minded individuals that make up their community of value are women.

Some of the other models are more relevant to this particular model because free content is essential to gathering individuals into a community of value. Other ways to attract a community of value include adding affiliates to create interest, generating a buzz in the community, and providing the community with one-hit wonders. The real issue will be whether or not the online community already exists, or is being created by the Web site.

Online communities do exist, but often they do not have a way to express themselves as a community. Large groupings, such as women or sport fans, have always clearly existed and have always had outlets for their collective soul, but some groups have just recently started to have a unified voice and meeting place. The Internet has provided the perfect medium for these groups, and new i-commerce companies are creating these online community environments every day.

Niching

Finding the "ties that bind" are quite easy to locate in today's early development of online communities. But as the main divisions start to get taken up, new companies will have to find new ways to redefine these groups. This technique is called cross-niching.

Cross-niching involves defining a population of people by either demographics or psychographics. The next step is to identify niches within these broad groups that you will initially target. Finally, these niches can be expanded by either promoting to new niches or by redefining the groupings. For example, let's say that I'm a divorce attorney, and that I want to start a Web site for divorcées. I can redefine the female population that may visit i-village by narrowing it to include women who have been or are divorced. I can further narrow the target, if I choose, into categories, such as women who are dissatisfied with their divorce and those who are satisfied with their divorce. We can use one of these niches to target women who are dissatisfied with their divorce and then expand the definition to include men and women who are dissatisfied with their divorce. Now I can go start up my Web site www.baddivorce.com and create an online environment with helpful advice, online forums, chat rooms, and links to other affiliates.

Market Niching

For more information on market niching, surf to `http://www.wilsonweb.com/articles/niche.htm`.

Divorce.com

We couldn't find `baddivorce.com` but there is a `divorce.com`. Surf to `www.divorce.com`.

Keeping Your Audience

The goal in trying to keep your audience is to ensure that the images and messages are consistent with your market. Occasionally, you may want to tweak the mix in order to expand the market by cross-niching, but caution must be exercised because the wrong image can alienate your audience and cause your traffic to decline.

The greatest advantage to building a community of value is the ability to tailor your image and messages specifically for this group. It also allows you to pinpoint their location both on-Net and ex-Net for promotional, advertising, and partnering opportunities. Allocating resources to encourage these users to try your Web offering will yield a far greater return on your investment, and will generate traffic that has a greater chance of growth, as long as your content and environment is what the market is looking for.

As an e-commerce company, you should tailor your offering or design your company to cater to your target market. The easiest way to stay focused on this task is to build and maintain a community of value. Building this community by using a user group marketing model will help you not only maintain traffic, but grow the traffic as more and more of the market becomes aware of your site.

None of the above marketing models will work better than the next, and in some scenarios, combinations of them all will be the best option. Your choice of model will depend extensively on your business plan and your markets. It will also depend on your resources and your milestones for implementation. Carefully evaluate all of these options, and the others that are out in the Internet marketing world before you start down the long path of Internet marketing.

The Least You Need To Know

➤ How to build an affiliate program.

➤ Why your content should be free.

➤ How to drive in the traffic.

➤ How to create buzz.

➤ What's a one-hit–wonder?

➤ What is a community of value?

Offline Marketing for Online Businesses

In This Chapter

➤ The benefits of face-to-face marketing

➤ Using promotions to build traffic

➤ How to spin great stories about your company

➤ How to effectively use public relations

➤ Keeping investors informed through investor relations

How Important Is External Marketing & Promotion?

There are 10 million Web sites of which more than 10% are estimated to be business Web sites. With that level of competition who needs to market? Anyone who wants to survive on the Net, that's who. In the last few chapters we discussed how to market your organization on the Internet and, in some cases, off the Net. This off Net or "ex-Net" marketing is a very important component of any e-commerce marketing campaign. Face-to-face meetings, promotions, public relations, and investor relations are all essential elements of any good organization. They are the key methods by which owners and executives communicate with the world, and meeting people is a vital piece of the e-commerce puzzle. However, like all good communication, you have to have something to say. You can talk about the weather, you can discuss sports scores,

Number of Web Sites

Number of total domains
10,910,997 Sept. 1999

Domainstats.com

but we all tend to gravitate to the person telling the great story over in the corner of the room. That's your e-commerce assignment, tell a great story to as many people as want to listen.

Spinning a Great Story

What makes a great story? It is characters, plot development, climax, and style. Any writer will tell you that the responses they get after they have written a story will be that some people hate it, and some people love it. And to make things more complicated, the "some" of the people who you were certain would hate it, actually loved it, while your strongest supporters may tell you to go back to the writing table. However, no matter how you write a story, not everyone will like it and not everyone will hate it.

Writing combines a wide array of potential styles, flows, images, subtleties, and impressions. It may flow logically, or it may flow erratically towards its completion. It may be concise, or it may be detailed. No one story is correct, and this is what the true art of creating a business story is all about.

Your Vision of Your Company

Your e-commerce story should be about your vision for your organization. A tale that begins, progresses in the middle, and even ends. It starts with an introduction and quickly progresses to an evaluation of where and who you are, your company's resources and strengths. It should move to identifying where you want to be with a clear direction and flow. It should include milestones, benefits, and goals. It should progress to a climax of future potential and establish a precision target, such as income, as its goal.

What Makes a Good Story?

Good stories are like fine wines, they start out smooth and end flawlessly. They have little or no downside, or the downside is dwarfed by the upside. If Amazon walked into your office three years ago, you might not have given them the time of day, but if you had listened carefully to their story, the risks would have been miniscule compared to the potential. A world market of six billion people served from one retail location. Even the harshest test criteria could not ignore the fact that even a small portion of this market equaled gigantic profits. So why do these companies lose money? That's the art of the story. When you invest in Amazon, you invest in a new way of doing business that intuitively sounds low cost, but, in fact, sets the standard so high that the margins have to be non-existent at the start. They will eventually attain profitability, but right now, building critical mass costs money.

Metronet

In 1999 Metronet communications was bought out by AT&T Canada in the closing of a tumultuous run-up of stock price that occurred over a period of four years. The company was an offshoot of a data transmission business between Calgary, Canada, and Houston, Texas that was in a perfect position to take advantage of the coming deregulation in the Canadian phone industry. Canada's telephone monopolies were following on the heels of the deregulation in the U.S. phone business. The founders of Metronet invited U.S. investment partners to fund the expansion of the company and under their direction grew the organization to a market capitalization of over $2 billion without ever turning a profit. The key to their success, according to management, was a great story. They were ideally positioned technologically to be a market leader in a growing "soon to be deregulated" market. Their only competition for the multibillion dollar Canadian phone market was from the incumbent phone companies. Large, old, comfortable with their monopolies, still tied into agreements with each other, and encumbered with antiquated infrastructures, they were minimally competitive. Metronet's great story was simple. Give us your money, and we'll build the most advanced network in the most profitable areas. They couldn't lose.

Most of the good i-commerce stories follow a familiar pattern. A company offers an application that is needed widely, and distributes it for free or at a loss on the Internet. Some examples of great stories are the following:

➤ Real audio for sending streaming audio and video

➤ Pointcast for streaming content

➤ Winamp/Mp3 for digital audio

➤ Yahoo as a search engine

➤ AOL as a community

➤ Shockwave for online gaming

➤ Java for Web language

➤ Netmeeting for Internet telephony with video

➤ Linux for an alternating operating system

➤ Amazon for online shopping

These stories were relatively clear and concise. All they had to say was that their application performed a function that had great potential over the Internet. Most anyone who has spent any amount of time surfing the Internet knows the great potential of these applications simply by trying them. But the same can be true even if you do not have a bunch of hot-shot app builders in your office to build you the next killer app. A lot of Amazon's success had nothing to do with a specific application, but had more to do with building a community and critical mass for their Web site. They, of course, are now on the defensive as established players like barnesandnoble.com (see Figure 17.1) or new start-ups come gunning for a share of the pie. But, they were originally unhampered because they were the first to market or at least the first to capture huge critical mass.

Figure 17.1

Barnes and Noble has a Web site that directly competes with the Amazon.com *Web site.*

Good Content Equals Good Web Sites

Even new content distribution companies can make a splash in the Internet world. You don't have to have a killer app—just a killer concept, which if it succeeds like Amazon will become a killer app in the eyes of the world. The key to future growth will be making the content unique enough to attract traffic, and that usually will require a couple of twists to the formula story. You may decide to deliver content to users through an online cooking Web site and tie it into a shopping database for kitchen wares. Although it may not be a killer app, the size of the cooking market is enormous and as long as you have unlimited recipes and cooking information on your site, you will attract lots of attention and with enough traffic, sizable sales (see Figure 17.2). Spinning a story about your idea for an e-commerce company is easy but takes some time and patience to get it right. However, the rewards of customers, investors, partners, and even your competitors will be worth all your effort.

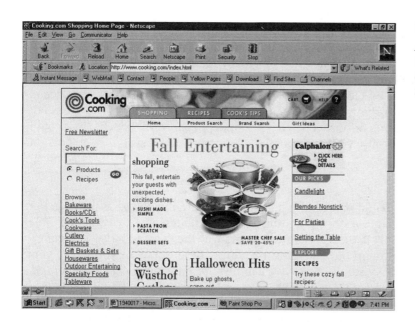

Figure 17.2

An example of a Web site that is taking advantage of the size of the cooking market is cooking.com.

Learnlots

When learnlots.com started on its long road to the world of i-commerce, they had to raise some money and get some major affiliates on their side. They raised their seed capital from family and friends and used this money primarily to travel to visit with affiliates like mySimon, investor groups, and potential key employees. The founders and initial employees only took wages that matched what they needed to live, and the balance was turned into the development and promotional budget. Thanks to a couple of initial contacts that they generated, meetings were established with some investor groups. Affiliates were cold called, and the road show began. They have recently secured second level funding, and are focusing on a successful launch.

Face-to-Face Meetings

What's not to love about a road show? Bad food, lumpy hotel beds, crowded airports, and a family who doesn't recognize you when you get back. Just keep in mind that it's only for a relatively short time. The power of the face-to-face meeting is an important thing. It's very hard for an organization or a group of investors to get a feel for your company if they can't meet you. This doesn't mean you have to go pounding on every door selling the company since that would be grossly inefficient or wasteful. What we suggest is that you call up the channel manager in those companies that you need to affiliate with in order to be successful and use a bit of soft persuasion to set up a face-to-face meeting. Remember that whenever you meet with your potential affiliates, always have a clear understanding of how your Web site or application will benefit their company. Don't hard sell because you're supposed to be getting partners.

The Road Show

The road show is an integral part of any organization's attempt to get its message out whether it is to potential investors, potential affiliates, the media, or customers. The advantage of a road show is that it significantly reduces the costs of travel and generates industry and investment buzz all within a narrow time frame. As you set up your organization and start to visit affiliates, you will need to raise some capital to get the job done. It's a bit of a catch 22; you can't *travel* without cash, it's difficult to get in the investment door without some buzz, you need to visit affiliates to generate buzz, you will need to *travel* to visit affiliates, and around it goes. Breaking the cycle with the use of seed capital allows you to split the balance of the funding between investor road shows and affiliate road shows.

Calling the small cap start-up areas of investment firms like Solomon or Deutschbank is the best starting point for setting up investor meetings. Affiliates can simply be called directly for appointments.

There are some simple tips to make the road-show task easier:

➤ Don't get too keyed up about the whole program. Relax and have fun. You will be more welcomed by these groups if you're professional and don't use hard sell tactics.

➤ Remember that they need good investments as much as you need money, and there are a lot of dogs on the road show circuit.

➤ It often helps if you can add a hired gun who has experience in this field. Some of the most arrogant and obnoxious individuals can make your company a success on the road show circuit. What counts is their enthusiasm, soft salesmanship, and the most important thing in a sales call—their ability to close the deal.

➤ Be prepared to tell the story in varying lengths from 15 minutes to three hours. It is important that you get across the main points in all presentations—the concept, the potential for the concept (either revenue or traffic forecasts), the benefit to the person or company you are presenting to, and the close.

➤ It is very important that you do not take their rejections personally. Remember that not everyone will get excited about your concept, and some people who say "no" will either come back or pass your name along to someone else.

At the end of your road show you should get some feedback from affiliates and investors. Be open minded and flexible; they may appear to be totally clueless about your idea, but they may bring some other element or piece of information to the table that may be essential. That information could be another competitor, a better piece of software or service for you to use, a twist on your concept that you never thought about, or business wisdom that is worth its weight in gold. Of course, most people won't have a clue at all, so smile politely, answer their questions, shake their hands, and leave. There is always another day, another investor, another affiliate, another partner, and another plane to catch. Most individuals you talk to will have at least one valuable piece of information to provide, and don't be shy about asking questions. Remember that people love nothing more than talking about what they've done and who they are. It gives us all a chance to brag.

You should always be wary of dubious individuals, investors who want voting control, affiliates who want money, and partners who want too much. Never give away the shop, and never sign on the bottom line unless you are comfortable with the individual you are dealing with. There are a lot of con artists and crooks lurking around Internet start-ups.

You should ensure that you do follow-up calls with those people who are wavering, if for nothing else than to give them the opportunity to say no and at a minimum to reinforce your company name in their minds. If you believe in your concept, so will others, and there is both a vast pool of money for investment and more new affiliate businesses opening on the Net each day. Always remember that your pool of resources will be limited so you will have to target your face-to-face contacts wisely. Major affiliates and major investors should be the primary focus at the start and never, ever turn down good media coverage.

Promotion

Promotion is a real art. Anyone can do it, but few do it really well. The art of promotion is a tangled mess of face-to-face meetings, carefully crafted stories and images, creative campaigns, and targeted delivery. The point of your first promotion should be to get the story out there. Spending thousands of dollars on a booth at Comdex in the middle of hundreds of other booths is probably not a good first step. Having your company van blown up accidentally by the U.S. military on the six o'clock news is getting there. Having the president answer questions in Congress about why he is surfing to your pornography distribution Web site is the ticket you are looking for. Promotion is quirky and twisted on the Internet, but it doesn't have to be. Sponsoring the last place team in the Daytona might not cost that much given their track record, but if it promotes your Web site fixcar.com, that would probably generate some significant press, especially if they win.

Promotion should reflect the beliefs of your target audience. You should not try to change them but rather try to attract them to your Web site or application. You may be able to attract them for things like curiosity, genuine interest, fake disgust, or out of sheer boredom. Of course, you can hire an expensive PR firm to create and execute a great promotion, but most companies will have limited resources for this task. A better use of the money would be to pay them for media distribution and interest gathering prior to an event built and executed by your own staff. An example might be a company that chooses to sponsor a promotional event and fundraiser by hanging a gigantic banner from a huge building for three days during a conference. If the conference is attracting delegates, most cities will comply with the wishes of an organizer to do some eye-catching promotion. In these instances, the PR money would be better spent on having the PR firm use their personal contacts to host a media party during the event inclusive of graft.

Delivering the Company Message in Promotions

All promotions should deliver the message of the company and its story. Some promotions are designed to attract traffic or interest, and, in these cases, promoting the name of the company will be the main goal—for example, hanging banners with only the company name on them. However, in the early promotional stages, the main goal should be to promote both the company and the story. Sending a banner unfurling hundreds of feet down the side of a building is interesting, but following it up with a speech at a conference or a special party will provide you with an excellent opportunity to get your message out.

Remember that new cool things or NCTs attract attention. Your staff should work to find that "new cool thing" that will get your message out there. Coffee mugs and key rings just won't cut it in today's world, but a digital watch with an easily attachable tracking device and a range of 100 feet to promote tracking your Web site, now that's cool. Even at Comdex they would line up around the block at your booth for that one. Of course, it might cost you a couple of million bucks, so a more selective distribution of expensive trinkets to media, investors, or real good affiliates would be the thing to do.

Free Content

You can obtain a wide variety of free content and affiliate links for your Web site at http://www.web-pageprofits.com.

What's in It for Your Audience?

Everyone is looking for a benefit. That's a good thing to keep in mind as you promote your story. In fact, you can practice this beforehand by asking what if the Microsoft reps drop by? What's the benefit to them? Or what if AOL asks what you are doing? Again, the response should indicate what's in it for them. Benefits are everybody's sugar. They can be traffic, advertising, promotion, partnering, commissions, micropayments, compatible offerings, or even competition. They are the grease that drives the Internet's e-commerce wheels, and they open the doors. Make sure that you clearly understand the deliverable benefits for each person or group whom you will talk to.

Public Relations

Public relations are a vital part of any e-commerce promotion, and are an ongoing part of any company's operations. Usually, the owners of small businesses will perform this function, as opposed to larger organizations that have individuals hired for the task. Public relations can include a wide variety of tasks from customer service to advertising. Different companies view public relations from different perspectives, and there is nothing to say that one structure is better than another.

There are, however, some basic principles that should be followed, especially for Internet start-ups. First, ensure that your Web site is functioning, even if only to provide some minimal information about the company. Nothing is more annoying than receiving a Web address that doesn't work. This also applies to having back-office staff who answer the phone when the principals are away. Too many start-ups send the primary staff out on the road without an adequate communications backup in the office. This could result in investor reps whom you talked to on the road calling your company for more information, but not receiving any. As well, the people who do answer the phone should have a professional manner and the technical capability to either forward a call or conference you in from a cell phone. These are basic functions that are almost universally ignored by even the most intelligent Internet start-ups.

What Do PR Firms Do?

The main function of a public relations firm is to get your name and story out to the world, primarily through the media. They can book interviews, schedule speeches, plan conference attendance, issue press releases, call the press directly, host events, plan promotions, design and produce advertising, create a media mix, and even develop a marketing plan. Their goal is to get you as much favorable coverage as possible, and in some instances, as much unfavorable coverage as possible. Whether you have the resources to hire these services will depend on your success at raising capital. If you are successful and your concept is sound, a good PR firm will take you to the market with a much better result.

There are a number of simple things that you can do to if you do not have the resources for a big PR firm. For example, you can create a mailing list of the e-mail addresses for the online news and technical services and find their requirements for submissions. Call these organizations beforehand and talk to one of the tech reporters about your story. Use this contact name as the reference for the press release. Issue an online press release to the media companies that you are targeting that clearly describes your company, you, and the concept. Don't wait for the phone to ring; follow up with the reporter and ask for her opinion on the story. Most opinions will be negative, but don't let that discourage you since you are not calling for anything but to keep the company name in their heads. Offer them your name as a contact and follow up with a mailing of your business card and promotional trinket.

Using Public Relations during a Road Show

A road show is a relatively easy thing to plan, but a complex thing to execute. You will invariably run out of time and run out of resources so careful planning will be essential to your survival. Never schedule meetings close together unless you think you can make them. Since a critical function of public relations is to handle any queries related to the organization or its concept, train someone who will stay behind and perform the task professionally while you are on the road. If you do not have the staff, forward your phone to your cellular; however, this may not always be the best approach if you are in a meeting with an important affiliate or investor. In this case, at least one onsite staff member is probably a reasonable investment.

The Big PR Event

PR firms also design and execute public relations events that can require a significant level of resources and can often be pulled off more efficiently by someone who has experience. However, it is not necessary that this be the case. You can plan and execute your own PR events, and some companies have individuals to do just this task.

E-commerce concepts come in very handy during the execution of public relations functions. Web sites can and should be used to provide the public with information. Call center and telephone systems can easily manage incoming calls, and customers, investors and affiliates can e-mail the company for information.

Investor Relations

Public relations pertains to the entire world of people who may contact you for various reasons. Investor relations is a subset of public relations, but with a particular financial undercurrent. In fact, understanding finance and stocks is so vital that investor relations groups are usually part of the finance or treasury department of large organizations. Their ability to talk about the forecasted earnings per share and how it will be affected by specific events makes their area of expertise rather unique. You can perform investor relations without a strong financial background, but we don't recommend it. Understanding your financial statements is an integral part of this task, and unless you can discuss ROE, EBITA, EPS and a whole bunch of other letters, we suggest you add a good Chief Financial Officer to lead your executive team.

Most of the initial calls that are received regarding investor relations will pertain to the story that is being told about your company. This implies that the individual picking up the investor relations phone line must be fluent in the company story you are telling to the world, and he must be confident and competent enough to deliver it to callers. The last thing that you want is a second level investor who is looking to silently bankroll a small e-business like yours, hanging up the phone in disgust when she can't get information about forecasted gross margins from "Binky," your wonder programmer. You must have individuals in the investor relations department who will instill a high degree of confidence and professionalism in the investor who is calling.

Publishing Financial Information

Using your e-commerce expertise, you should be able to now see how you can use the power of your Web site to publish financial information. Most online companies recognize the importance of investors and give them a separate home on their Web sites. These investor relations areas should contain the following information:

➤ A short version of the company story

➤ A detailed version of the story

➤ The corporate business plan

➤ Analysis of the markets

➤ Information about unique company strengths

➤ Inside information about key employees

➤ Risk mitigation factors like insurance

➤ Financial information

➤ Stock price

➤ A variety of other pieces of information

Ensure that when you release data to the public on a Web site that you are not breaking any rules of the existing stock exchange where your shares are listed.

Releasing Financial Information Online

Another way to use e-commerce technology is to release data to the financial media through e-mail. Services such as zdnet.com, yahoo, CNET, newswire.ca, cnnfn.com, and a variety of other online information companies can receive company announcements through the Internet, making the distribution of information extremely easy. When combined with products like Adobe Acrobat or Microsoft Power Point, you can produce entire multimedia packages, complete with video clips and sound bites. In fact, all potential investors should have the opportunity to receive online investor information packages through downloads from your Web site. The package can include a short video message from the founders, as well as a brief sound and slide presentation that explains the company story and provides general information about the company and documents on financial performance and press releases. You should also offer the option to have these packages mailed to individuals at their request.

The Motley Fool

One of the best online investment information sites is the Motley Fool at www.fool.com.

The goal of investor relations is to provide the information that the investor requires to make a decision to purchase the stock. They also attempt to mitigate any negative information pertaining to the financial performance of the company and work closely with the public relations department in providing coordinated external communications. Investor relations are a fundamental piece of any public corporation or even private corporations that have a significant number of shareholders. Performing the task well will result in favorable buzz about the stock and assist the company in attaining a stable growing stock value.

The Least You Need To Know

➤ Why face-to-face promotion is important.

➤ How to make and promote a great story.

➤ How to do a road show.

➤ How to do great promotions and why they are important.

➤ How to do public relations on your own or with a PR firm.

➤ How e-commerce can assist you with public relations.

The Marketing Goldrush: Data Mining

In This Chapter

➤ Capturing data and storing it

➤ Databases and storage area networks

➤ Extracting data from a data mine

➤ Neural networks

➤ Analyzing data

The Old Days of Mining

Remember those rooms with the raised floors and special ventilation systems that everyone had years ago for their mainframes? Well, at least I heard Grandpa talk about them. They were the storage areas of millions of pieces of accounting information and after month end reporting was complete, a tape was made and put into storage never again to see the light of day. All that effort for so little return.

Today, things are significantly different. Information is stored in data warehouses or distributed over a Storage Area Network (SAN), and both architectures have the capacity to store trillions of pieces of information. These new data architectures combined with new applications allow us to extract this information instantaneously and perform complex analysis used in e-commerce decision making. Back in Grandpa's time, he says they used to have to reload the tapes every time someone wanted information, and then a programmer would have to create a special program to extract and

IBM SAN Information

You can get more information on SANs and other storage methods at www.storage.ibm.com.

report on the information. Thousands of pounds of paper would be printed, burst, collated, and then delivered through a raging blizzard, three miles in bare feet. Of course, Grandpa does tend to exaggerate. I mean who would actually believe a programmer would actually program a report?

Data mining really didn't take hold until customer information started being stored in a way that users could easily look at it. By accessing customer account information, a marketer could sometimes tell what a customer's personal likes and dislikes were and what they might be ready to purchase, but only if the customer had an established account. Plus, general trends could be identified from the generic sales data that was stored in the accounting system. It wasn't until the mass installation of laser-enabled, point-of-sales terminals and barcoded customer shopping cards that retail companies really started to capture extensive databases of customer shopping preferences.

POS

Point-of-sales systems or POSs are the laser readers and cash registers that you see in almost every retail location. By scanning a customer card, the laser will store such information as the product purchased, the time of day, the location of the store, and the method of payment. This data can then be used to analyze such things as which customers are most likely to buy a particular product based on the buying trends of other customers who have purchased that same product. The analysis is used to create promotional campaigns or to direct advertising efforts.

Retail stores gather an extensive wealth of information and combine it with personal data to run a variety of analyses. For example, they try to determine what products you have purchased, which ones you are likely to purchase in the future, what you have recently stopped purchasing, your average expenditure per trip, the location of where you shop, etc. All this information is extremely valuable to savvy marketing analysts. They can develop mailings to encourage you to buy specific products that you may need, create in-store advertising for the market demographic that shops at a specific location, etc. The depth of the information is amazing. By running award program systems on a desktop, an analyst can tell when you will likely leave your house to shop, how long it will take, and how much you will spend. They can also tell that you don't like broccoli, have kids, need to floss, and like Madonna. A bit scary, isn't it?

Loyalty Group

Loyalty group introduced the concept of a customer going to a retail store and presenting a card that can be scanned by a point of sale (POS) system or electronic cash register to award points. These points can then be assigned to the customer's account based on the volume of purchases, and the customer can redeem them at a later date for airline tickets, hotel accommodations, or even electronics. The information that is captured by the POS system is stored in large databases for use by the retail organization to determine such things as customer preferences and tastes.

Capturing Data

Point of sales systems, combined with customer loyalty cards, are an excellent way to capture information about a customer. Automated supply chain systems also perform the same function. When a customer sets up an account at your online company, he is, in essence, building the foundation of your data mine or a way for your analysts to track information on transactions back to that customer. Unlike a regular mine in which the ore is haphazardly scattered and mixed with other minerals, your data mine should be carefully crafted to store information for later retrieval. When storing information in a data mine, you will have to consider where the information is coming from, how that information is to be extracted in the future, and what type of analysis is to be performed on the data once it is extracted.

The real success of capturing data and putting it somewhere for future reference will depend a great deal on how you tag and bag the information. If you tag information incorrectly, it won't necessarily mean that you will not be able to extract it at some point and run an analysis, it just may be a more difficult process. The phrase "more difficult process" should always be read as "costs more money." Remember from the prior chapters of e-commerce automation that the goal of your business should be to streamline operations as much as possible. Storing information is no exception. If you tag every piece of information you store, you will be saving and managing a lot of tags. If you group like information and tag it, your storage and retrieval process will be much more efficient.

Sit back and think of all the information you could capture about a transaction and then think about what type of information you would like to get out of the analysis. For instance, you may find that each customer's purchase can provide a valuable volume of information. From that information, you would like to see a report that shows the type of product purchased so that you could group all the information by product and then narrow the search by age in order to produce a mailing list. For this task, you will need a way to differentiate customers and items purchased (two static codes), and each customer will need to have his or her age stored (no code required). You can run this same process over and over to identify all the flows of information that you require and the reporting needed. The result will be a storage map that will guide the developers in building your information systems.

Navision

Software packages that have the right structure to be easily mined are Navision at www.navision.com, SAP at www.SAP.com, and Oracle at www.oracle.com, with SAP and Oracle adapted to i–commerce businesses. Or, you can get a better picture at www.excelco.com and follow the "huge comparison chart" link.

In Grandpa's time, accounting systems were custom developed for each organization or purchased off the shelf and pushed and crammed into an organization. Currently, systems such as Navision come with some simple customization tools that easily allow you to perform this customization without a staff of high priced talent. Of course, if you have the resources, then the big systems like Oracle are what you need to really add power your world (see Figure 18.1). Most older systems followed traditional accounting structures that forced organizations to align their internal operations along sales divisions or some other form of accounting measure. The problem was that organizations wanted to align their operations in other ways, such as by product category or customer group. The ability to gather operational data from these various divisions proved difficult, and often resulted in different pieces of accounting or operational systems for different areas.

Today, organizations are built for e-commerce, and the flexibility required to succeed in this world implies that the accounting and operational systems must now flex to meet the organization. The problem is that very few do so. Often, the underlying architecture of today's software has firm roots in the structures of the past. In choosing any solution, the first question out of your mouth to the vendor should be "How do I change it?" If the answer is "No problem" or "You can make any changes you want," then you have a system you can at least work with. If the answer is "Why do you want to change anything?" find a new vendor. In Chapter 8 we discussed real-time systems, and in Chapter 9 we talked about the automated supply chain. These concepts should form the basic foundation of any e-commerce operations system, and should incorporate the most current technologies available (see Figure 18.1)

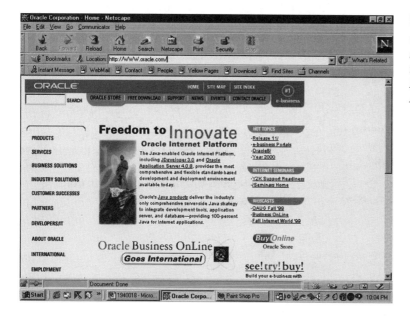

Figure 18.1

Oracle Corp. provides the software that is used by many of the leading Internet companies like Amazon.com.

The storage of information that is captured by your operational systems can be done in a number of ways. Relational databases are the standard method for capturing and storing information. A relational database is simply a series of tables, each with one or more indexes or keys. Think of it as a spreadsheet with multiple pages. The more indexes in the database, the faster the data can be extracted, but the longer it will take to load.

OK, so now you have chosen a database and had Binky the wonder kid build a hot application that captures every piece of information flowing through your company and stores it in some manner that allows you to know where it is. The next step is to get the information and analyze it. Most every database engine has a query and reporting capability built into it. You can, however, use third-party reporting tools such as those created by Seagate.

Free Tools

Seagate software provides some free data analysis tools on their Web site. Surf to www.seagate.com and follow the Seagate Software link.

ODBC

Open DataBase Connectivity is an important standard that you should ensure is available in your database. It ensures that the builder of the database has provided or built in the tools that allow the database to communicate with other software programs and databases, primarily Microsoft products.

Leveraging Your Data Mine for Marketing Information

You should now be able to use tools like Crystal Reports to dig into your data mine and start pulling useful data. For example, you should be able to access information by using your static and dynamic codes and their associated information to run reports on particular data (such as the area of the country that made the most and the fewest purchases of a particular product or the number of member hits on your Web site by gender). How would this information be obtained? Very simply and quickly, assuming that we have applied our identification codes correctly. For example, keeping customer information in accounts or userids allows us to link back to specific stored data about gender that we may have stored with these codes.

Objects

Grandpa tells a wild story about building programming code that would perform a single function just for a particular program and then repeating that code in the program every time it was needed. He proudly says that one program of his took up an entire file cabinet when it was printed. Today, we build one piece of code to perform a process on pieces of data, regardless of the value of that data. This way, every time we have to do this process we simply call that piece of code or object to process the data. When the "data" became complex, we built more complex objects in languages such as Java. Now we are storing little pieces of information with "data" that tell users what object to use. Put it in a database, and you have a pure object database. If you run it through an interpreter and store it in a relational database, you have an object/relational database blend. Isn't Grandpa a hoot?

Getting information from individuals, however, is becoming more and more difficult as people are becoming more and more annoyed with the time they have to spend entering the information. This is even more evident when they receive nothing in return. For example, some companies literally demand demographic information from their customers and then turn around and wholesale it to anyone who knocks at the door with a check. There is a growing discontent and resentment among surfers who are beginning to question whether they need to enter the information. In most cases where there is no benefit, they are entering bogus or false information. Using some innovative techniques, companies are attempting to turn the tide of resentment.

Yahoo Privacy Policy

Yahoo has implemented a privacy policy that clearly explains what information is captured about you and how it is used. Surf to www.yahoo.com and follow the "Privacy Policy" link at the bottom of the page.

Companies both on the Internet and off have long understood that one of the best ways to get information from consumers is to gather it by offering something in return. Contests and free give-a-ways are the best way to gather demographic information (see Figure 18.2). For example, a grocery store that has a contest can ask and usually receive an answer to questions such as age, gender, and income range. Higher response levels can be obtained by avoiding personal health and financial data and by using generic ranges as a choice instead of an exact number. Gathering data can also be performed when special services are used, accounts are set up, or an online help center or i-center is accessed. In these instances, users perceive they are going to receive some benefit from providing the information so they will be more open to providing it.

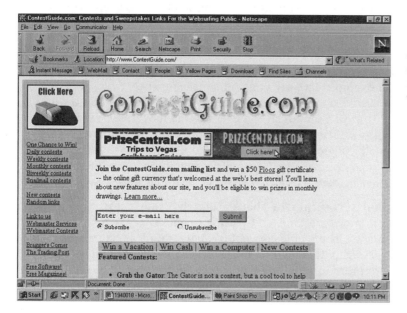

Figure 18.2

There are a variety of online contests available on the Internet such as the ones on www.ContestGuide.com.

Many organizations gather data and then quickly resell it to others. If we follow the model of the killer app, this information may even be distributed for free one day. Until then, your company will have to decide if it will sell the information to third parties or not. The benefits are revenue, especially if you have a large membership. The disadvantage is that a spammer can infuriate your customers. A second option is to collect the data and only distribute it to your affiliates or partners. Once again however, they could sell it to any e-mail bulk mailing company they want.

The most promising data mining model that we have seen is to distribute the information only in a generic form to your partners or third parties. This way, they are buying your analysis but will have to do individual promotion through your Web site. This method benefits you by allowing you to control whether the application is something that you want to supply. For example, you could supply a demographic breakdown of click-throughs to your partners without names, addresses, or email IDs. Your partners could decide that they want to run a promotion to your community, based on the mined information. You could evaluate the offering on behalf of your community to decide if you would like to offer it. The benefits can be ranked, and a delivery mechanism chosen such as a direct link, a banner ad, or an information notice. In some cases, you may not want to accept the offer at all. For example, if you were a family-oriented site, and the offer was a link to a pornography site, you could decline the affiliation.

Niche Marketing Using the Mine

Niche marketing is the concept of taking a large demographic or psychographic profile and breaking it into smaller units called niches by using multiple divisions. For example a larger demographic that you may choose to promote to, such as males between the age of 30 and 35, can be broken into successively smaller groups, such as those within that group that like sports and drive a truck. The advantage of niche marketing is that you can promote to a portion of your competitor's market, sometimes without them even knowing. For example, let's say you and your competitors sell the same products but your competitor's market is young kids between 13 to 18-years-old and yours is 18 to 30-year-olds. If you run an ad to target their demographics, you will invite immediate competition. The alternative is for your company to run an ad targeted at your 18 to 20-year-old subgroup that promotes and uses images that the 16 to 18-year-olds aspire to. If your competition isn't swift, and we know they aren't, you will successfully bleed their market before they have a clue about what has hit them.

Cross niching is even more successful. The above example is called cross niching, and is the process where promotions are targeted by using images that apply to two distinct demographics or niches. The whole concept of demographics was created to allow companies to more efficiently and effectively target their promotional budgets. However, with the cost of promotion falling to almost nothing thanks to e-commerce and the Internet, the concept of niching and cross niching will become more essential in the new millennium. The biggest use of data stored in e-commerce businesses will be for marketing new products and services.

Advanced Math and the Neural Networks

Remember calculus? What do you mean it's a mental block? Advanced math and all that stuff that we never thought would ever be used in real life is actually being used to analyze mined data. Yes, no kidding. These advanced mathematical and statistical tools are now being incorporated into data mining tools so that past information is used to mathematically predict future events.

This type of analysis is used extensively in the world of finance, derivatives, and options to predict future prices of things like currencies or the price of oil. In a regular data mine, they are used to predict such things as future buying behavior. A simple application of this technique would be to look at the historical buying behavior of customers who have recently purchased a new product. If the majority of them exhibit a specific behavior, such as they had just recently purchased another compatible product, then these advanced models should be able to identify this behavior based on the data in the mine. Then the database can give you a list of your customers who are most likely to purchase the new product. Now, you can target those customers in a special promotion for the new product.

A neural network is an extension of this concept. A neural network mines data in data warehouses or SANs and analyzes the data using many of the same mathematical and statistical concepts. The difference is that a neural network measures its guesses and attempts to learn from its mistakes. In most cases, it uses the equivalent of a very advanced averaging formula and adjusts the formula to account for the degree by which it missed its original guess. In this way the software appears to be learning from its mistakes. Neural networks are great for predicting behaviors that tend to follow something of a consistent pattern, like load volume in the i-center, in order to plan staffing levels. The problem with software that predicts trends is that computers lack intuition and gut instinct. They probably would have told Jeff Bezos that he should sell books in a store.

Do you need all this advanced stuff? No. You can get by without it. But, in the future, if it is implemented properly, you can probably use it to great advantage. For the time being, you should keep it in mind when you are loading data into the mine. If you see certain historical data that can be used to predict future actions, then that will likely be the best place to start advanced data mining when you choose to do so.

What to Look for in the Data

Now you have captured the data in some form of database and located the tools to extract and report it. What are you looking for? You are looking for information that you can use to find opportunities with your customers, make better use of your vendors, make your internal operation more efficient and effective, etc. Information that is properly "tagged and bagged" can be easily extracted and analyzed by your executive team. Remember that historical information is just that—historical. As a business leader, you stand on the precipice and look ahead at the future—don't dwell on the hill you just climbed. However, it helps to have a map that shows the ground you have already covered and what you might expect ahead. The map can't tell you how the landscape has changed, but it can give you a pretty good idea of what should be there.

Customer demographic and psychographic information coupled with purchased items' information can indicate the color, preferences, and size for existing customers. This is valuable information to have when ordering an inventory of new product. For example, if your vendors' mined data indicates that a particular sweater is purchased primarily by women 20 to 30-years-old and 50% of your 20 to 30-year-old female customers prefer red in a size 8, then you may bulk up the orders of this sweater in this particular color. If you use advanced data mining techniques, it may help you predict a movement towards a new color or size based on trends within your own market (for example, your market leaders are starting to buy a different color so tone down the order numbers of red sweaters by 5%).

Vendor information can be coupled with item sales' trends to indicate falling turnover rates by customer group. For example, let's say that you ran the sales numbers for the past twelve months on a particular product by age group.

What if it showed that sales for 20 to 25-year-olds had started to drop? You can use this type of data to ask the vendor for a new promotional effort, or you can use the information to clear out inventory and reduce future ordering quantities. Advanced analysis might indicate the same subtle percentage adjustments were occurring in the younger demographic in front of the 20-25 demographic and inventory orders should be further adjusted downward by 10%.

Both of these examples assume that you actually carry an inventory, but if you can provide information like this to vendors, they may be willing to carry the inventory for you through a direct connection to their own systems (called Just In Time). The advantage to the vendors is that they can fine-tune their own inventories thanks to your advanced information analysis effort. The advantage to your company is that you may not need to carry any inventory or may need to carry only a very small inventory. Eliminating the need to finance an inventory is an immense cash saver for the company since an inventory that is purchased usually never returns the investment until the business is sold or closed (for example, you pay for the inventory and when it is sold have to re-buy it). Inventory has to be the lousiest investment in any business.

There are hundreds of ways to use internal historical data to assist in decision making as long as you remember that it is historical data and that your focus should always be on the future, not what has happened. Some trends to look for in your data mine include the following:

➤ Sales by age group by product

➤ Sales by psychographic division (i.e., interests) by product

➤ Item turnover by age group

➤ Response to promotion by psychographic division (i.e. favorite music or 20% of country listeners responded)

➤ Average order completion time by vendor

➤ Forecasted item purchases by age and gender

➤ Reduction in production inventory after new, "just in time" ordering is implemented

Data is by far one of the most valuable resources available to the firm. So much so that blue chip executives have been overheard to say they would give up all the traditional manufacturing infrastructure if they could keep the data. Even American Airlines once said they would give up the airplanes as long as they could keep the Sabre Reservation system (see Figure 18.3). However data, like ore, is not very valuable in a mine. It is far more valuable after it has been extracted, separated from the junk, and turned into a final product. That's the goal of data mining—to take your data and turn it into a shiny piece of gold. There really is gold in them thar hills of data.

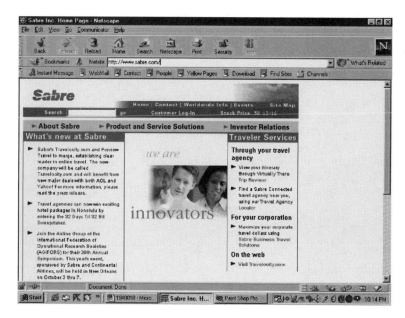

Figure 18.3

Sabre Reservations Web page.

The Least You Need To Know

➤ How to store data in a data mine.

➤ What the difference is between relational and object databases.

➤ How to extract the data.

➤ How to analyze the data.

➤ What specific data you are looking for.

➤ How to do niche marketing.

Part 4

e-Strategies: Managing the e-Corporation

In this section, we will start to discuss how all of the information in the prior sections hangs together. e-commerce is complex and requires a new way of thinking about business so we will try to highlight some of the things that you will have to consider about running an e-business.

First, we'll look at planning your resources for your new business, including outsourcing considerations and developing a Web presence. Then the management of your knowledge assets will be covered. Your corporate knowledge base is one of the most essential ingredients of any e-business, and managing them for this new high tech world will be critical to success.

Leveraging your e-commerce assets is the process of making more out of less. Your resources are limited, and leveraging these resources to get customers by using affiliates and partners is an excellent way to bring growth to your company.

At the end of this section, you will have the necessary pieces to build and manage a successful e-business, but wait, there's one more section.

e-Commerce Resource Planning

What Is Resource Planning?

Resources are anything that an organization needs and uses to complete its operations. Resources include capital, cash, employees, raw materials, inventories, technology, market intelligence, and anything else that goes into producing a good or a service. The primary push behind e-commerce was both a need to capitalize on the fundamental changes in communications because of the Internet and the need to capitalize on the realization that with the assistance of technology, businesses could much better manage all their resources. ERP or Enterprise Resource Planning was a key paradigm in the last half of the 90s and had some of the largest players explaining how their software was the only one that could provide true ERP. This quickly vanished into the paradigm of e-commerce. So, rather than just jump on the latest buzzword bandwagon, let's look at what these concepts were really all about down in the trenches where a paradigm was the extra 20 cents you needed for the next Starbuck's hit.

Businesses in the early 90s were running flat out in the world of technology trying to keep pace with the problems noted by Moore and Metcalf. Their internal operational systems had to be replaced to take advantage of the newer technologies and to pass the Y2K testing hoopla. In the process of upgrading software, companies abandoned the large internal development areas in favor of "off the shelf" solutions that would magically be upgraded by the giant software companies. The savings were immense and allowed companies to focus IT resources on networking and the new emerging technologies of the Internet.

On the top of their wish list to the vendors of these operational systems was a request to integrate the various pieces of software so that manufacturing systems would talk to the general ledger and human resource systems would communicate with the project planning software.

This complete integration of operating systems was called Enterprise Resource Planning because it was based on the concept of providing systems that would better plan and utilize the resources of the organization through integration. The goal was originally to automate the supply chain process in manufacturing environments, but it quickly spread to the entire organization. Now ERP has been rolled into the wider concept of e-commerce, and the big ERP developers, such as SAP, have shifted their focus to remain at the forefront of the latest paradigm.

Tracking Resources

Down in the bowels of the development labs, the app wizards found the 20 cents they were looking for and started a caffeine-induced redesign of the way operational software interacted. Now, companies could install a piece of software that could track everything from raw inventory to how much time an employee had spent on a project. At the end of the 90s, software companies were still trying to complete the missing pieces of their ERP developments when along came the Internet.

Companies like Germany's SAP or American-based Oracle are rapidly redefining themselves for the world of the Internet and e-commerce. As the subtitle on an Oracle Web page clearly indicates, the Internet "Changes Everything" (see Figure 19.1). Now those systems have to be retooled to communicate over the Internet and even run applications over the Internet. The problem is that the foundations of these systems were never built to even consider the way a business will work in the world of e-commerce. Virtual companies with virtual employees who communicate over vast networks and need instantaneous access to information, are still an area under immense construction, as far as the software companies are concerned, and just when you thought it was complicated enough, throw into the mix the fact that standards are constantly changing. Will Windows continue to dominate or will it implode, will the public Internet continue to grow or will privatization kill the growth, will XML and the growing complexity of technology outpace the skill sets of the work force that have to use it? Ahhhh! I love the smell of change in the morning.

It is literally a war. Companies have to manage runaway technology budgets, keep pace with rapid change that is altering the entire way they do business, stay ahead of the competition, and still manage to conduct business. They need to better control the way they manage their limited resources, and one wrong move can cost millions and millions of dollars. So companies attack the world of technology by gaining beachheads in the battle with Java development staff and HTML coders. The goal is to try and map out a strategy to move inland.

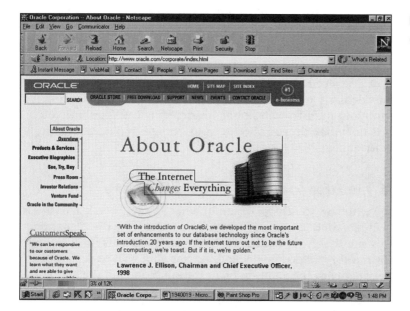

Figure 19.1

Oracle states the obvious.

Choosing an e-Commerce Strategy

Choosing an e-commerce strategy involves making tough decisions, but some have already been made for you. The Internet and distributed computing environments or net-working models are already here and chances are that you are either using them or need to. Every organization can benefit by putting a logo on the Internet if only to give the location to your real store. Evaluating the cost of an Internet site isn't much of a task given that a single business phone line itself costs between $400 and $800 per year. The fact that you can put a Web page up on the Internet for free should make the decision to create a Web presence quite easy. Of course, the vast

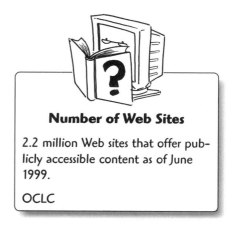

Number of Web Sites

2.2 million Web sites that offer publicly accessible content as of June 1999.

OCLC

majority of businesses will hire Web designers to create the page and ISPs to host the site. It is surprising to find out that of the millions and millions of business in the United States, fewer than two million have Web sites.

So what is going to be your e-commerce strategy? What will be the main goal or mission, what will be the smaller goals along the path, and what will be the schedule to completion? The answer will depend on the nature of your business. You will probably have to have some sort of presence on the Web, and you will probably have to have some sort of technology, not because you want to but because your suppliers and customers will demand it.

You could grow vegetables in your backyard and sell them at a farmer's market without any need for technology, but eventually you'll need to use some form of technology to do your banking or else face the higher costs that come with the old ways of doing business. So, some decisions are already being made for you. In most cases, what the standards are for your industry will not be impacted by the decisions you make. The big question is how then do you allocate your limited resources to use these standards to your advantage?

Choosing the Best Technology for Your Strategy

The choice of technology will have to fit your vision of what you want your e-business to be. If your business will remain traditional but with an outlet to the Internet and an integrated operational system, then your traditional business strategy may still suffice. For example, you may own a shipping company and have as your goal to do business as you have always done, only with the addition of an information Web site and a new internal system.

However, if you want to accept shipping orders over the Internet and manage your logistics better, then the development of your technology or even partnering with an Internet shipping killer app, will require that you rethink your strategy and how you allocate your resources. You may need to set up regional shipping hubs and collection outposts, or you may change from a local shipper into a statewide shipper by adding affiliates to the hub network. These strategies may or may not be vastly different from your current strategy

There are a number of steps that you can follow in deciding what strategy is best for your company. Start by defining what you are going to do or what your concept will be. For example, you may decide that you will develop a Web site that will offer the use of an online software for free. Define what benefit you will receive from the application, such as revenue, traffic to your traditional business, greater operating efficiency, or critical mass. Then set a long-range target for your business, such as to continue current growth rates, to become a leader in your market, to be a global boutique, to become a standard, etc. Now you can start to define what the foundation of your organization will be.

Spending Carefully

Investing in technology is a tricky business and is becoming more so every day. Organizations can spend thousands of dollars to upgrade systems only to find that they are out-of-date the following year and unusable in five. Making the correct choices will require research either by you or from a third party. Some companies choose to outsource the technology to organizations that are more capable or have better resources. For instance, you can say that you will create a Web site of "how to" information and rather than create the entire site including the posting of information, you add a link to Learnlots and other information sites. This will still require that you have resources for Web site construction and management and promotional costs for the site, but it is an example where you have outsourced the content and technology to Learnlots. If the standards of the Internet change, Learnlots will have to bear the burden of upgrading their technology, and you will only have to deal with your Web site. This same technique can also be used for hard technology assets like internal systems. The choice will be to decide if you are going to take on the burden of technology, or if you are going to outsource it.

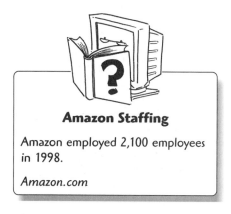

Amazon Staffing

Amazon employed 2,100 employees in 1998.

Amazon.com

Human resources are the most costly of all your resources, but they provide the greatest opportunity for a return. For example, just imagine the return on your stock if you had hired Jeff Bezos to run your bookstore, or if you had hired Bill Gates as a partner in your fledgling software company way back when. Which employees you hire and how you utilize their talent is one of the most critical resource management issues you will ever face. The answer is directly affected by what you choose to do as a company and how you choose to use the technology. Linking to Learnlots is not a very complex process and may not even require any staff. Building an information network or e-commerce retail site will take considerably more people.

Resources Hard and Soft

Hard resources such as inventories, investments, plants, and buildings are an integral part of any strategy. So are soft resources like intelligence, skill sets, information, and marketing ability. If the strategy is the map to achieving your goals, both hard resources and soft resources provide the fuel to get you to your goal. Step on the gas too hard, and you might not make it to your goal before you run out of fuel, but be too cautious and you might miss the goal altogether. Managing these resources is what business truly is. Whether it's taking your tomatoes to market or building cars around the globe, the choice of how to invest in resources, how to efficiently utilize them, and how to direct them to achieve your goals is what you as a business owner will have to decide. Deciding how to use hard and soft resources in an e-commerce strategy is no different than any other business strategy, but in some situations getting rid of or not needing hard resources is the end result.

Building an online retailer does not mean that you have to own any hard resources. Constructing an online community of value may only require a Web site. On the other hand, you may want to expand your tomato distribution efforts to include trucks, plants, salsa factories, and juice retailers. The major difference between traditional business strategies and e-commerce strategies is that the choice of and the implementation of resources will depend heavily on the e-business plan, technology, and human resource strategies of the organization.

e-Commerce Is Not for the Faint of Heart

Got a heart condition? We're not sure we would recommend e-commerce as a hobby. Imagine learning a new technology only to find out that it's obsolete before you finish the class, or how about partnering with a small company that supplies vital information to your Web site only to find out that Disney has bought them and the service is no longer free. Welcome to the hurricane-powered ocean of the Internet where a business that is up one year can be wiped out the next and where traffic patterns can change overnight with the next big wave.

Parts of e-commerce are manageable, such as internal automation. For example, overhauling your technical structure in three-year increments makes the process a whole lot smoother than getting the latest upgrade installed as soon as it is released. Also, partnering with established organizations provides a certain level of comfort even if you do miss a couple of trends and opportunities that you would have had with the smaller companies.

Investing in Change

Technology changes extremely rapidly and putting all your eggs in one technology basket is risky. On the other hand, avoiding change is even riskier. You will have to strike a balance between studying and investing in new technology and holding development steady while your operation has a chance to run. Ongoing research and development into technology is probably the best investment that an organization can make as long as the expenditures don't get out of control or take too many resources away from the task of making money. Also smaller organizations may not be able to justify the resources required to participate.

For example, if your systems person has available time during the day to learn Java, then this may be an effective investment, particularly if you would like to provide some Web-based functionality to your customers such as a mortgage calculator or game. On the other hand, if your function is to sell items and you are contracting out your Web site and i-commerce functionality, then the expenditure on Java research may be inappropriate and wasteful. However, allocating your technology resources should always include some type of technology strategy of which ongoing research and development are a part.

Another way to limit your exposure to changes in technology is to outsource the function entirely. Some companies currently outsource their computers and networking function to companies such as Futurelink (see Figure 19.2). This places the burden of training and IT resource management back on the outsourcing firm. It is their responsibility to train their staff and upgrade the leased machines periodically. The problem is that the costs of these arrangements are usually much higher than if you performed the process yourself, especially for smaller companies. Also, relying on other organizations comes with its own inherent risks (see Chapter 5 on the Virtual Corporation).

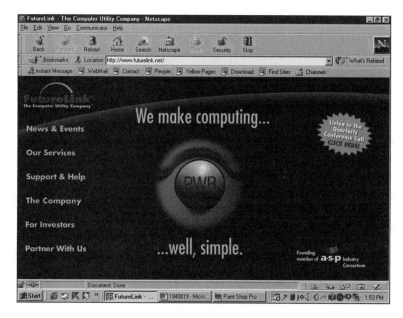

Figure 19.2

Futurelink is a company that leases access to software such as Great Plains Accounting to other companies that don't want to purchase the software.

Making Your Company Stand Out from the Crowd

What if you build a site and no one comes? Public relations is a very expensive task, as are promotion and advertising and the ability to not blend in with the millions of other Web sites, which can be a challenge. In fact, some search engines are charging to separate the business sites from the personal sites. Although this runs counter to the concepts and rules of the Internet, these companies just may succeed if they narrow the access and get rid of the junk.

However, currently most of what they have is sales junk. Of course, in true Internet fashion, someone is bound to come out with a free app that can get the best of both worlds. "Limited linking" sites that only provide links and limited searches to valuable information or "controlled content" sites like Learnlots are the wave of the future. These online companies will succeed as people try to get better information without extensive searching or advertising.

What if you build a site and the wrong people come? Imagine that you open a little coffee shop in a new trendy mall. You sell specialty coffees and some treats and put a few cool magazines for people to read. One day you arrive at your shop only to find that Chapters has opened a mega bookstore on the opposite side of the mall, and they put in a Starbucks. The same thing can happen to an i-commerce company on the Internet. The big boys may like your killer app so much that they'll reproduce it, add a lot more offerings, and promote directly to your customers. Pretty soon, thanks to their unlimited bank accounts, they'll be ringing the NYSE bell, and you'll be trying to find the new killer app. The other threat is that a multitude of other companies open Web portals just like yours, thereby confusing the community.

Branding

The best thing you can do is to define a brand image for yourself that the big boys can't copy without a huge copyright infringement lawsuit. The goal should be to build something that their money just can't buy. It could be an image or a community, but try to build on something that you have that the big companies can't get for any amount of money. Then you can position yourself right beside their Internet front door and pick off their best customers. Nothing infuriates a big company like a smaller one that can pick off the cream of their market. It has long been a tradition for restaurants to open up right next door to the most popular restaurant in town in order to get instant traffic and recognition. The same thing can be done by opening up a toy store and linking to the "Disney site." In this way you become an indirect retailer for Disney whether they want you or not. In fact, you could link to a bunch of different shopping sites and sell advertising space on the main Web page.

Shopping Link Site

Shop.com provides a centralized listing of shopping services from their Web page. Surf to www.shop.com.

Automating Your Company

The automation of your business is another area that can keep you up at night, especially if you are converting from a traditional operation to an automated operation such as a supply chain or a back office. Employee resentment and fear, contractors and resellers that leave your business with limited support or high-priced consultant's bills, existing technology that has to be replaced or upgraded, or implementations that go ahead without any understanding of the dynamics of the business are all factors that can also directly impact your business. However, change is a manageable process, and doesn't have to include massive risk. Here are a series of steps to follow to implement new systems:

➤ Identify the direction that you would like all of your technology to take (technology strategy).

➤ Understand and document what you do, right down to step-by-step instructions.

➤ Work with your software vendors to identify the solutions that are best for your business.

➤ Decide how much you can afford to spend and make sure that you have someone dedicated to managing the project from start to finish.

➤ Develop a plan to implement the system(s) and what changes are required.

➤ Train your employees.

➤ Make any required changes to operations.

➤ Implement the system.

➤ Test the system.

The goals for implementing and integrating technology into the organization should be the same as any strategy. Identify where you are (what you do), where you want to go (technology strategy), and the path to get there (project management). The better you do these tasks, the better the result will be with less disruption to your existing operations. If you can, it is sometimes better to implement pieces of systems, as opposed to entire wholesale system overhauls. For example, you can start by implementing a network, then add a server, a back-office system, proxy, etc., etc. Or you can either gut the company and retool entirely, or open a brand new location with new systems and slowly migrate your existing operations.

The world of e-commerce is fast-paced and full of risks and rewards. Keeping on top of all the changes is a full-time job. Learning and using the technology is even more than a full-time job. Picking and choosing your battles and tools carefully will help you survive the stress of playing in the world of e-commerce. It is definitely not a place for the faint of heart.

Outsourcing Today

Outsourcing today has taken on a whole new meaning, thanks to the incredible growth of the Internet. Today, virtual corporations with virtual staff no longer need to risk investment in infrastructures like offices and technology. With enough operating cash flow you could marshal the resources required to build an e-company without doing anything. For example, you could hire a Web designer to build a portal to the Internet that your contract channel manager could then fill with links to affiliate sites. Your online site management company would control the technology (see Figure 19.3) to run your Web site, and your PR firm could manage your customer and investor communications through an i-center. Finally, your online accounting firm could process your e-bank deposits and accounting and email your financial statements to your virtual CEO working from his home office. He can analyze the information and report to you at lunch.

Figure 19.3

Web hosting at firstsource.com *allows companies to have a Web presence without all the technological headaches.*

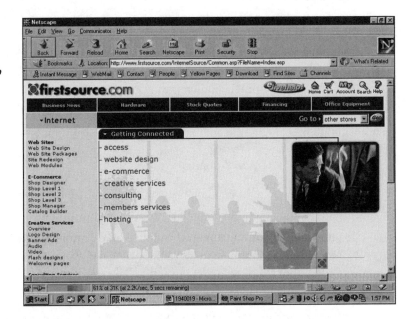

Of course, you probably won't be able to lounge by the pool while the millions roll in, or maybe you will, depending on how good your e-business is. The reality of the situation is that you will have to work very hard to create the brand image that can carry a virtual organization. So for now, unless you are already independently wealthy, you will have to perform many or all of the operational tasks needed to launch your company including promotion, back office, and systems. However, as you grow, your most critical decision will be to decide what functions you want to outsource and how you will do this. Simply outsourcing the accounting of a mid-sized organization is a major undertaking. The advantage will be that so many online services will be opened in the next ten years that the idea of successfully running a truly virtual organization is not just a pipe dream. It can be done today.

Outsourcing Tomorrow

Outsourcing in the near future will be a unique experience. Massive organizations will have small executive offices and almost every service will be farmed out. Even as employees with very specialized skill sets start to market themselves to the online world, they will be establishing home offices for their specialty with Internet-capable communications for work with their clients.

The ability to select the organizational operations that you need from a smorgasbord of online functions will be the wave of the future, and will significantly redefine the way all organizations do business. Starting to prepare for this world today can save you an immense expenditure of resources later on when your corporate ship, the Titanic 2, has to make a quick turn in the technology ocean. You can prepare by doing the following tasks:

➤ Study the new technologies even if at a high level.

➤ Set aside time to review the online technology e-zines.

➤ Surf a bit each week.

➤ Start using technology that is proven (such as email).

➤ Attend seminars and conventions.

➤ Start talking to potential partners

➤ Hire young talent and give them some e-toys to play with.

➤ Develop a Web presence.

➤ Map your current internal operations

➤ Think about how you will capitalize on an increased ability to communicate with an entire world and how you might make your voice heard above the millions of others.

Get a Web Presence

We think that the key to ongoing corporate growth is to develop a Web presence and start marketing it in your own world. A simple Web page and domain name are not very difficult to do. Get an ISP contract for an Internet service, one that can host a Web site, and surf to www.networksolutions.com registry home page (see Figure 19.4). Then start typing names until you locate the domain you want. Surf to the trademarks office at www.uspto.gov and verify that you can use the name for your purpose. Start thinking about image, function, and content that you could provide on your site and how you can gather a community of value. Build the site, have someone build it for you, or use one of the online services. This will start the process of becoming an e-commerce company.

Allocating your resources whether they are cash, employees, technology, or plant and equipment is a difficult task and is the true essence of being in business. Choosing the correct strategy will help you efficiently perform the allocation process. Capitalizing on those resources is what will make your e-business a success. The world of resource planning and utilization is changing right down to its fundamental core, and the way we do business will never be the same. The Internet and e-commerce systems have forever changed all organizations and those that choose the correct mix of change and risk will ultimately be rewarded for their vision. Unfortunately, many businesses that do not understand change will fail, as will many online businesses that do not understand the dynamics of sailing the Internet oceans.

Figure 19.4

*Network Solutions'
Domain Registry search is
the place to register your
.com, .net, or .org domain
name.*

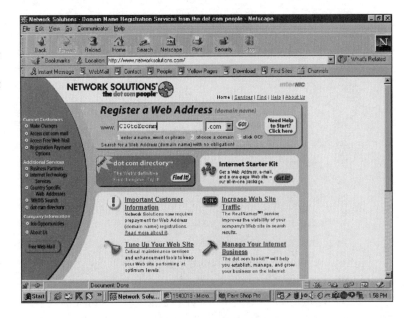

The Least You Need To Know

➤ How to use e-commerce to plan your resources.

➤ How online resources are available for your company.

➤ How to choose an e-commerce strategy.

➤ Why e-commerce can be risky.

➤ How to outsource the needs of your business today and tomorrow.

Knowledge Management

The Rapid Speed of Technological Change

Trying to clock the speed of technological change is like trying to figure out how high is up. We know it's fast, so fast in fact that by the time you finally load a software package, it's time to upgrade. Keeping pace with technology used to be easier because there were not as many standards to learn. There were a couple of operating systems, a couple of flavors of office suites, a couple of networking systems, and a couple of graphics packages. Then came the Internet and a whole variety of new standards. Now your operations require that you not only know about operating systems and networks, but also how to connect to the Internet, implement real-time operational systems, build an Intranet, HTML, XML, Java, e-commerce systems, streaming content, etc. Given that you can successfully find and keep the staff you need to manage a specific software, trying to find people with enough experience in all these standards as well as your company's operations will be almost impossible. Your staff and your content make up your knowledge resources and managing them in a world of fast-changing technology will be immensely difficult.

The problem is that to gain the depth of skills necessary to program Java is not that difficult, to install and administer an NT network is a piece of cake, and to create and operate an Internet portal is no problem. You may even find someone who has lots of experience in all three technologies; however, the ability to pull them together and manage them to the benefit of the corporation is a skill set that is very rare. It may require an understanding of fundamental programming, mathematics, system analysis, finance, systems engineering, electrical engineering, corporate operations, logistics, design, marketing, database administration, network administration, Internet Web site construction, and a variety of other technologies both existing and emerging.

Understanding Technology

You can, of course, hire specialized organizations to perform these functions. However, to effectively manage this resource, you must first understand what it is that you are outsourcing. The more you understand the technology, the better you will be at using it to successfully grow the company. Too often the CIOs don't understand the fundamental principles behind the newest technologies presented in all those professional looking reports from underlings. It's always a "must have," and it invariably costs far more than it should. This problem arises from the fact that people are political by nature, and decision makers rarely have enough technological depth to make an informed decision. When you hire staff you should not be looking exclusively for specialists who will present their narrow view of the world, as is the case with most technology organizations HR practices. Instead, you should seek to mix a couple of generalists into the pot to provide an "out of the box" or "forest as opposed to trees" perspective.

Information on Technology Change

You can find some interesting writing on technology changes at http://www.contract.kent.edu/change/.

Our point is simple: you have to understand technology just as you would understand mining in a mining company, stocks in a brokerage, or logistics in a delivery company. Technology has become such a fundamental part of our business world that it has crossed from being a tool to being the very foundation of our e-businesses. If you do not understand it, you will make poor decisions about it, regardless of how many top-notch technical specialists or consultants you have on staff.

Keeping Pace with Technological Change

The ability to keep pace with changes in technology does not imply that as CEO you should dedicate the majority of your time to learning the intricacies of Java. However, unless you understand the principles of what Java is, how it works, why it was developed, what the competing technologies are, how it would benefit your organization, what it will cost in resources, and what return can be expected, you will be making decisions that are meaningless gambles. In larger organizations, the management of your knowledge resources may be as simple as encouraging your staff to communicate their knowledge on a company Intranet or to present their findings in a weekly corporate team meeting. The problem is that the majority of people, like organizations, protect their expertise like it was a personal fortress, rarely willing to bring their peers up to their knowledge level and invite competition. This is directly impacted by the corporate culture and environment. If the leaders of the company encourage and reward sharing, then the knowledge will spread among workers. This should sound very familiar to the concepts discussed in Downes & Mui's *Killer App* book (see Chapter 6, "Killer Apps"). Hoarding information both internally and externally should be discouraged and replaced with assurances that positions will be secure and internal politics punished.

Knowledge Resources

Your employees are only one piece of your knowledge resources. Another significant piece is the knowledge resources of the entire organization. As staff come and go, the corporation gains from gathering and storing expertise in its systems and operations. This is primarily a function of the way knowledge and expertise is passed from worker to worker. If this free flow of information is not performed in the organization, the knowledge asset attributable to the organization will not grow. For example, let's say that you hired a Linux expert to obtain a Linux distribution and test its capabilities for the company (see Figure 20.1). That individual can spend months becoming the corporate expert in Linux, but unless he or she shares this expertise with others in the organization either through collaboration or reporting, the organizational knowledge base will not grow in this particular area. Many would argue that to spend resources such as assigning two people to study a technology is inefficient and in some cases this is true. As a business owner or manager, you will have to define how much information should be shared and how much should be kept at the individual level.

Knowledge is the most critical asset of any organization, and by investing in and expanding the knowledge base of the corporation, you will earn a return on your investment. This return will be in the form of your ability to perform your operations more effectively and more efficiently than your competition. This is especially true in e-commerce, since the complexity of the multiple systems will require an extensive and varied knowledge base. Your company will have to not only obtain this expertise, but also the expertise to make all these diverse systems work together to the benefit of your organization.

Building a Portfolio of Knowledge Assets

What about a virtual corporation? Virtual corporations that operate without hard assets, such as employees and equipment, still require the knowledge of e-commerce

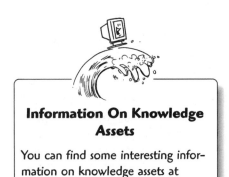

Information On Knowledge Assets

You can find some interesting information on knowledge assets at http://www.aiai.ed.ac.uk/~alm/kamlnks.html.

and i-commerce so that their organizations can be designed and built to take advantage of these technologies. Could you outsource this knowledge as well? Yes, with enough cash anything is possible, even having your virtual knowledge resources recorded. However, a person could achieve the exact same result by simply investing in organizations that have an extensive knowledge base and the ability to use it. Some examples are Sun Microsystems for Java, Microsoft for NT, Red Hat for Linux, Amazon for shopping, and the associated support organizations like FedEx, UPS, Winamp, Real Networks, etc. You could build a portfolio of knowledge assets and get the same benefits as building your own complete e-commerce organization. However, as any investor knows, knowing what you invest in is as important as knowing how much to invest, or the old card counting theory of investment—counting cards at the black jack table improves yours odds significantly and improves your gambling return.

Figure 20.1

Linux is a computer operating system that is available for free.

The Two Classes: Technology "Haves" and "Have-Nots"

There is definitely a new class distinction occurring in society. The technology "haves" and the technology "have-nots." Young techno savvy individuals are about to enter a world where even their own capabilities will be pushed to the limit. No longer can individuals leave a post secondary school with a technology degree and expect only to return for the occasional refresher course. Now technology skills need to be updated constantly. For example, spending the day administering a network has to be followed up with a couple of hours at home on technology study just to keep up. This has caused a noticeable rift between the technology "haves" and "have-nots." The "haves" own one or two computers personally and have one or more at work. They, on average, have two Internet connections, one at work and one at home, two e-mail IDs, and a personal Web space allocated to them by their ISP. They will have at least attempted to load a Web page, be involved in technology at work, will be thinking about networking their home, and will surf the Net regularly for both work and pleasure.

The "have-nots," however, do not necessarily come from a different socioeconomic background, although there is a direct correlation between an individual's technical capabilities and the ability to purchase a computer and obtain an Internet account. The majority of those people in low-income groups who do not have direct access to the technology are starting to fall behind those with the ability to purchase personal computers and Internet connections. Even within the same socioeconomic group as the technological "haves" are a large group that is not technologically competent enough to keep pace. As well, children from technologically advanced parents have a greater statistical head start over those whose parents are not technologically advanced. This is because these parents understand the power and benefit of

Home PC Usage

July 1999 54% of all homes in the United States have a PC. 38% have an Internet connection.

Source: Arbitron NewMedia

technology, and are surrounding their kids with it. That, of course, takes money and since not everyone can afford the latest version of Windows, they start to fall behind.

The Growing Shortage of Technological Workers

Although this differentiation has been viewed as nothing more than a curious anomaly in our currently expanding economy, this division is growing greater as the speed of technology accelerates. It has a direct impact on our lives since as the technology becomes more complicated, technology organizations will try to attract talent that understands both how to create and use the technology and how it relates to their new e-business. The shortage of this particular skill set and the demand that will be created in the next few years will drive up the price of this type of talent, making a new class of technology worker that is significantly higher paid than the general population. Already e-commerce contracting rates for top site builders with HTML, Java, and e-commerce have risen to above $125.00 per hour inclusive of stock options for the sites they are building. And companies have rewarded these techno employees generously because of the huge returns they are capable of producing and the limited talent pool that has this capability.

At those rates, there are a lot more people driving new SUVs and sports cars in the upper middle class areas of town. Meanwhile, the line employees at the plant are lucky if they haven't had their wages cut over the past ten years. This is a vast division that is likely to grow as more and more technology workers update their skill sets, and the demand for technology workers drives up the wages. The problem is that this division is a cycle because higher wages start putting pressure on the rest of the economy, and the race to beat the competition drives software companies to make new advances in technology for such areas as faster streaming content and delivery of video. Technology workers with the capital to upgrade systems will stay ahead of this wave in technological change, and the "have-nots" will fall even further behind. Governments are aware of these impending skill shortages and have started programs to train the youth of their respective countries in the advancing technologies. However, in most cases, the government workers designing the programs and the teachers who are teaching our children are members of the "have-not" knowledge population.

Career Auction

You can search for talent in a talent auction at http://talentmarket. monster.com/search.asp.

There Is Opportunity in Technology

So what does this have to do with e-commerce? Opportunity. Lots and lots of opportunities to help the technological "have-not" companies and individuals keep pace. Online training such as Learnlots (see Figure 20.2), or online services like Firstsource.com assist organizations and individuals to become competent in technology. Of course, this doesn't mean that everyone will start building Web sites, but it does mean that people with skill sets that are not technology based can still capitalize on e-commerce technology by using the online educational services or online e-business services. Now you can take generalized information, such as that contained in this book, find additional online resources to fill in the gaps, then start to build your e-commerce company or adapt your existing company without having to hire expensive e-commerce specialists. Of course, if you want to jump way up the technology learning curve, then spending capital resources to gain knowledge onsite may be your best investment.

Google Search

A Google search on the phrase "education resources" returned 17,041 references for the exact phrase in 1999.

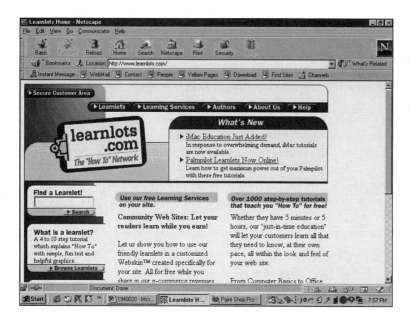

Figure 20.2

The Learnlots Web site provides online information to help individuals learn about new technology.

The Rising Backlash against Change

You can't see it. It isn't getting press coverage. It's more of a rumbling, or more correctly, a grumbling of discontent. It's discontent that companies and individuals have to spend so much in resources just to keep pace with the change of technology. Companies that finally figured out how to share files over a Windows network and eventually grew to use NT are now faced with the changes presented in Windows 2000 and whether to upgrade to Office 2000. Seat licenses, incompatibility, high prices, and the need to upgrade or put in patches and fixes every few months is probably driving the economy to newer heights as workers move toward the technology sector and away from traditional service and manufacturing sectors. But resources have their limits, and the completion of upgrading for Y2K has now lead to the push to rationalize capital expenditures on technology infrastructure. Luckily, this

Hold on to Your Seat

A seat is another term used to describe an installation of software. If I have a network that has five active computers or clients and I install Office 2000 on all of them, then I will need to pay Uncle Bill for a five-seat license; otherwise, the software police will introduce me to Bill's extensive legal team.

push is still falling on deaf ears as business owners and boards of directors realize the fundamental changes that are currently shaking all industries thanks to the Internet.

Some business leaders are starting to question why a move from Office97 to Office 2000 is essential to their organization or why NT 4 will not suffice for the next few years. This type of attitude is new and unusual in a world where the frantic pace of change has caused companies to abandon their entire IT departments in favor of IT outsourcing. When Microsoft first released its Office 2000 software, the rush from businesses to upgrade was decidedly lower than the movement to Windows98. Of course, the difference in price was significant, plus there was a concerted need to keep operating systems consistent with the new machines that were purchased and loaded with Windows98 (or that Y2K spoof thing). But many people question the benefits from the minimal additional features in Office 2000. The same is true of the faster and faster chips being released. Many organizations that moved from 486s to 333s with each change as soon as it was out have started to draw the line in moving to +500 MGhtz chips by forcing IT departments to justify the costs. This resistance is likely to continue into the future.

Do We Really Need To Go Faster?

Individuals are also starting to question the need for speed. Gaming is one of the biggest users of PC power, but with the +300 chips and 56K modems, most users are content with the functionality of their machines. Couple this with the human's tendency to avoid change, and you have a recipe for slowing the growth of technological development. Technology will always grow and change, but the pace will slow slightly as software companies find a divergence in their user groups and pressure to make all upgrades compatible. This can be seen in the Office 2000 software that has backward as well as forward compatibility (a file created in one version can be seen in the other, although specialized functions may not work). This will also be more prevalent as the technology "haves" push harder for improvements while the vast majority of new users, the "have-nots but changing" need to keep the pace of change within reach. Complicating the issue will be companies like Amazon that will forever set the benchmark exceptionally high.

This does present outstanding opportunities to the Net savvy people to create the support mechanisms that will help bridge this widening gap between the two groups. Online information and online help, technology change management, application service providers like Corio Inc. (see Figure 20.3), and better technology strategies are just some of the areas that will grow rapidly in the first few years of the millennium. These companies can help stem the rising backlash against too rapid a level of technological change, but they will be unable to stop it. As new applications are released on the Internet for free, more and more individuals will turn from the traditional "buy because it's new" mentality to one of "Do I need it right now or can I get by with what I have for a few years?" decision making. The advantage is that companies that are more wise about accepting change will become the norm, and this could have a significant dampening affect on technology vendors.

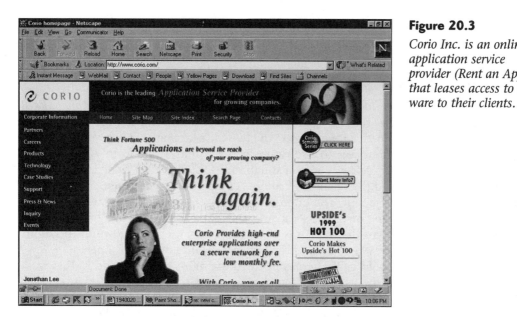

Figure 20.3

Corio Inc. is an online application service provider (Rent an App) that leases access to software to their clients.

Convergence to the Rescue

There are a couple of very bright lights on the horizon that could change this impending scenario. The first is convergence. When someone builds a piece of software, they can create it in such a way that other software manufacturers can easily share data or use the functionality of the application. This sharing and interrelating is called convergence. For example, if you build an application such as an online order-taking system and then make it compatible with some sort of standard like ODBC (open data base connectivity) or JDBC (Java Data Base Connectivity), then you will be able to use other software such as a particular database that is also compatible with the same standard. This means that purchasing a particular software should not require the purchasing of a whole host of other software from the same manufacturer just to gain the compatible functionality you require. For example, a Netscape Composer document can easily be posted to your Web site or intranet by saving it as HTML. This means that Netscape Composer is compatible with HTML, and you don't have to run out and buy a separate software package for converting the Composer document into HTML. That's convergence.

As more and more software and application companies seek their own piece of the e-commerce world, you will find more and more variety available. As long as the software is convergent around a specific standard, you will not be required to learn two different individual software programs or separate applications. You will only have to learn the one you are using and convert it to the standard. This level of convergence between software and application (either e-commerce or i-commerce) is likely to grow as the pressure from companies and individuals becomes more intense due to falling upgrade sales and lower purchases of new software.

Convergence and e-Commerce

Convergence is also vital to the new world of e-commerce. Functions such as automated supply chains will require that all operational software communicates with each other. One way for this to happen is for everyone to have the exact same software. That, however, would provide a monopoly to a software company that would further reduce competition and force up prices. The best situation is for the market to define non-proprietary standards and then allow any and all competitors to use these standards as the basis for their development. The Internet was designed on such standards and as long as no single company owns the standards, the market will grow and prosper. The minute one company owns the standards of a market, and they lock down distribution in favor of profit, growth stagnates, and the market becomes divergent. Imagine how different the Internet would be if Microsoft owned the rights to HTML and XML. One very good example that shows the difference between open and closed standards is the battle that erupted between the VHS video standard and the Beta video standard. The result, as we know, was the success of the VHS format that was open to the world of electronic manufacturing while the Beta standard was closed and proprietary.

Convergence around standards has always produced growth in the past, and it can be argued that standards are a true maker of market efficiency. The Internet luckily is one large open standard as are Linux and Java. This imbedding of a proprietary property as a standard only succeeds because the companies are able to create critical mass through free distribution. During the birth of the PC, it was Bill Gates who captured the standard for operating systems, first with wide distribution of DOS and then with a comparable agreement to distribute Windows. Microsoft's goal has always been to get more copies of its software into the hands of users, thereby creating critical mass, and now that everyone else knows the trick and has less capital invested in infrastructure, software like Linux and Java are poised to become the new standard. The key to their success will be convergence with the standards of the Internet and with each other.

Ease of Use Standards

The complexity of software is growing each day and with fundamental changes to the operating systems, it is getting more difficult for the average user to figure out the technical details of installation and troubleshooting. More and more software manufacturers are making the process of installation easier by working with hardware manufacturers and other software vendors to make easy installations the norm. This creating of "easy to install and use" systems is becoming more of a standard as customers want to spend less time doing installation and maintenance and more time operating the software. As well, working seamlessly with other systems is also becoming a requirement as customers demand compatibility.

Ease of use lowers the cost to customers in training, installation, maintenance, knowledge transfer, and the costs of making incompatible software communicate. It also allows the organization to focus resources on those tasks that are value added. The difficulty has always been that software manufacturers were always focused on the production of the application and its compatibility with Windows. Compatibility with other peripheral devices was not always considered high on the priority list. Therefore, customers usually had to answer what appeared to be a series of skill testing questions about their peripheral devices in order to successfully install the software. Installation of drivers, choice of IRQs, varying standards such as ISA & PCI made it difficult for a technical novice to interpret what was required. Even today, trying to locate drivers for the installation of a new device like a DVD player can be challenging. Some software manufacturers, especially game software builders, have added installation routines that are not only easy to use and comprehensive but also entertaining. Plug in the device, stop the Windows Plug and Play function when it starts, put the CD in the drive and select "install," and that's it. The software detects the configuration of the machine and installs itself without interaction from the user.

Ease of Use and the Internet

This concept of "ease of use" is also extending to the Internet. Manufacturers are using the standards inherent in the Internet to install plug-ins to browsers that provide the functionality necessary to use a new Web site with little or no intervention by the user except to start the process. New technologies already in use allow the user to create a "tunnel" to the Web server and run applications on the e-business Web site without extensive downloads or installations (see Figure 20.4). This process is very similar to the distributed network environments in our own offices, but will require some solutions regarding bandwidth and other Internet related issues.

Bandwidth

You can think of bandwidth as the amount of space on a road. If the road is full, you might have to wait to get on or go slowly once you are on. The question of bandwidth and the Internet relates to how much traffic the backbone or infrastructure can manage. It will get better as more bandwidth capacity is added and newer technologies make more efficient use of existing bandwidth. New functions such as streaming video or servlet architecture will take up large amounts of bandwidth, and must be addressed before we are all stuck in a big Internet traffic jam.

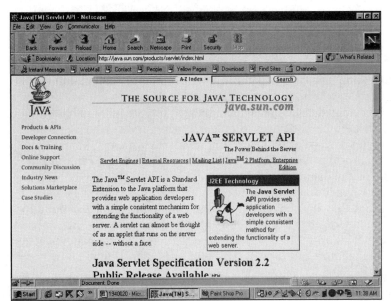

Figure 20.4

Java servlets are applications that can process information sent over the Internet in HTML forms.

As the technology becomes more and more complex, the pressure to take away some of the technical aspects related to software and hardware installation and administration is beginning to disappear. The evolution of plug and play to new USB (Universal Serial Bus) architecture and even the "easy to use" standards of the Internet are helping reduce the technological knowledge gap among individuals. But for e-commerce companies, ownership of this knowledge is still a fundamental part of being able to build a successful online business. This means that companies that intend to move with the technology must gain the depth of knowledge to understand this new world, while individuals will have an easier time as new online information sources coupled with easier to implement technologies take hold. One of the greatest benefits of going to Windows from DOS was the ease with which files could be deleted, moved, and copied all in an easy-to-understand graphic world. Of course, Apple users had known this all along.

New Knowledge Models

Knowledge of technology is becoming more and more vital in this ever increasingly complex world. The information needed to attain this high degree of knowledge is becoming easier to obtain thanks to the Internet and the dissemination of information. However, companies that currently have a resource of information about their products or services are facing increased competition from other Web sites and conversely, users are having a more difficult time in trying to locate useful information. The new knowledge model, such as the one implemented by Learnlots, takes the concept of online education for the masses to new levels. Now anyone with a computer and an Internet connection, even one at a public library, can become technologically knowledgeable in the most intricate details of a software. Content providers like the authors of this book are embracing the new distribution techniques like e-books and online tutorials to provide users around the world with access to clear and concise information. The hoarding of information is being dismantled throughout the online world thanks to these new models in much the same way that people who had access to books became well read and knowledgeable.

Technology is not the only thing you need. The hottest Java programmer in the world isn't nearly as valuable as an experienced Java programmer and database specialist combined. This is simply because knowledge is a lot like critical mass, the more you have, the more you will obtain benefits from the total volume and depth of this knowledge. Humans have long since known that a depth of knowledge or how much and how varied your education is has benefits to your life. That is why most universities force new students to take a general studies program. Concentrating all your knowledge in one specific area is not as beneficial as studying a variety of disciplines with a concentration in one area. For example, business managers who have technical expertise tend to succeed more than business managers who only have business management expertise. The well-rounded individual is usually a more valuable resource to an organization because of his or her ability to think "outside the box." A concentration of knowledge in areas such as technology is good, but employees should also be able to understand accounting, operations, politics, philosophy, math, and life. The Internet is already starting to create these individuals as more and more information becomes available in customized learning communities.

So, knowledge is a key ingredient of anything we do and e-businesses are being presented with a once-in-a-lifetime opportunity to grow their business by helping others. The key ingredient of building a community of value is providing value. A community of sales information with no discernible benefit to the surfer is not a community at all, it's a Web site. A Web site that provides a benefit to the users, like knowledge content, starts the process of creating a community of value. Unobtrusively adding sales content to the site is the way your company grows.

The Least You Need To Know

➤ What are your knowledge resources?

➤ How to manage your knowledge resources.

➤ What is causing the technology knowledge gap?

➤ How can this gap be reduced?

➤ How to distinguish new opportunities for online content.

HOW MUCH?

Customers: Leveraging Your e-Commerce Assets

In This Chapter

➤ Reducing transaction costs

➤ Increasing your supplier reach

➤ Leveraging your partnership

➤ Leveraging your systems

➤ Leveraging your traffic

Reducing Transaction Costs

You could go to the library and use an Internet connection to create a free Web page, get a couple of online partners, add a couple of links to your Web site, spread a few rumors in the newsgroups about a new Web site, and away you go. An instant e-business for free. What are your transaction costs? Zero is the correct answer unless you count the bank account you may need to cash commission checks, and there is even a way around this. For the guys manufacturing the product, the costs to the loading dock will probably not change significantly, unless they have added e-commerce functionality. However, beyond the loading dock, the manufacturer's costs associated with sales and marketing will have dropped to represent only those costs related to the Web site. This is the greatest benefit of e-commerce—the ability to lower your transaction costs to zero.

SpiffStorm

We took two 10-year-old kids without any e-commerce expertise to the library one afternoon and gave them the URLs of a free Web site, free email, and a couple of partnering sites. Then we watched as they created an e-company for selling toys and electronics on the Net. Surf to www.geocities.com/ spiffstorm/spiffstorm.html to take a peek.

Although not all companies can achieve this level of cost reduction, most companies can gain significant benefits from using pieces of the e-commerce philosophy. Automating all or part of your supply chain, creating a Web presence to reduce calls to your office, or building an online store to capture order information are just some of the things an organization can do to start reducing the costs of operations. The trick is to use the low cost of communications that is available from the Internet to lower your own transactional costs. These cost reductions can come in the form of reductions in staffing levels, or more appropriately the redirection of staff to value-added services, or the reduction in the future growth rate of staffing levels as a result of expansion. Other forms of transactional cost reductions are in the hard costs of operations, such as supplies of paper, pens, office space, computers, benefits, parking, cleaning, and phones. Using the Internet can help reduce, eliminate, or redirect all or most of the capital spent on these costs.

Using Technology To Lower Transaction Costs

The goal of reducing your transaction costs can also be achieved by using technology to implement a combination of systems that create the virtual organization that best meets your current business requirements. Leveraging off your existing assets can provide your organization with a specific advantage over your competition, but only if you are willing to change the way you view your suppliers and competitors. Remember the example of the American Airlines CEO who stated he would rather give up the planes than the Sabre reservation system. He understood the great value of being a standard in the market as opposed to the small individual pieces that operate the market. It was more beneficial to sell all the travelers their tickets than it was to actually transport them to their destinations. The business was run by an IT infrastructure that was a sunk cost with a very low operating overhead compared to running an airline. Yet the small profit generated from these information-based operations was worth far more because the cost per transaction was exceptionally low, and the volume of transactions was exceptionally high.

Of course, the Internet has changed the dynamics of the online ticketing world, and many larger organizations have created online travel agencies (see Figure 21.1). Now customers and travel suppliers can connect directly together over the Internet without having to pay fees in the middle. And to rub salt in the AMR wounds (and their Travelocity Web site), Microsoft's Expedia is one of the faster growing travel sites.

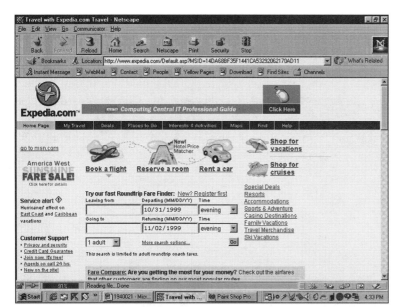

Figure 21.1

Microsoft's Expedia Travel Web page offers visitors the ability to book holidays online.

Lowering Your Marketing and Sales Expenses

The true underlying rule still remains—faster, wider, and cheaper electronic communications systems lead to a significant reduction in transaction costs. Obviously, one of the biggest reductions comes in the form of lower marketing and sales expense. The old traditional operating infrastructures required a significant amount of resources to grow organizations to a global scale. Just to reach the world's population with sales and distribution channels was such an incredibly large task that even organizations such as General Motors or MacDonalds needed the investment of others in a franchise distribution network designed to create critical mass. The car manufacturers even took this principle back down the supply chain by contracting parts and inputs to companies like Magna International. It's almost to the point where anyone can build a car simply by ordering all the parts and having them placed together at the automobile assembly company of his choice. But that would require an excellent communications model where the masses could easily produce their own cars online and communicate these wishes to the automobile company. That'll never happen, right? (See Figure 21.2.) It would give a whole new meaning to the phrase "pick-a-part."

Now let's say that you could order a car over the Internet and then have it delivered to your door. No salesmen, no pre-dealer inspection, just shipping charges. Naturally, you will still pay the same for the car as you do now, but without all the hassles, haggling, and you can do comparative shopping. How much would that add to the profit of the car company, especially if they had outsourced the assembly process back to Magna? The answer is the profitability of these companies would grow considerably.

311

The other option would be for Magna to bypass the car companies altogether and build finished cars for anyone who walked through the front door of the Web site. Of course, they would have to establish a favorable brand image, which is a very difficult task.

Figure 21.2

The Magna "Parts Included" Web page offers visitors the chance to see which parts of their car are manufactured by Magna.

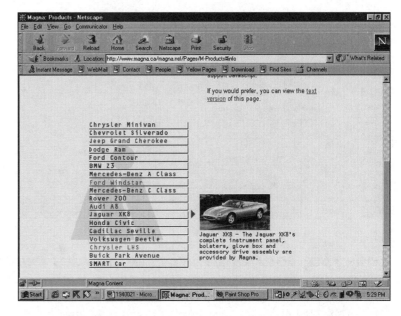

Figure 21.3

Autoweb.com *is one of a number of Web sites that offer car buyers information about new cars.*

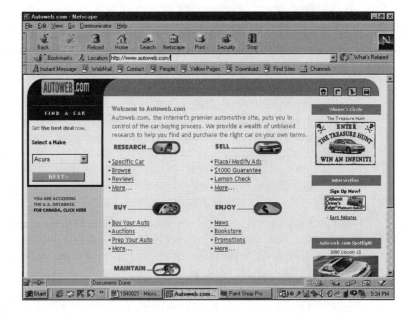

Competition and the Internet

The price of raw materials and the expense of turning the raw material into a finished product used to be so expensive that only companies with deep pockets could compete against each other. Companies that could lock up the distribution channels or overpower the tastes of the market with extensive promotion of their own brands further tightened their grip on an exclusive marketplace. In the future, this scenario may still be evident, and there are currently threats of just this sort of thing happening to the Internet as large companies seek to control the entry costs of new e-businesses. For now, however, anyone can start a Web company for almost no money (and in some cases no money at all) and start the process of building brand awareness for his brand of product.

At this point in the history of technology, there will never be a better time to open an i-business or capture all the advantages of e-commerce and still be able to effectively compete with the biggest companies in the world. If you don't think that Microsoft, currently the world's most successful technology corporation, isn't just a little worried about the idea of having every techno geek think that they are the next Linus Torvalds (the creator of Linux), then think again. They are seriously concerned that the knowledge contained in books like this will filter out to the common man and if just a handful of those people make it to the top like Jeff Bezos and Amazon or Linus Torvalds and Linux, the competition would be unbearable for Microsoft. If you don't believe us, then go to your local high-tech development shop and ask them if they had to choose between Microsoft C++ and Java, which would they choose? Our small, unsophisticated survey showed unanimous votes for Java. Of course, that could change when your killer app hits the e-commerce world, and trust us, there is a lot of room for improvement in the current product spit out by the big guys. However, when you do go to the Net, remember that the sophistication of some of the hot new software on the drawing boards of the new techno generation is undeniably awesome. They all seem to be "gunnin'" for Bill.

Control of the Internet

The one thing that could change all this is if one or a handful of the big corporations managed to wrestle control of the Internet away from the multitude of companies it currently needs to make it a success. Microsoft could continue to grow if it gains the upper hand in content so that access to the Internet is essentially regulated. The main controlling weak point today is the search engines. It used to be that anyone could submit a URL and have her Web site show up on the Web. Now many search engines charge a fee that is certain to rise and most of the ISPs present these "pay per view" search sites to get a click-through micropayment. Try to submit your own URL to your favorite search engine to see if it charges a fee or not.

The downside of charging fees is that you will automatically exclude Web sites that are not willing to pay a fee. This means that if you are searching for information on technology, you may not get all the Web sites that are available, but just the ones that paid a display fee. We all know that the problem with that type of model is that it will *not* guarantee the best information, and in some cases will lead to substantially poorer information than if the search had included all sites. The greatest benefit of the Internet was that it provided a way for everyone to communicate and share their best information. The downside of this was that there is a lot of really lousy information to share.

Saving Users Precious Time

So what does all this mean? What it means is that there is a growing opportunity to narrow down the search for good information while still allowing for the free exchange of all information. The goal is to turn back the tide that is costing users their leisure time by providing quality information while still keeping the opportunity for a free information market. If you can succeed in providing this to your community, you may succeed in beating the big guys at their own game. Of course, managing information can be a costly venture if you are trying to run your own search engine and superlinking site.

A better solution is to partner with existing organizations that can provide you with quality information or online services like `Learnlots.com`, `Ivillage.com`, `parentsplace.com`, `autoweb.com`, etc. By giving customers exactly what they want, the best product available, or the greatest variety, you will beat the big guys who only offer the content from those providers willing to pay. In other words, provide a section for edited, top-quality information and a section of open and free information, and you will succeed in creating a sticky site.

Can you supply all the information yourself? Probably not, and why would you want to duplicate all the other knowledge sites that are out there when you can access most of them for free? Of course, `Ivillage.com` is a network for women so accessing it may cause you to lose traffic in your female demographic if they feel they belong in the Ivillage.com community more than they belong to your community. In general, the rule is that the more partners you have, the better your offering will be to your own community, and the more they will stay with your site and not stray elsewhere.

Sticky

If your site is sticky, your customers not only come back, but they also stick around. That means that they will look at other pages on your Web site or use your site to access other Web sites. Your i-commerce goal is a sticky site.

e-Commerce Partnering 101: Supplier Reach

Any business starts life with capital and invests in procuring the supplies it needs to produce a product or service. For example, a mining company purchases or leases the land that has the ore underneath it and then buys everything from mining equipment to pencils for the office. Eventually, hundreds or even thousands of suppliers can supply these inputs. A football team invests money in joining a league and hiring the talent of the players and coaches as inputs, as well as pencils for the office. An e-commerce company also has to invest in technology to build a Web presence, but a Web presence may be all that is required. No pencils are needed.

How do you successfully build a business without inputs? You build it solely as an outlet for the supplier of the only input you need—content. At any point in time, you can start to move backward through the supply chain to provide content or even go so far as to manufacture the products that are sold on your site. This is one of the great equalizers of the Internet—anyone can join the i-business world at any point along the supply chain, from suppliers of base inputs to creators of an online community. The key to the entire process is partnering.

Evaluating Partners

We have extensively discussed the importance of partnering for the i-business and even how to go about partnering. We haven't yet discussed how to evaluate your potential partners or what the partners gain from a relationship with you. Your e-partners may not be as critical as they are in a traditional business environment. For example, if you manufacture a product and you have one shipper who handles your unusual products and for some reason this supplier cannot get your product to market, your business will suffer financially. If the same thing occurs on the Internet, you will simply change online shipping companies. As long as there are ample suppliers of the product that you carry, you should have a relatively low risk from suppliers who are defaulting, thanks to the ever-increasing reach of your supply lines.

The Internet also allows both manufacturers and online suppliers to extend their own supply lines globally with very little effort. A plant in China that manufacturers a component for your product can now sell directly to you through its own Web site and ship using an international courier. The importers and distributors would be wiped from the equation, given that the details of the logistics, such as customs clearance, will likely be managed by an online customs brokerage (see Figure 21.4). This allows for a truly global supply reach for manufacturers or retailers who want to offer more variety to their online community or reduced costs.

Figure 21.4

Online custom brokerages provide assistance to vendors and buyers trying to import foreign produced goods.

Embassy World

You can contact various embassies online to get more information about products manufactured in different countries at http://www.embassyworld.com or for North America try http://directory.hotbot.com/Business/Industries/Manufacturing/.

Supply Reach for Gathering Content

The concept of "supply reach" also holds true for information or knowledge. The ability to gather content supply from anywhere in the world is extremely evident, thanks once again to the global reach of the Internet. Writers, authors, companies, communities, or anyone can supply content on the Internet. E-commerce businesses can obtain the content for minimal up-front payments in exchange for royalties back to the authors. As long as the content is linked or can be supplied online, the reach of the supply line for the business can be global.

Learnlots.com

`Learnlots.com` has implemented this concept for gathering its tutorial content by providing authors with the opportunity to participate in revenues that the site generates through commissions. This way, anyone in the world can contribute to `Learnlots.com`, making the company's supply reach truly global.

Choosing a Content Supplier

When choosing a supply partner, as opposed to a traffic or distribution partner, you should look for a couple of specific things. You should partner with organizations that have a clear concept of what they do and what they want to be. Vague linking sites and questionable product offerings mean that your potential partner might not understand i-commerce well enough to survive. They should also be professional. This does not mean that they are in class "A" office space on the good side of town and wear suits. They can be two kids in their basement as long as they have the drive and desire to see the project through to the end. They should at least be aware of the concept of doing business on the Internet and have a clear plan as to how they are going to provide you with content.

The content that your supplier will provide should be professional and of the highest quality. We are not talking Shakespeare. The information does, however, have to be clear, concise, and well written for the target audience. If it is written above or below the level of the audience, they will either lose interest or lose trust in the information. You should also get the intuition that your partner organization is actually going to stay in business. However, don't get too hung up on this because there are lots of content providers on the Net.

e-Commerce Partnering 201: Affiliate Partnerships

Affiliate partnerships are those where both companies gain an advantage by partnering together. These types of partnerships can provide a range of benefits to both parties. Affiliate partnerships tend to be stronger because it is in the best interests of both partners to work for the common good including, but not limited to, survival. Let's face it, way back during the beginning of human existence our ability to partner with each other was the basis of our survival. Communities could more efficiently gather and produce the food that was required to live, and they could combine together in times of crises to defeat enemies or save the village from disaster. The same holds true for the Internet—the combining of groups into affiliated partnerships adds mass and bulk to the participating organizations, making them far less vulnerable to large corporate predators, although not entirely immune. We still operate independently within our own operations, but collectively as a whole, affiliates benefit each other.

Communication among Affiliates

We discussed the importance of affiliates and the way to go about contacting affiliates in prior chapters. The communication between your affiliated partners and your business must be clear and concise. You must spell out responsibilities of both parties and the deliverables. For example, if your site depends on their content, then they should be willing to ensure that your community will have access 24 × 7 (24 hours a day, 7 days a week), and they should clearly stipulate their fail-over and disaster recovery capabilities. They should clearly indicate what, if any, payments will be made, the method of paying those amounts, and a schedule of payments. Finally, they should indicate how payments are to be tracked and verified. If it is a mutual exchange of traffic, they should stipulate what is to happen if the balance of "traffic generation" shifts too much to one partner. Whether you use lawyers to draft the document, use standard partnering agreements, or just trust the company is purely your decision. However, legitimate companies will understand the necessity of fair agreements and will satisfy your requests. Remember that if the benefits are marginal, then agreements may not be necessary because there is little to protect.

Fail-over

Fail-over is what happens when a network or server fails to operate. The server or network connection will immediately correct itself or use an alternate delivery mechanism such as a secondary backup server or alternate pipe. You cannot control the fail-over of the Internet backbone you are connected to, but your ISP and your affiliates should be able to tell you specifically what fail-over systems are in place to protect your affiliated business partners.

Managing Affiliate Relationships

Your affiliate relationships are important, and they should be protected and managed. Usually, specific individuals are assigned the task of establishing partnerships. They spend a great deal of time phoning and traveling to partnering companies to obtain specific information regarding the partnership, including negotiating agreements and establishing milestones and deliverables. They maintain contact with the partners ensuring that deliverables and milestones are attained. They monitor such things as performance, payments, and traffic measurement. They also manage cooperative promotional programs that divide the cost of advertising, promotion, or public relations. A healthy relationship with your partners not only helps both businesses function more effectively, but it also helps both businesses grow.

The greatest benefit of partnering is that you can build a virtual corporation for very little capital expenditure. This is essentially leveraging your assets and your ideas by utilizing partnerships to get those pieces of your organization that you require. Traditional businesses use leverage by raising capital to purchase assets and then use those assets as collateral to raise more funds. For example, if you raise capital to lease a retail location and purchase an inventory, you can then pledge the inventory as collateral to raise funding for operations and advertising. In the virtual corporation, you raise capital to build a killer app and use it to generate traffic. The traffic may be the result of partnering, or it may be passed on for revenue generation by click-throughs or commissions. The revenue and partnerships can then be leveraged to raise capital that can be turned into advertising and promotion to further increase traffic levels.

Amazon.com

Amazon started with a shopping Web site to sell books. They used this application to pay commissions for sales generated by click-through traffic. With this model, they were able to attract thousands of Web sites to become partners by placing a link to the Amazon Web page on their Web site. The result was a significant jump in traffic to Amazon. They were then able to extrapolate or forecast traffic growth rates for the Web site. These potential growth rates attracted the attention of the investment world for the IPO. The result was significant funding for investment in systems and promotion or an $11 billion leverage against a simple Web site.

Leveraging Your Systems

Internal systems can also be leveraged. If your systems are incompatible or need to be upgraded, then the investment required to do this may be significant. Raising funds to replace systems can often provide a return in reduced costs. However, in general, the return will be relatively low compared to investment opportunities available for value-added areas such as promotion. A system that costs thousands of dollars can often be outsourced to a partner, but the operational costs and risks in these arrangements will be higher than if you had purchased the system. The advantage, however, is that the capital can be used to grow your business either traditionally or online. In the 80s and 90s, established retail organizations like Safeway Stores used a similar concept when they sold a significant number of the stores they owned, and used the funds to expand and upgrade the existing facilities. The result was an increase in traffic to the stores and an increase in sales volumes.

Leveraging Your Traffic

Leveraging is the act of pledging something of value to gain more value through investment of the proceeds. We are pretty generic in this definition because leveraging does not have to apply only to money. You can also leverage things like traffic. Pledging traffic essentially means that you agree to send your traffic to a specific site in exchange for something you can invest or an actual investment itself. Something to invest is more traffic or actual funding.

An investment itself can be the use of an application or use of advertising or promotion. In the Learnlots.com examples, sending traffic to the Learnlots.com site will provide both a return in the form of commissions and click-through and the use of the content contained in their application. This content can then be leveraged to attract more visitors to your Web site. More visitors will generate more revenue, and higher revenue and traffic can be used to raise capital for investment in advertising and promotion. It's like a snowball rolling down a hill—it will gather more snow, and as it does, it will grow in size.

The Least You Need To Know

➤ How to reduce your transactions costs.

➤ How to gain supplier reach.

➤ How to leverage your affiliate partnerships.

➤ How to leverage your systems.

➤ How to leverage your traffic.

Chapter 22

Land Mines Lurking on the Net

In This Chapter

➤ Diminishing hits

➤ Lawyers alive and well on the Net

➤ Overvaluation of Internet stocks

➤ Commercialism

➤ Privatization

➤ Divergent standards

Diminishing Hits

There are a lot of people who have never had Internet access and with the price of PCs and the cost of connecting to the Internet falling, there will be high growth rates in the total volume of Internet traffic in the coming years. Over the next few years, there will be increases in the numbers of people who make purchases over the Internet. However, there will also be millions of new places for them to go. Let's say the Internet was composed of one million users and one Web site. If the entire online population surfed, you could expect most, or all of them, to belong to the community of that one single site. If a second site was opened, then the number of people who would "belong" to your community could be expected to fall by 50 percent, assuming

Revisits

4 out of 5 users never revisit the average Web site. (1999)

Nvision & Engage Technologies

TV and the Internet

Less than 2% of those with Internet access trade time watching TV for usage of the Internet. (1999)

Burke Information, MTV, and Turner Broadcasting

that the two Web sites offered essentially the same value. Some experts estimate the current ratio to be approximately 10 users for every Web site. Of course, the vast majority of Web sites get very few hits, and a small handful of Web sites take the lion's share of visitors. As well, visitors tend to visit many different sites.

The Thrill Is Going

The problem, as we noted in previous chapters, is that users will tire of the thrill of the Internet and usage will eventually taper off as the Internet moves from a technological tool to a utility. How many of us actually pick up a phone and use it just because it's a phone? We use it because we have to talk to someone at a distance. If the Internet was to generate the same level of intense interest, like just after you buy a new car, then the level of usage would be starting to have a significant impact on the level of time spent on entertainment such as the TV.

However, anyone who has surfed the Internet for leisure has noticed how the hours of usage are declining at home, although the hours of usage at work may be increasing. This trend will continue as good information becomes even more difficult to locate, and the average user loses interest. The result will be that the Internet will become a utility of sorts for users to gather knowledge on specific technologies, read their e-mail, get updates on their real-time news delivery sites, or purchase a product at one of a handful of shopping sites. The total volume of users will continue to increase as access is granted to more people throughout the world. The thing that will stop this trend toward decreasing repeat usage and present a number of opportunities is the creation of communities of value that save the average user time in their already hectic lives.

Making Sticky Sites

The key e-commerce question is how do you make seasoned Internet users visit your site continually, given this information? The answer is that you make a conscientious decision to act like a utility. That means your users will generally return to your site to make their surf quick and efficient. There are other things that users value in a utility, such as the convenience of use and reliability of service. These same principles should be the underlying foundation of your own online Web presence. Providing a reliable source of knowledge, an application, or a community will start the process of having regular users return to your site. People will tend to take the easiest and most certain route since it is an inherent thing in human nature to make things easy. That's why TV is so popular. It has to be one of the easiest forms of entertainment— point and click. Before the Internet will seriously start to dent TV viewership, it will have to capture the ease of use that TV now enjoys or provide significantly more value (see Figure 22.1).

Figure 22.1

Web TV is one way that the Internet is trying to compete with TV for viewership.

If you were to take a quick poll of your Internet using friends you would probably find that the number one use of the Internet, for hit generation (for example, what causes you to surf to a new site), is probably information gathering. The searches would be performed because Aunt Ethel has a pain in her side and needs information, or your goldfish has turned blue and you are uncertain why, or you don't trust the $18,000 worth of work your dentist wants to do on your teeth and that your mechanic wants to do to your car. The second biggest use will probably be entertainment, such as games or music or reading news. Then you might find shopping or downloading software in third place.

Repetitive Value

e-commerce is not about building a great app and then watching users beat a traffic path to your Web site. It's all about trying to get customers to consider your site as something of value that they should return to again and again. This means that your Web site must provide "repetitive value." Without repetitive value, your customers will not return, and you will be forever spending money and resources on promotion and advertising to get new customers to visit your site. It's far more efficient to build repetitive value and promote less and less as your critical mass continues to grow. However, since more and more Web sites will be gunning for your customers, you will have to continue to work at keeping your customers loyal. Now loyalty building becomes a part of the mix. You could start by offering rewards for click-through or sales (see Figure 22.2).

Figure 22.2

Internet reward programs help keep visitors coming back to a Web site.

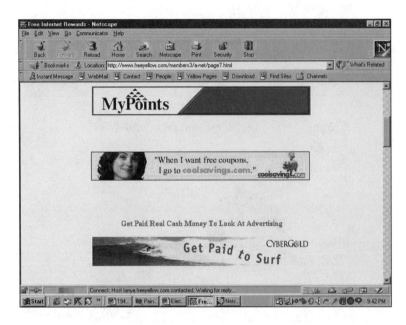

Lawyers—Alive and Well on the Net

Internet Law

There are a number of great resources for Internet law on the Net. The Web site http://www. lawguru.com/ilawlib/ is just one of them.

Affiliate partnerships, links, click-through payments, commissions, content agreements, trademarking, cybersquatting, and intellectual property. You can almost hear the battle cry from the hoards of lawyers making "Internet law" their specialty. Many law firms currently have individuals dedicated to studying the Internet and its legal ramifications. There are, in fact, a wide variety of online law resources and online law firms dedicated to Internet law.

The Growth of Internet Law

The Internet is drawing lawyers like moths to a flame, and it is becoming increasingly difficult for commerce to occur on the Net without a lawyer lurking somewhere nearby. Part of this is a simple function of protecting the rights and responsibilities of e-commerce organizations and their customers. The other part is pure opportunistic malice. The Internet has been called the equivalent of the business "wild west." All the traditional rules have been set aside in favor of a flexible and rapidly changing environment, and lawyers have had some difficulty adapting to this constantly changing target. More than one major technical partnership has been scuttled by delays in the agreement phase of the partnering program.

Lawyers have learned to adapt to this world of "easy to understand" short agreements and semi-handshake partnering deals by drawing up agreements that avoid extensive legalese and by fast tracking on-the-fly business partnerships. They have done this unwillingly because they understand the risks and consequences of taking short cuts in documentation. e-commerce businesses and in particular i-businesses have forced the issue with a blistering pace of development and stratospheric growth rates. The ability of traditional law firms to keep pace was just not there. However, organizations that require partnerships are now drafting fast, simple agreements that provide the opportunity to close partnering deals quickly, or they are using standard agreements that are provided by one of the partners (see Figure 22.3).

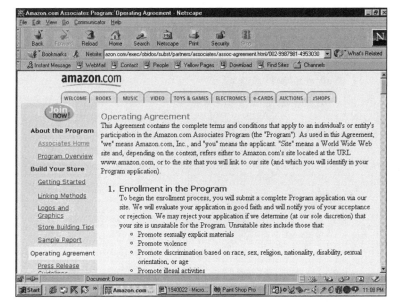

Figure 22.3

The Amazon Associates Agreement is a standard form online legal document used by all "Associates."

The Rise of the e-Lawyer

There is a vast amount of legal territory to cover for the average law firm trying to get a handle on the Internet. Content providers are seeking protection for their copyrights so that their work cannot be freely distributed on the Internet. This includes authors, musicians, artists, and the big content providers like Time Warner or Disney.

Another task of Internet law is the protection of partners to ensure they receive click-through and commission payments and more importantly to define what constitutes a payable transaction and how these transactions are measured. The principle here is to protect the smaller sites and individuals to ensure they are paid for their traffic.

Problems related to site content are also becoming an issue, not just for copyright infringement but also for illegal use of trademarks in domains. This also ties in with the act of cybersquatting or stealing customers from legitimate sites by trying to mimic those sites. Obviously, if you set up an Amazon duplicate, there are grounds for legal action. But what if you own the domain to a traditional company like www.jcrew.com (online clothing retailer) and are using it to direct URL calls to your own site www.buymyclothes.com? Is that considered cybersquatting?

There are also a wide variety of other legal issues on the Internet that are drawing the interest of lawyers and lawmakers. The distribution of pornography and hate litera-ture, the always-sensitive area of defamation, and the growing work in fraud and hacking. It has created so many new areas of law that combining it into one area called Internet law or e-commerce law is definitely a step in the right direction. This will allow lawyers to focus on some of the unique aspects of the Internet and how to manage the legal aspects while still freeing clients to move quickly with new develop-ments and partnerships. The question is whether the law profession can itself change to meet the challenges of e-commerce without being driven to it by their clients.

The Legal Impact on e-Commerce

The whole issue of e-commerce and i-commerce and the legal questions surrounding it are going to be one of the most significant hurdles to the growth of commerce on the Net. If simple partnering arrangements turn into long formal legal agreements, the creation of barriers to business will have started on the Internet. Hiring a lawyer at $300 per hour is a significant disadvantage for smaller businesses trying to formal-ize a partnering agreement, and it is especially hard on low or no resource virtual cor-porations.

Creating barriers to the free flow of small business commerce is one of the best ways to take control of the Internet. We need to lobby Congress to have laws passed that regulate the Internet through the use of formal registration processes, set up rigorous certification programs, force a strict adherence to set of standards or attempt to other-wise control the free flow of ideas, partnerships, and innovation. Obviously, there are limits as to what a democratic society can or should allow and luckily that's up to the politicians and not the authors of this book.

The problem is that if I am a small e-business that wants to offer an application that could terminate the existence of a large technology company, should they have any right to stop me? For the Internet to flow smoothly, the answer should be "no," but the legal landmine lurking in the distance is that the large company can now legally strangle my ability to partner through the use of exclusionary practices. There are a variety of these exclusionary practices starting to occur on the Internet, such as charging fees for search engine placement or locked-in distribution of software with new computers. As more of these exclusionary tactics occur, you will start to see more private actions arise that will provide e-law firms with a significant amount of work long into the next millennium.

Overvaluation of Internet Stocks

There's nothing quite like an overheated stock market. In the good old days of stock trading, the market lost big in an October 1987 losing more than 20% of its value. It fell in spite of the fact that assets of the vast majority of the largest companies were hard assets or asset that had a marketable value, such as trucks or equipment. Imagine what would have happened if those companies didn't have hard assets?

The problem with the stock market today is that stocks are trading on historically unheard of price earnings ratios. There is no single individual who can clearly explain whether these inflated values are justifiable or not simply because no one has ever lived during such a period of technological change. Is technology powering the growth of our economies to new heights, or is the hype just hype? Is the stock market a huge bubble waiting to burst, or has it only just begun to grow given the potential of today's global economy? There are so many dynamics at play, such as the globalization of the American economy, the rapid advances in technology at the end of the 90s, and the low-cost instantaneous worldwide communications capability of the Internet. With all these variables, it is little wonder that the pros on Wall Street haven't a clue where the existing market is going over the next two years.

They do, however, have a clear view of where solid i-commerce IPOs are going. The direction is up, as in through the roof, the clouds, and into space. Are the IPO values justified? We can look at some simple statistics to do the math. If you sell a book and make 30 cents gross margin, then selling 2 million books will net $600,000 in gross margin before operating expenses. If you have to pay for the retail overhead required to sell 2 million books or approximately 50 stores, you would have approximately $12,000 per location or $1,000.00 per month for rent, utilities, overhead, etc. You can see that at 30 cents gross margin, it's going to be pretty tough to make a living. Now, let's say you raised $30 million and built a state-of-the-art online e-business and warehouse. Your current attainable market is now 100 million people. At 30 cents a book profit, how many customers do you need to provide a return to the guys who invested the $30 million?

Two percent of the market returns 2% and 10% returns 10% before operating expenses for warehouse and office space. Increasing the mark-up per book to net 60 cents drives the return from 10% to 20%. The average retail markup on books is significantly higher that 60 cents.

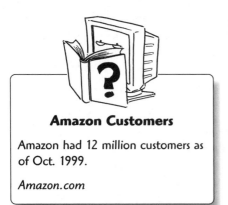

Potential Growth and Profit

Let's say that Amazon never got another customer and each of its existing customers purchased one book next year with an average markup per book of $1.00. The gross margin on the sales of these books would be $12,000,000. Assuming an investment in systems of $40 million, the return is 30%. Now factor in the growth in new online areas such as electronics and auctions, or the growth of the sales base given the lack of comparable competitors. What you will quickly realize is that the potential profitability of this concept is phenomenal, regardless of whether there are enough hard assets to protect your investment. Also, let's not forget about some of our e-commerce principles, such as critical mass, first to market, or the killer app rules. All of this makes a company like Amazon.com an extremely valuable property for investors.

Amazon Customers

Amazon had 12 million customers as of Oct. 1999.

Amazon.com

Can the Market Keep the Value Up?

Although there is some merit to the high value of on-Net organizations, the next big question has to be can the market sustain these values? The answer is it's anybody's guess. However, the impact of a sell-off of Internet stocks would have significant implications for e-businesses that were positioned incorrectly. Since most of these organizations do not have any substantial hard assets to support their valuation, anything that might slow the growth of the Internet, such as a recession, would seriously affect these inflated valuations. Already some companies are having trouble successfully executing an IPO to "spin off" new Internet offerings backed by traditional businesses. In this case, a traditional retailer who decides to enter the i-commerce field might find the competition daunting and numerous. If the company is considered by the market to be lacking the sophistication necessary to compete in the new online world, it will have difficulty raising the capital it needs through an IPO.

Raging Bull

You can get information on IPOs at www.ragingbull.com and follow the IPO Center link.

Providing Real Value

Although the future potential of the Internet probably more than justifies the stratospheric prices of online companies, a hiccup in these valuations could make it difficult for your organization to raise capital. So there are two pieces of advice. Hurry and try to provide real value. Providing real value is giving the investor a reason to hold or want your stock. It won't protect you if the market decides to tank, but it will cushion the fall. When you do go to market, providing real value should help to ensure the success of your offering, although this is not always the case. IPO investors can be finicky and sometime a company with little in the way of value but with a great story will capture the hearts of the investment community ahead of one that provides real value.

Providing value, however, is a long-term growth model. It can be done by owning proprietary technology that gives your Web site something unique, or it can be through an investment in infrastructure such as a distribution chain. Real value can also be provided through the ownership of the content of your site (but not hoarding). This value can be intellectual or entertainment property, and an application or an online service that is difficult or impossible to duplicate. Real value can also be the strength of the online community that you create.

Hurry, don't wait and don't dawdle. If you try to go to the market to raise capital past January 2000, you will be playing blind. Let's face facts, recessions happen, and no one can predict when they will occur or how deep they will be. In fact, we may be only at the very start of the longest period of economic growth ever. Or maybe we are at the end. The best thing you can do is go to market before anything causes Internet funding to falter. You don't have to shoot for the tripling of your stock, just try to raise the funds you will need to grow your business over the next few years. Your aim should be slow steady growth if your goal is longevity but if your goal is short term gain, then give it all you got, hype it to the roof, cross your fingers and hope that it holds until you get out. Of course, companies with a short game plan often fall short in the IPO world and wind up pulling the offering at a high cost.

Commercialism

The Internet is full of advertising. It's so full of advertising that finding useful information is becoming more like finding a needle in a haystack. Of course, the great value of the Internet to businesses isn't information provision, it's sales. In the old ancient days of text-based "freenets," there was almost no information about companies unless it pertained to some sort of technical product. Now the Internet is awash in promotions and advertising. Banner ads, Web sites dedicated to sales, contests, come-ons, and hoaxes are all aimed at trying to wrestle away sales from traditional retailers near your home. The rush of e-businesses is going to be immense in the coming years as the concepts contained in this and other e-commerce books start to filter into the offices and boardrooms of the millions of businesses that have not started the migration to the Net.

This mass commercialization of the Internet is going to once again change everything. As each new business sets out a virtual shingle, the volume of clutter will grow on the Internet. Let's say you hopped in your car and went over to the local power center to purchase some electronics but instead of seeing one or two electronics stores, you were faced with 3,000. Which one would you go to? They will all claim to have the lowest price, and they will all claim to offer the best service. Some will

The Shakeout

A shakeout is where a large group of companies all trying to compete for business in the same market eventually start to fail. They fail because the customers will cluster around a few companies with the right image or product offering. These firms will use the windfall of proceeds to buy up smaller firms in the market or promote and compete hard against the existing companies. Eventually, only one or two remaining companies will exist in the market.

provide information and help on how to use the products, some will let you try the product first, and some will provide financing or someone to install it. But 3,000 choices—who has the time? You will likely choose one or two retailers that you feel most comfortable with or that were recommended and forget the others. If enough people do this, then you will see something called a shakeout.

How To Survive a Shakeout

There is no real solution to a shakeout because it's almost like a "catch-22." If you don't grow fast enough or take on more risk, you will eventually be taken out of the market by those organizations that grow substantially, thanks to the dynamics of the shakeout. However, your best protection in a shakeout is to not overextend your organization by taking on the added risk of large expansion, unless of course you are headed for the top. There are a number of survival options available such as "niching" a market or guerrilla organizations.

The massive growth in the volume of commercial Web sites that is looming is certain to create an environment for a shakeout, as some online companies that are competing in an ever increasingly crowded market find partnering doors closed and promotion expensive. Some other pitfalls might also include declining surfing habits of users, as valuable information becomes more difficult to locate. Another landmine could be a corporation the size of Microsoft obtaining a technology or standard that provides them with control of the market. For example, the amalgamation of Sun and Microsoft would position a super organization to control many of the standards that are the basis for the Internet. A concentration of ownership of the key software and Web sites that control the Internet would create a significant threat and add potential barriers to entry. However, legislation, the speed of technological change, and some of the new applications and business models currently under construction promise to fundamentally change the structure of e-commerce, significantly mitigating this type of threat.

Privatization

Imagine if you had billions of dollars, and you were able to privatize the Net. Not likely to happen, you say? How about if we tell you that to exercise control on the Internet you don't have to own control of everything, just some of the key pieces. In fact, most of the key pieces that make the Internet work are already owned by a handful of companies. Luckily, it is in their best interests and in the best interest of their shareholders to capitalize on their ownership as soon as possible. Very few investors are farsighted enough to sacrifice today's gains for long-term control. If a maniacal CEO wanted to control the Internet, he would always be up against a boardroom that wanted immediate and maximum returns today.

The privatization of the Internet is a real concern for the e-business of tomorrow simply because privatization can close access or make it costly to operate. Search engines that charge for listings, presentation of controlled information, high fees for the use of critical applications or standards, and charges for access to information are all land mines on the Internet that can increase the barriers to entry or limit a new companies ability to access the market (see Figure 22.4).

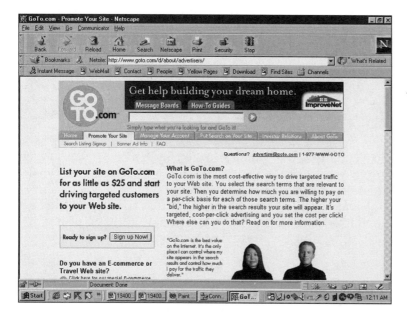

Figure 22.4

`Goto.com` *URL listing fee is an example of the move away from free listings to pay listings.*

As companies become more sophisticated about the Internet, some will attempt to capitalize on their position in the market. Sun may distribute Java for free to the Internet community for now, but eventually some sort of corresponding return will be required (see Figure 22.5). It will likely come in the form of compatible products such as Web server software, publications and training, or other products. However, there is nothing to stop Sun from charging a fee for future releases of Java, although they would probably do this at their own future peril. The good news about privatization at this point is that most of the large companies are not only driven by their shareholders to perform in the near term, but they are also deathly afraid of the next whiz kid and his annoying little system. Imagine the person who creates the ability for all households and businesses to communicate without an ISP, telephone company, or operating software.

Figure 22.5

This Sun Java Web Server advertisement is one way that Sun is trying to capitalize on the free distribution of the Java language.

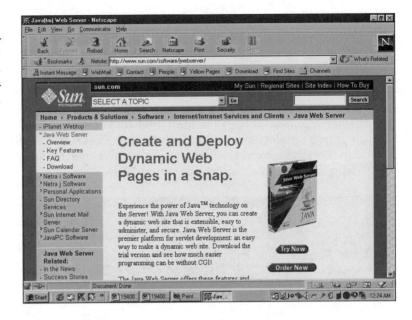

The best protection available to the new e-commerce company is to avoid dependence on a single supplier of technology. You can always run one technology as your main "in-house" standard, but experiment and be ready with other technologies or do what Microsoft is doing and diversify your investment so that you are a partner in the new technology of tomorrow. Also ensure that you partner with those cutting edge corporations that may be creating the next standard for the industry, such as Linux.

Divergent Standards

Nothing would do more harm than a movement away from standards and toward divergence. However, this scenario is not impossible. Software companies that become the standard may abandon other industry standards or attempt to scuttle emerging standards. The goal is that by creating divergence in the market, no clear standard will emerge. This was the concern that Sun raised when Microsoft attempted to alter its release of the Java software. If Microsoft had been successful, then the Internet would have had to deal with two versions of Java that might not have been compatible.

A more likely scenario is the divergence of standards for proprietary gain. Some companies believe that if they produce a product that has wide acceptance, then the standard should be what they dictate. For example, there are currently two main browsers, Netscape and Explorer. Netscape used to command the vast majority of the browser market and has since fallen behind Explorer, thanks to the free distribution of Explorer with new computers. The two technologies use the current standards of the Internet so they both operate effectively and efficiently. However, if a gaming company wants to create some sort of new browser plug-in, it may have to work with two different standards. As well, if one browser becomes the single standard of the Net, it may have the clout to change the underlying standards of the Internet or force companies to meet whatever standard it builds into its product. This could result in the gaming company having to pay a fee for the privilege of interfacing with the dominant browser.

There is very little an e-commerce company can do to avoid this scenario, but there are a couple of bright spots. The first is that technology is rapidly changing so that standards of today may eventually be completely wiped out by the developments of tomorrow. Secondly, the young techno generation is very keen to ensure their place in the future of tomorrow. The Internet was not given its massive push from obscurity by the established corporations; it was pushed by a small subculture of people who built bulletin board systems and eventually grew into the local ISP of today. The attitude that led to the creation of Linux is the same attitude that will likely keep a limit on the privatization of the Internet.

So there are a lot of risks and landmines out there, and there are a lot of options and opportunities. Where you position your e-commerce organization is critical to its future survival. Knowing which options to select or which paths to follow is the $11 billion question. Keeping in tune with the world of technology whether by hiring techno savvy staff or learning it yourself is a critical component of divining the future direction of the business world. Avoiding the above landmines or the ones that are certain to crop up will be a regular task of managing and building an e-commerce organization and also critical to its long-term survival.

The Least You Need To Know

➤ How to manage diminishing hits.

➤ What the impact of lawyers on the Net will be.

➤ How market overvaluation can impact your IPO.

➤ What are some commercialism problems and opportunities.

➤ How to avoid the privatization land mine.

➤ What divergent standards mean to your e-business.

Part 5

Pulling It All Together

It doesn't do you any good to just get bits and pieces of sporadic information, so in this section we will bring it all together in the definitive e-commerce model. We'll cover what you have to do from start to finish to build an e-commerce empire.

This model is applicable to small and large businesses, as well as traditional businesses that are going to update their traditional operations for the new era of technology.

Pulling it all together completes the process of moving you from an e-commerce idiot to an e-commerce professional. At the end of this section, you will know more about e-commerce than most e-commerce experts. But that can be our little secret.

HERE WE GO!!

The Definitive e-Commerce Model

In This Chapter

➤ Know where you are

➤ Know where you are going

➤ Building your app

➤ Partnering

➤ Building a community

➤ How virtual is your corp?

➤ Funding your company

➤ Going on road shows

➤ Managing growth and change

Knowing Where You Are Is Important

In order to implement any business model, you first have to understand and appreciate where you are. Imagine trying to travel somewhere, but you're lost. How would you know which way to go? You couldn't choose a location to head towards or a path to get there or even decide how much you would need in supplies. Like any strategy, the first starting point is to find out where you are. Then you will know how far you have to go and which direction to head.

Information technology is the foundation upon which the e-business model is built. The fancy doors and windows of the company are important to the outside world, but the foundation has to be rock solid. Therefore, one of the first things any company, individual, or organization should do is an IT inventory. This isn't about counting the number of computers that you have or the bandwidth of your fiber pipe. It is vital to know both of these statistics, along with the following information:

➤ What the depth of your technical knowledge resources is.

➤ What your current technology standards are.

➤ What your infrastructure is composed of.

➤ What technology needs to be upgraded.

➤ What technology must stay.

➤ What your technological philosophy is.

  (Internet based, in-house systems, outsourced technology, direction of technological change, etc.)

The goal is to create an itemized list of your technological resources along with your future technological direction. This will at least indicate where you are now and the direction you are headed from a technological perspective.

The Corporate Inventory

Just as you would analyze where you are from a technology perspective, you also have to analyze where you are from a corporate perspective. This includes identifying your corporate knowledge assets, as well as your proprietary strengths and weaknesses. You should evaluate the strength of your corporate culture by trying to define what the culture is and how it should change. Obviously, you should also identify your real assets, including capital and hard resources such as inventory, as well as any and all risks that the current corporation faces.

You should also look at what changes you need to make to the existing corporate resources in order for the company to change its operations. These can include the addition of transitional staff, a research and development lab, or more investment in a subsidiary. For example, if you have a traditional warehouse operation, you may need more warehouse space, a new configuration for the existing warehouse space, changes to shipping and receiving methodologies, etc.

The goal of the corporate inventory, like that of the IT inventory, should be to identify where exactly the corporation is in its world so that you can understand your starting point. For example, if you are a medical test lab that is going to use national shipping but you only have accounts with local couriers, then you will have to plan on establishing national courier accounts and dedicate resources to understanding how to change your shipping procedures.

The Competitive Inventory

It is pretty difficult to fight a battle if you don't know anything about your competition. You need to identify who your competition is including indirect competitors, such as companies that supply a product that can impact your sales. For example, the automobile was indirect competition to the buggy whip manufacturer. Knowing the size and potential impact on your operations as a result of your competition is also important. If they are further ahead in the development of an identical application to yours, they stand a higher chance of becoming the standard before you can reach them.

It's important to understand where the competition is relative to your own organization. If they have comparable resources and size to your company, including their knowledge assets, they will be a formidable threat. If they are significantly smaller, and in some cases larger, they might not be a threat at all. You should also try to identify which markets they operate in and any proprietary advantage they may have.

> **Knowing Your Competition**
>
> For more information on competitive intelligence programs, surf to http://www.brint.com/papers/ciover.htm

The Industry Inventory

The industry inventory should indicate where your particular industry is on the e-commerce curve. Are they far down the technology learning curve or back at the start? In some cases, an industry in the early stages of an e-commerce evaluation presents numerous opportunities, but in other cases if you exceed the technological capability of your suppliers, they may not be able to meet your goals for an automated supply chain. This may require that you take a leadership role in moving your industry forward, or it may require that you take a more supportive role and search for other opportunities.

All of these inventories are nothing more than a simple session of information gathering and documentation to identify the strengths, weaknesses, and opportunities for the organization. These tasks should not take a great deal of time or resources, but should take enough time to produce some documentation for the business plan that will be included in publications such as a prospectus. Your goal should be to produce a few written sections like:

➤ Who is the company?

➤ What are the company's strengths?

➤ Who is the competition?

➤ What is the state of the industry?

➤ What are the opportunities?

Know Where You Are Going

Once you have decided on where you are, then you can decide where you want to be. This is essentially giving your organization a target to head towards. Often, these targets are spelled out in annual goals, five-year plans, business strategies, or mission statements. The point is that it is very difficult to move an organization if you don't have a clear idea of where you're going. You may change the target as you go, but at least have something to head towards initially.

The Business Plan

You have already started formulating a business plan in the last section. In fact, you should have been able to formalize and create the first few pages of a draft business plan. Now, the next step is to expand on the opportunities section by choosing one or two targets and creating a long-term corporate goal. We say goal as opposed to mission because mission statements are far more general and philosophical than goals. For example, you may choose to fight a war to protect the principles of democracy, but your actual goal may be to eliminate your opponent's weapons and infrastructure in the first few weeks. Defining a goal gives your organization a target to head towards. Now you know where you are and where you are going.

The next step in the process is to define all the smaller goals that have to be accomplished to get you to the main goal. These goals can include changing your infrastructure, updating your servers, installing a T1 line, purchasing software, and hiring consultants. Each of these goals should be clear and concise. There should be no ambiguity, and you should always be able to identify a clear path to the main goal that indicates how far you have yet to go. For example, you can state that your main goal is to supply "how to" information for free on the Internet like Learnlots.com. Your sub-goals could include something like get four major sponsors or partners by October or have a functional Web site online by August. They should not be fuzzy or soft goals, such as define metrics methodologies or establish base priorities, or our favorite—define interfaces that lead to the effective implementation of strategic initiatives. Like that actually means something!

Strategy

Some interesting information on strategy can be found at `http://home.att.net/ ~nickols/three_forms_of_ strategy.htm`.

Now that you have defined where you are, where you are going, and all the milestones in-between, define a schedule of when these goals will be accomplished. Again the date should be clear and not soft, such as December 20, 9:22 AM, as opposed to by the end of the first quarter. These dates are essential because they indicate the progress of the organization and should result in a graduated level of rewards. For example, if you miss a target, but it's not really your fault, you get a cookie. If you just barely miss the target, you get two cookies. If you make the target, you get two cookies with a stock option agreement sandwiched in between them. This combination of goals and schedules is called a goal map or sometimes a strategic map.

The strategic map is usually not published in a widely distributed business plan. Instead, a page or two outlining how your company plans to capitalize on the opportunities noted in the industry section of the business plan should be enough.

Staffing Up

The next step in the process is to start defining the structure of your organization and the executive staff who will be required to run it. You will then need to locate those staff members, and the best way to do this is to steal them from other organizations, although we recommend that you always mix in some of the best young talent from the schools. Your most senior staff should bring either an extremely high level of talent or some other significant benefit, such as contacts, salesmanship, reputation, etc. These individual talents should be documented in an executive's list and included in the business plan.

It is vital that if you hire your friends for moral support that their role be backed by others with talent or reputation. Some of the most successful companies that we are familiar with were the product of two or more partners. Defining the founding partner roles and responsibilities and ensuring a very selective hiring policy from that point on is essential to ensuring that you get the right individuals on your corporate team.

The Technology Strategy

Just as you set goals for the organization, you should do a sub-map just for technology. This is critical because of the nature of our new businesses. Technology is so vital to any business plan today that a separate set of goals should be established to define such things as which standards are going to be used over the short term, what technological partnerships will be developed, what proprietary technology you will develop, and what technologies you will have tested for future applications. This particular map can still use the corporate goal as the main technological target, but the sub-goals should all be clear, concise, and related to technology. Installing a new server is a good goal, but defining corporate direction as it relates to emergent structures is not. It is important to note that in some case the technology may not yet be in existence and may require development. This fact also can be noted in the strategy.

Once again the technology strategy and its strategy map should include hard target dates for measuring the performance of the corporation and for giving rewards. As well, a single page technology section should be added to the business plan that identifies both the existing technology and the new strategy. Both the main strategic map and the technology map may have to be altered at a later date if the resources are not available to meet the goals.

Resource Map

The resource map is the same as any other strategic map except that it deals with the amount of resources that will be needed to achieve your goal. It should first of all identify what resources the organization actually has to play with. This includes financial, knowledge, and technical resources, as well as hard assets. The next step is to identify what new resources you will require and how much they are going to cost.

Once again you will have to establish milestones as to how you are going to achieve your resource goals. These should include such items as the amounts that you will require from the different levels of funding along with some pro-forma financial statements. If you follow professional accounting guidelines in the production of those statements, you will be able to move easily to audited statements at a later date. These statements along with financial notes and a comprehensive statement of the risks facing your firm should also be added to the business plan.

Business Plans

Surf to just about any company and look at a prospectus. You will see a stock business plan. Look at a lot of them, and you will see a pattern.

At this point, you should essentially have 95% of a comprehensive business plan drafted. It will change as the organization moves ahead, but for now you have performed the most difficult task, the rough draft. The business plan that you have drafted is your story, and the story is what you sell to the world.

Building Your Killer App

Now you have spent enough time on the planning and those off-the-wall brainstorming sessions. Itís time to get to work. You can do one of two things, prototype your concept on a shoestring, or you can go directly to your seed investors with your business plan. Either way, once the money is in the bank, the real work begins. You will have to locate the resources that you will need to complete your app. This could be systems, software, people, or partnerships, and obtaining these resources may include travel and promotion. You should spend the time to practice presenting the story that you just drafted so that you are very prepared. Remember that rejection is just a part of the game.

You must clearly understand why and how your application will become a killer app. Of course, you can still be profitable if your application is not a killer app, but it probably means that someone else is becoming the standard, and they will eventually wipe you out. There is no sense in picking a direct head-on fight with the leading app unless you have a reasonable expectation that you will eventually come out on top. Part of this is that you must understand what makes your application different from your competition's application.

You must also understand how your application will earn revenue and establish your goals, so that eventually your organization will be profitable. This is a growing concern because some of the high-tech stocks are under careful scrutiny for expected profitability. Their revenue is not in question, but their profitability is. Therefore, you should anticipate some hard questions from your investors about when your company will become profitable. You must not just understand how the company will be profitable and set your budgets accordingly; you must also set financial performance goals so that you know how you are doing. These goals will also indicate if you can afford all the resources you require, or if you will need more funding.

Partnering

You must first identify a target list of partners who are essential to the operation of your business. These partners must be located, identified, contacted, and then visited. Agreements must be negotiated and signed, and the technical requirements for linking the two organizations must be completed. You should be expecting from your partners the same level of enthusiasm for your application that you have. If they reject your idea wholesale, you may have to re-evaluate the potential of your application.

Rejection

Investors and partners have rejected almost all successful online organizations at one time. Some of these companies have gone on to become some of the largest technology companies in the world. Just imagine what would have happened if you had jumped on board financially with Microsoft or Amazon very early in their corporate lives. They received rejections along the way just like everyone else, but their perseverance is what eventually won the day. Just remember that someone rejected Bill's and Paul's little DOS idea as having no value. Ouch.

The next step is to identify the secondary partners. These partners are not critical to your business, but they are just as important because they will supply you with traffic, content, mutual promotion or advertising, etc. They should also be identified, located, and visited if their contribution is significant enough to warrant the cost. Don't forget that they may also provide industry buzz depending on who they are.

Finally, you should establish stock agreements for the general partners with which you exchange a mutual benefit, such as linking sites. Depending on the size of the site, it may justify traveling to visit these partners or having them visit you.

Building a Community

Now that you have started building the application, you have to start building your community of value.* The first step in this process is to define your base target customers. Then you will start defining any sub-classifications of this group, such as a

*From the book Killer App *by Larry Downes and Chunka Mui by Harvard Business School Press*

niche. The result will be an identifiable group, although it may not be identified by pure demographics, but may instead be defined by attitudes. Be aware that these groups may change as you further develop your application.

The next step is to define the image that you will portray to the world, and, in particular, to your customers. This is a bit of a chicken and egg argument since some will argue that you can't define an image without knowing the market. Others will argue that you can't define a psychographic niche without knowing the overall image. In general, just pick the market, define the niche, and choose the image; then reiterate the process until you locate the right mix. You can always choose the image first and try to define the market later.

Identify what repetitive value you will provide to your customers and how you will keep the value repeating. This may mean that you will require a staff who will update the content on your site, or it may mean that you will link with a site that provides updated information on a regular basis, such as a news service. You may also require a development staff to change your application or an onsite e-commerce specialist to keep your product offering constantly changing.

You will also have to decide what type of advertising you will need to reach your customers. This will include the type of medium that will be used to deliver the image as well as the media mix that will be used. You must choose the targeting for the ads by carefully selecting sites and develop a schedule for distribution to ensure the correct timing of the delivery. How much of the task you will outsource is also a consideration at this point.

At the same time, you will have to decide what type of promotions you will require. This will include the delivery method of the promotion whether it is face-to face meetings, a road show, news event, or bulletin. You will also have to identify media contacts and choose the best method for delivering your message to them. Scheduling and outsourcing are also two critical pieces of the promotion strategy that will have to be decided at this point.

Finally, you will have to choose the marketing model that is most appropriate for your company and your customers, as noted in Chapter 16. The most important step in the marketing process is execution, and you will have to start that process as soon as possible.

How Virtual Is Your Corp?

Another step is to start defining the structure of your organization in more detail. Identify which functions you will partner out and which you will keep in the company. For those that are partnered out, identify the companies that will perform the function and ensure that adequate agreements are in place if the function is deemed critical to your business. For functions that are staying in-house, map the tasks that are to be performed, identify systems that are to automate the task, and try to define staffing requirements. Implement and test the structure of the organization prior to opening.

For those tasks that are to be outsourced, carefully choose the organization that you will work with and test their references. Define how the two organizations will connect technology and identify such factors as pricing, security, disaster recovery, etc. Ensure that there are adequate testing and negotiated agreements prior to the commencement of online business.

You will have to define those employee functions that will be outsourced, those that will be made virtual, and those that will be essential and left onsite. You will also have to define the company's policy regarding offsite employees. Choosing the location of the company and building the environment to handle the mix of employees will also be necessary whether it's a traditional environment or a virtual style environment.

You should clearly map out any existing back-office process and any existing systems. Then you should identify how the back office will change according to the corporate and technological strategy maps. The systems will have to be purchased and implemented, and the new policies and procedures will have to be defined. As well, employees will have to be trained on the new systems.

Funding

Funding will be the single most essential piece of your start-up costs. You will have to map out a quick strategy as to how you are going to gather capital. This should include a list of individuals who are likely to support the project in the seed stages without requiring control of the organization. It should also establish some form of tracking and keeping in contact with these investors. Regulatory requirements should be noted, and legal agreements should be drawn up to ensure all parties are protected.

You should be using your pro forma statements as an indicator of how much funding will be required and on what dates. You will have to map a strategy to start creating investment buzz by visiting investors and their representatives to present the story of your company. The good news is that you will have already completed most of a prospectus that can be used as a brochure. You will require assistance in this funding process, and that will require that you contact the start-up funding specialists at the brokerages. This will mean scheduling and travel. Once again, you will use the goals of the corporate plan to indicate how much funding will be required and by what date.

Finally, you will have to start the process of preparing for the IPO. Review the business plan, fill in any of the missing gaps, and verify that the information is still accurate. Identify those individuals in the brokerages and banks who can assist in taking you through the IPO and allow them to do their work. While this is occurring, you can still continue work on developing the application and growing the organization.

Road Shows

You will have already performed some road shows during the start-up phase, but now they will change. The first question you will have to answer is do you have the resources to do public relations effectively. A good PR firm with a track record for your type of organization can easily get you through the doors of the media firms that will spread the word about your organization. Usually, these funds are well spent, since your initial media public relations can make or break your firm. Choosing the correct PR partner is essential.

You should start creating buzz in the market through the use of road shows with your industry and your partners. These do not necessarily have to be planned by your PR firm. Instead, they can be managed very early in the process by identifying which industry partners are most likely to be receptive to your application or product and visit with them to obtain their sign-on. Some very small organizations have had a great deal of success, thanks to relationships established with larger partners.

Choosing the investor for your road show is usually best left to the start-up pros in the bank, brokerages, investment firms, venture capital funds, etc. Although a PR firm can provide some assistance in fine-tuning your presentation, the best resource to present the company is you. They can, however, provide support in the investor relations area by assisting in managing the entire investor relations program if needed.

Where your PR firm will have its greatest impact is in your dealings with the media. They will choose the media best suited for your company, establish contacts, set up interviews, create and manage press releases, choose the type of media, schedule the presentations, create newsworthy events, and execute those events. They will manage the verbal presentation of your image, and can usually go the next step by designing your entire corporate image.

Managing Growth and Change

Finally, your little concept has started to grow into an e-commerce success story, and the next task is certainly not covered in this book. It's the process of managing the growth and change of your company. All we can say is hang on because the ride is very fast and very bumpy.

Enjoy your e-commerce success.

The Least You Need To Know

➤ How to implement the definitive e-commerce model for your company.

Glossary

24 × 7 A reference to something that is open 24 hours a day, seven days a week.

Affiliate An organization or individual whom you have formed a formal or informal agreement with to either sell or receive products, services, content, traffic, etc.

Animated Gif A graphical interchange format (image) that appears to move or change as a result of multiple layered images.

Applet A small piece of Java code that can perform functions such as moving images or providing a lookup list. This software is sent to and works inside browsers.

Backbone The term used to describe all the wiring and routers that make up the Internet.

Backoffice All of the functions in a company that occur behind the scenes away from the public such as accounting, service work, warehousing, and management.

Bandwidth The capacity of an electronic transmission medium, such as a cable, to carry electronic signals.

Banner ad The long thin ads usually located at the top and bottom of Web pages.

Browser A software package that displays HTML (Hyper Text Markup Language) documents primarily from the Internet.

Buzz A term used to describe conversations and general discussions about a particular company or technology.

Certificates Electronic security forms or documents that verify the authenticity of a Web site.

Chat Room   An online place for people to post and read electronic messages.

Click-through   The term that describes when a visitor to a Web site uses a link to access another Web site.

Client   An application used to access the Internet, which is resident on a user's machine. For example, a browser is a Web client.

Community of Value   A concept where the visitors to a Web site believe they belong to a community of people who share the same interests and that membership in the online community has a value to these visitors.

Content   Anything contained on a Web site such as files, software, information, graphics, etc.

Convergence   The movement of various types of software toward common standards.

Critical mass   The gathering of enough users of an application to make the application viable and necessary.

Cross niching   Finding commonality between two or more subdivisions of the customers in a market after they have been divided into niches.

Cybersquatting   The act of trying to divert customers from a Web site by using a similar name and identical look as another site or the act of obtaining and holding domain names for resale.

Data warehouse   A large electronic storage area that is structured so that the data stored in divergent formats is converted to consistent output, such as the same type of database.

Data mining   Locating, reviewing, and analyzing stored operational information to assist in decision-making.

Distributed computing   The technical architecture where the network clients, as opposed to central processing and storage areas, perform some or all application processing or information storage.

Domain name   A plain-language name for a Web site. This is translated into an Internet Protocol number that is used to locate and access the site on the Internet.

e-bank   An online bank that provides regular bank services over the Internet.

e-commerce   Business conducted exclusively through an electronic format.

EDI (Electronic data interchange)   The transmission of electronic data in a specific EDI format or series of EDI standards.

EFT (Electronic Funds Transfer) An electronic transfer of information that equates to moving funds from one financial institution to another.

Electronic cheque A type of electronic funds transfer that can be given an online company for deposit at an online financial institution.

Encryption The scrambling of digital messages in such a way that only the sender and receiver can read the message.

ERP (Enterprise Resource Planning) A model for building software in which all the operation processes that impact resource management use integrated software.

FAQ (Frequently Asked Questions) A listing of questions that have already been asked along with the answers to those questions.

Firewall A piece of software that regulates who can access a network from outside the network via a modem or router.

FTP (File Transfer Protocol) A standard used to transfer large files or large amounts of data over the Internet.

GIF (Graphical Interchange Format) A file format for electronic images and pictures used on Web pages.

GPS (Global Positioning System) A series of low-level satellites that transmit a signal used by devices on the ground to indicate the longitude and latitude of the device

Hit A visit to a Web site by a Web surfer.

HTML (Hyper Text Markup Language) A standard markup language created by a worldwide consortium and used to format Web documents.

i-center An online customer service center that may or may not allow interaction with humans via video, sound, or electronic messages.

i-commerce Business conducted through an electronic format on the Internet.

Integrated systems The concept of having software that communicates and operates as one seamless unit.

Internetwork A connection of networks usually connected through routers.

IP (Internet Protocol) Address Internet Protocol address is the numeric address used to locate physical or virtual computers or sites on the Internet.

IPO (Initial Public Offering) The first public offering of a stock.

ISP (Internet Service Provider) A company that has a connection to the Internet and charges the public a fee to use part of that connection.

Java   An object-oriented programming language created and distributed for free by Sun Microsystems.

Keys   Alphanumeric codes that are used in encryption to ensure that other computers on the network cannot read encrypted information without the keys.

Killer app   The concept identified by Larry Downes & Chunka Mui in their book *Killer App* as "a new good or service that establishes an entirely new category and, by being first, dominates it, returning several hundred percent return on initial investment."*

LAN (Local Area Network)   A network that is confined to a specific, single physical area (i.e., ***not*** connected directly to any other network via a router).

Link   Also known as a hyperlink, a link is an address embedded in a Web document. The browser transfers to that address when the link is clicked.

Linux   A free, Unix-like operating system for computers created by Linus Torvalds.

Logistics   Shipping and distribution functions in an organization. Sometimes used to define a role that manages all the company's resources.

Metcalf's law   Utility = (number of user)^2 where ^{2} denotes the square.

Micropayment   A very small payment that is accumulated and paid once a specified threshold is attained. Usually used for traffic or click-throughs.

Moore's law   In the 60s, Gordon Moore, Intel's founder, predicted that every 18 months, chip processing power (as established by chip transistor density) would double while the costs would stay the same.

MP3   A digital file standard for recording sound. The files can be sent and played on the Internet.

Network   A series of computers connected together in some way to allow for the sending of electronic information.

Neural Network   The storage and retrieval of data by systems that have the capability of making changes to their methodologies through the use of statistical and mathematical algorithms.

Niche   A small subdivision of a large market demographic.

Outsourcing   The contracting of work to another company.

From the book Killer App *by Larry Downes and Chunka Mui by Harvard Business School Press*

Packet A small piece of data that has addresses appended to it to allow it to be sent from one computer to another.

PC Acronym for a personal computer.

Plug-in A piece of software that is "plugged-in" to a browser for running special objects or content over the Internet.

Point of Presence (POP) An Internet Service Provider's point of connection to the Internet in a specific city or community.

Pop-up windows Windows, other than the main browser window, that open when you open a Web site.

Private placement Raising money through invitation to a select few individuals or organizations.

Prospectus An information document provided to investors that identifies information about the company. Usually provided to raise money through the sale of stock.

Protocol A standardized way to transfer data so that computers on a network can communicate with each other.

Psychographic A way in which members of a population are differentiated by action, moods, identity, etc.

Public Key Infrastructure The provision of public electronic security keys for use by companies and individuals who want to send encrypted messages.

Push technology The delivery of content to users periodically as opposed to when the user requests it. Primarily used to deliver time-sensitive information like stock market quotes, news, or sports scores.

Real-time systems Information systems that instantaneously process a transaction and all associated information about the transaction.

Red herring A preliminary prospectus used to provide information prior to the real prospectus. So named because it has red lettering on the front.

Relational database A structured table of data, where data in records are keyed or related to data records in another table or tables.

Rich media Online advertising that has some form of functionality that allows the user to obtain objects, such as video or sound, or interact with the ad by providing information, choosing information, etc.

Roadshow A series of presentations used to gather interest in a company or an application.

Router   An internetworking device that determines the route a data packet will travel between nodes on the Internet.

SAN (Storage Area Network)   The storage of data in various storage servers on the same network.

Search engine   A Web site that allows a visitor to enter a search phrase and have the engine search all the shared files on a network.

Second-level financing   Private funding for an organization that bridges the gap between the seed capital and the IPO.

Seed capital   The initial funding of the organization.

Server   A computer that acts as a central control point for a network to manage applications.

Spam   Unsolicited email usually sent to try to sell or market a product or service.

Spoofing   Deceptive identification of an address or point of origin on the Internet.

Surfing   Using a browser to visit sites on the Internet

SSL (Secure Socket Layer)   A security measure in which encryption is used to make a secure connection between a Web server and a client so that others cannot see the transfer of information.

Streaming   The sending of a repeated stream of packets from a server to another computer connected to the same network or Intranet. Usually used for sound or video broadcasts.

Supply chain   The entire process of accepting a customer order through to the delivery of the product to the customer inclusive of supply procurement and production of the product.

Technology template   A series of standards that the corporation has decided will be the long-term technological environment of the organization.

Telecommuting   Working away from an office and using a PC to communicate with the organization.

Thin client   A client computer on a network that has limited peripheral devices and storage.

Traffic   Visits to a Web site.

Uniform Resource Locator (URL)   The full address of an Internet service, including the protocol and domain, for example, `http://www.20ants.com`.

Virtual employees   Employees who work offsite or away from their organization

WAN (Wide area network)   A network over a wide physical area and usually connected through high speed phone lines or wireless devices.

Web page   A series of HTML or XML files that can be viewed by using a browser

Webcast   A webcast is the streaming of electronic data between a server and a client computer.

XML (Extensible Markup Language)   The next generation of standard Internet presentation language created by a worldwide consortium.

Zine   An online magazine.

Index

O

objects
databases, 274
object-oriented code, 121
ODBC (Open Database
Connectivity), 192, 274
offline marketing, 216,
257-258, 260
on-demand customer
service, 143-146
online operations
banking, 167
credit card purchases, 77
investor data, 267
meetings, 182
retailing, 26
shopping, 77
online help desk, 148-149
operations mapping, virtual
corporations, 72
optical storage, 128
options, 111
Oracle
ERP tools, 284
Web site , 272
order/entry flow,
automated, 138
outsourcing, 80-82, 184-185,
291-293
overvaluation, Internet
stocks, 327

P

packet sniffing, 64, 163
part-time virtual
workforce, 179
partnering, 15, 108,
315, 343
affiliates, 245, 317-318
choosing content
suppliers, 317

global, 17
stock agreements, 343
payments
credit cards, 156-158
processing, 159
in-receipt of
payments, 157
payments out, 167
security, 162
types, 157
PCs, 8
performance evaluation,
virtual workforce, 178
personalized
promotion, 217
pipes, 219
pitfalls
killer apps
advertising, 96
asset owners, 92
avoiding, 97
clutter/garbage on
sites, 92
commercialization of
Internet, 94
corporate control, 95
disinterest in Web
sites, 91
duplicate
functionality, 94
fragmentation of
Internet, 93
Internet usage drop, 90
virtual workforce, 186
PKI (Public Key
Infrastructure), 165
Pop-up Killer Web site, 231
portfolios of knowledge
assets, 298
POSs (point-of-sales
systems), 270-271
preferred shares, 33
presence on the Internet,
31, 293

presentations, stock
offerings, 30
privacy policies, Yahoo, 274
privatization of Internet,
330-331
promotions, 209, 212,
263, 289
ads, 234
banner ads, 214, 227
link ads, 215
data mining, 195
locating customers, 211,
226-227
newsgroups, 213
off-net, 216
targeting customers, 210
prospectus, 34
protocols, 64
psychographic analysis, 212
public relations, 13, 219,
265-266
publishing financial
data, 267
purchasing mined data, 220
push technologies,
Webcasts, 230

R

Raging Bull Web site, 328
RAID, 128
real-time systems, 119, 124
back office options, 125
data mining, 126
storage, 125
red herrings, 34
registering
domain names, 59
e-company name with
government, 58
rejection of business
proposals, 342